Legacy on the Land:

A Black Couple Discovers Our National Inheritance and Tells Why Every American Should Care

To Miguel
with love
from
audrey.

by Audrey Peterman
& Frank Peterman

Earthwise Productions, Inc.
Atlanta, Georgia

Published by:
Earthwise Productions, Inc.
450 Piedmont Avenue, #1512
Atlanta, GA 30308 U.S.A.
www.earthwiseproductionsinc.com/legacyontheland

Cover photograph of the Petermans © Ken Karst
Photo credits: Photographs © by individual photographers (Ken Karst, Eric Metzler,
Peterm (Germany), Audrey Peterman, Frank Peterman, Frank Peterman, Jr., and
Mike Theiss) and the National Park Service

Publisher's Cataloging-in-Publication data
Peterman, Audrey.
Legacy on the Land: A Black Couple Discovers Our National Inheritance and Tells Why
Every American Should Care / by Audrey and Frank Peterman.
        p. cm.
        Includes index.
        ISBN 978-0-9842427-2-6

1. National parks and reserves – United States.
2. Natural history – United States.
3. Environmental justice – United States.
4. African-Americans – Monuments.
5. African Americans – Civil rights.
6. Social justice – United States.
7. African Americans – History.
8. United States – Race relations. I. Peterman, Frank. II. Title.

E160 .P48 2009
917.304/931 —dc22
Library of Congress Control Number: 2009936800

Dedication

To our children, grandchildren and great-grandchildren, and all who come after us. To Audrey's mom, Avenel; and to the memory of "Mama" Ida, Mass D, Veta Mae and Frank Peterman.

Contents

Part Three
It's Time to Discover Our Parks

Foreword

I spent my entire professional career in the National Park Service and the Department of the Interior, and I couldn't be more proud to be a steward of America's natural and cultural treasures. I've had the pleasure of knowing Frank and Audrey since the mid-1990s, and the passion and enthusiasm they bring to the issue of connecting the national parks and the American people fits perfectly with the vision and goals I have pursued.

It is uncanny that the book is coming out at the same time that we have a new Administration that is racially and ethnically diverse. One of the chief mandates of the Obama Administration in which I serve is to connect the American people with their heritage on the land. It is a healthful, life-enhancing opportunity and the future of the publicly-owned lands system depends upon it. I do believe that this book, *Legacy on the Land: A Black Couple Discovers Our National Inheritance and Tells Why Every American Should Care*, will be a great help in accomplishing this mission. Few people know the parks as well as Audrey and Frank, and the excitement that they bring to the issue is inspiring and contagious.

Robert G. Stanton, *Deputy Assistant Secretary in the Office of Policy, Management and Budget, Department of the Interior; Director of the National Park System, 1996–2000*

Acknowledgements

To the Divine Spirit who we see richly manifested in the natural world.

To our agent, publishing advisor and dear friend, Janell Walden Agyeman, whose faithfulness, love and devotion played a vital role in getting this book done.

To our editor and friend, Carolyn Finney, who "has a Ph.D in Peterman" and brought her considerable editing talents to bear on this work.

To Midge Hainline and her family, Lee and Jimmy Cross, whose friendship and generosity assisted us in doing much of this work.

To the original team: Cathy & Neil Ritter, Eloise Davis and Keith Conzett who encouraged and assisted us to produce *Pickup & GO!*

And to legions of friends and colleagues with whom we've worked side by side including: Kim & Jim Anaston-Karas; Don Barry; Francisco Morales-Bermudez; Diana Blank; Al Calloway; Keith Clayborne and the *Broward Times*; Charles Fulwood; Iantha Gantt-Wright; Senator Bob Graham; Congressman Alcee Hastings; Bobby Henry and the *Westside Gazette*; John Huey; Gwen Ivory and the *Palm Beach Gazette*; Charles Jordan; Kenny Karst; Kevin Kelly; Kathryn Kolb; Cynthia Laramore; Dr. Wilbur Leaphart; Congressman John Lewis; Doug Lyons and the *Fort Lauderdale Sun-Sentinel*; Congresswoman Carrie Meek; Minuteman Press, Ft. Lauderdale; Dorrit & Wilfred Nelson; Letitia Owens; Nan & Britt Pendergast; Garth Reeves and the *Miami Times*; Jerome Ringo; Laura and Rutherford Seydel; the South Florida Community Partners; Alan Spears; Bob Stanton; Stuart Strahl; Sonny Wright and *South Florida Newsweek*; Julia Yarbough; Cy Zaneski and the *Miami Herald*, and posthumously to our beloved MaVynee Betsch, Leola McCoy and Brenda Lanzendorf. From the bottom of our hearts, we thank you!

Prologue

Integrating the Environmental Sector and the Great Outdoors

When President Barack Obama and the First Family moved into the White House in January 2009, they effectively integrated the National Park System at the very top. The White House is among 391 units of the System described by those in the know as "the Soul of America." The system includes a peerless collection of world-class natural wonders such as the Grand Canyon National Park, Mesa Verde National Park with its remnants of ancient Native American civilizations, and Independence National Historical Park where the U.S. Constitution was debated and signed. The natural wonders are also known as our "Crown Jewels," and while the British keep their Crown Jewels under heavy guard in the Tower of London, ours are spread out in plain view for the entire world to enjoy.

But as late as 2008, in the pre-Obama years, the system remained "hidden in plain view" to the masses of Americans. Very large, very public, they were an unknown quantity among Americans of color and millions of other Americans who mostly kept to the developed urban areas. A visit to any of the vast, scenic landscapes such as Yellowstone National Park might reveal less than one percent of non-white Americans enjoying the spectacular views and wildlife, or working among the staff. In 2008, according to the 2009 Diversity Task Force Report, National Parks Conservation Association, an astonishing 72.7 percent of the workforce in the National Park System was white!

My husband Frank and I "discovered" the national parks in a round-the-country adventure in 1995, when, with our last child having just graduated from college, we decided to explore our country. From the top of Cadillac Mountain in Acadia National Park in Maine to the mesmerizing formations of the Badlands National Park in South Dakota to the rainforest wonders of Olympic National Park in Washington State, we marveled at the astonishing richness and diversity of the natural landscapes. I felt like someone who had lived in an opulent mansion for years and had only seen the kitchen, then accidentally opened the door leading into the grand ballroom. The sheer beauty extending as far as our eyes could see awakened a deep feeling of spirituality, as if we were literally seeing the face of God, His handiwork untouched by human hands. It was hard to believe that these places exist in our own country and we hadn't known about them.

That life altering experience made us resolve to do everything in our power to lift the veil that shields these places from the masses of the American people. For the eight weeks we were out, we saw less than a handful of African Americans, Latinos, Asians or Native Americans among the hundreds of thousands of visitors in the parks. When we found out that the National Park Service (NPS)—which manages the National Park System—is prohibited from advertising, we began working to combat the lack of information in communities of color and urban communities by publishing the periodical, *Pickup & GO!* featuring the parks and the wonderful experiences to be had in them. We've collaborated with a plethora of national, regional and grassroots groups to combat the perception in the mainstream environmental segment that Americans of color and urban people are somehow unsuited to appreciate the great natural bounty of our country, and be part of the solution for our environmental challenges.

In 2008 this fact was particularly incomprehensible since, as early as 1994, the influential *National Parks* magazine (published by the National Parks Conservation Association) outlined the problem and the solutions needed in an article titled, "Designing for Diversity: Ethnic minorities are largely absent from most major national parks, a problem the Park Service is working to correct." Written by Jack Goldsmith, it stated:

> The National Park Service (NPS) has a proud history of welcoming special groups to the parks. Visitors older than 61 carry Golden Age Passports that remove entrance fees. People with disabilities have benefited from enormous improvements in access, and foreign tourists are likely to find brochures written in their native languages. Our national parks host Sunday services for several religious denominations, as well as programs that draw equestrians, bicycles, shutterbugs, even wine tasters.

But one segment of U.S. Society is still largely unseen at the national treasures their tax dollars help to maintain: ethnic minorities.

Studies show overwhelmingly that America's fast-growing black and Latino populations are effectively absent from major parks. In a nation that is 12 percent African American, Texas A&M researchers found in 1992 that only 0.4 percent of Yosemite's visitors arriving by car and 3.8 percent of those arriving by bus were black.

At Grand Canyon National Park in Arizona, African Americans accounted for 1.5 percent of those who arrived by car and 2 percent by bus, and the representation of Latinos was not much better. In a state with a large Latino population, this ethnic group accounted for 4.7 percent of visitors traveling by car and 1.4 percent of those traveling by bus. The Bureau of Land Management (BLM) stated in its Recreation 2000 Report on California that Asians and Latinos had a lower average rate of participation in wildland outdoor recreation activities.

Although an accelerating movement for ethnic diversity in the park system has begun with some encouraging plans and programs, much more is needed.

We are not achieving the goals of the National Park Service (NPS) if the treasures of the park system are not being enjoyed by all elements of society...

The article provoked a backlash. Five of seven *Letters* in a subsequent issue of the magazine were in response to Goldman's article and included the following statements:

Your recent article by Jack Goldsmith, "Designing for Diversity" (Forum, May/June 1994) is way off target. To modify the National Park System to lure ethnic minorities would be a disaster and one more facet of our country that would be changed to please a few, ignoring the desires of the majority.

Bringing more minorities into the parks would probably raise the crime rate when the rangers are being forced to spend more of their time in law enforcement than ever before.

If minorities do not like going to the parks, it is their loss. But please, don't let us be duped into thinking it is our loss. Many of us look to the parks as an escape from the problems ethnic minorities create. Please don't modify our parks to destroy our oasis.

With visitation having plummeted and more foreign visitors in the national parks than Americans, one writer who was outraged by the racially charged comments, asked in a letter to the magazine's editor:

…what would happen if those of us from mixed-racial and ethnic minority families should begin to feel that the parks are only for an elite group and not for us? What would happen if nothing is done to encourage those who have not yet had the opportunity to visit the parks to do so? What will happen if, by the year 2000, when one-third of the nation's school-age children are ethnic minorities, these children do not have the opportunity to experience the parks first hand? Is there any guarantee that when they grow up they will want to continue to safeguard them from exploitation? How can we expect people to respect and protect something they know very little about?

The atrocities perpetrated against our public lands system in the eight years of the Bush administration show the writer's worst fears being realized. The national parks and forests, as the largest unspoiled ecosystems in the U.S., are both a barometer of our environmental health and the key to solutions for many of our climate change problems. Because they have been the purview of such a restricted slice of the population, the parks have been subject to exploitation and abuse by an administration that saw them only as a source of wealth for the few, at the expense of current and future generations of Americans. Few in the cities can care passionately about what drilling will do to the Arctic National Wildlife Refuge when they have no idea what this place is and what it means to America.

The Park Service and mainstream advocacy organizations, having failed to engage the increasingly racially diverse population of our country, now bemoan the predictable results, commission more "studies of the problem," and charge the declining interest in our world-class resources to "apathy" when, in fact, they have not done what their own multiple studies showed was necessary: inform the public. In a topical report published in 2003 titled "Ethnic and Racial Diversity of National Park System Visitors and Non-Visitors," African American and Hispanic respondents cited "lack of information" among the two top reasons why they do not visit the parks.

While we and thousands of others around the country have succeeded in creating a crack in the door, the election of an African American to the Presidency throws the Great American Outdoors wide open. Old ideas of limitations based upon racial identity and what African Americans or Latinos "don't do" no longer apply. Today, almost everyone is interested in "living green," and nothing is more "green" than the natural abundance in our national parks and other publicly-owned lands such as the forests and wildlife refuges. From the moment we first experienced the great outdoors, we became sensitive to the fact that wherever we are, nature is all around us. Now, we can feel that deep spiritual connection to nature whether we're in a Yosemite or in our own backyard. Time spent in the outdoors has been proven to be an antidote for stress, depression and anxiety, as well as the Attention Deficit Disorder (ADD), hyperactivity and other disorders that plague our children. Nature-based programs have been shown to turn teenagers and young people away from delinquency and towards finding their place in the world.

Now is the time for Americans of all races, including those who fear what might happen in places where they *think* they "don't belong," to throw off those mental shackles and embrace our collective natural legacy. It is time for mainstream environmental groups to abandon the old excuses of race as a determinant of who is capable of enjoying, conserving and protecting our natural world. In addition, these groups, which are largely funded by government, corporate and foundation dollars, have remained implausibly white in staffing and supporters and today look alarmingly like the Republican Party in the 2008 elections—overwhelmingly older, and white. If we had a dollar for every time one of our colleagues working to diversify this area has said of the white leadership, "they just don't get it," we'd be incredibly rich. I've taken to quoting Upton Sinclair in response: "It's difficult to get a man to understand something when his livelihood depends upon his not understanding it." At this late date, it is just indefensible that people are clinging to the same old justifications even when they have been proven to be outmoded and destructive, both to the changing population that doesn't get to enjoy the benefits of the system, and the public lands that need popular support.

"He or she is a better citizen, with a keener appreciation of the privilege of living here, who has toured the National Parks," said Stephen Mather, the first director of the Park Service.

Frank and I can certainly attest to that. Discovering the Park System launched us on a magnificent and unending journey of self discovery, of citizenship, and the understanding of what all Americans owe to our forefathers of every race and color. It's time to explore and take ownership of the stunning natural, cultural and historic treasures that make up the totality of the American experience, in its continually evolving state. Knowing who we are, and where we have come from, is the simplest and most effective way to unite us as Americans. Our national parks were set aside for this very purpose.

Part One:

Exploring America Coast to Coast

Laws change; people die;
the land remains.

—Abraham Lincoln (1809-1865), 16th U.S. President,
cited in Peter Blake's *God's Own Junkyard*, 1964

Chapter 1:
"We're off to see the wizard...!"

It was a Friday night in August 1995 when Frank and I pulled away from our apartment in Fort Lauderdale for the last time. In our newly-acquired, lightly-used Ford F-150 with the double gas tank, we set off like kids on a camping trip to explore our country from coast to coast for a full three months. We had no particular destination in mind. Our general plan was to explore the "Great American Outdoors" making certain to hit world-famous sights such as the Grand Canyon, Yellowstone and Yosemite, and most especially the dramatic scenery of the Badlands which had been the setting for Frank's favorite cowboy movies growing up in the '50s.

We got the idea two years earlier when Frank returned from Belize, Central America, where we were dreaming of relocating and opening a bed-and-breakfast. On his last day there, he was in a bar having a beer with a couple of locals when one asked,

"Say, man, have you ever been to the Badlands?"

"No. Have you?" Frank said, in between gulps.

"No, but I know you've traveled a lot. I just thought you might have been there."

"What made you ask about the Badlands, though?"

"Oh, the kids and me look at a lot of old cowboy movies, and you always hear something about the Badlands. Where is it, anyway?"

"Way out west, in South Dakota."

"I bet it's something to see. How about the Grand Canyon? Have you ever been there?"

"No," Frank answered.

So when he came home, Frank had a different agenda.

"Honey, how would you feel about us taking some time and traveling around the country? You know, millions of people come from all over the world to see the beautiful natural places in America, and most people who live here never see them. We live here and we've never seen them."

"Well, when are we going?" was my response.

Our friends teased us - if one of us said, "Jump!" the other one said, "How high?"

At that point, we'd been married only three years, though we had been close friends for more than seven. Frank and I met shortly after I moved to Fort Lauderdale from upstate New York, when he came to the secretarial service where I worked to get his manuscript edited and retyped. I was captivated by his energy and vitality, and impressed by the fact that he'd written a book. We were attracted to each other and immediately became friends. He was newly divorced and I tried to set him up with my most eligible girlfriends. When it finally dawned on us that we were the main attraction for each other, we got married in less than six months.

"Oh, the places we shall go and the things we shall do!" Frank told me on our wedding. I had no idea what he meant, but I found him so exciting and dynamic, and our times together had been so much fun, that I looked forward to what our new life would bring. Now we were taking off on the biggest adventure of my life.

When we told our folks we were going to drive around the country just for the fun of it, and that we planned to spend time in the woods enjoying nature, they thought we'd lost our minds. Who ever heard of black people just taking off with no particular destination in mind, and with no certain return date? Both our mothers tried to "talk sense" into us, but we'd made up our minds. We couldn't tell them where we'd be at any particular time, so we bought cell phones and promised to keep in touch.

Our friends were apprehensive about the dangers we might run into. Their chief fear was that we didn't know what to expect and anything might happen, especially in the woods where, as black people we'd definitely be in the minority and out of place. Some of Frank's friends brought out their guns and offered him his choice. But he refused to arm himself in order to exercise his rights as an American citizen, and I totally agreed.

Excited and a little nervous, we were taking the first giant step when, driving two hours north on the Florida Turnpike, we ran into our first hurdle. An accident had shut down the entire turnpike, and the back-up extended so far that people had left their vehicles and were socializing by the side of the road. I'd lived in Florida for 11 years and traveled the turnpike from end to end, and I'd never seen anything like this. As the wait dragged on I wondered, was this an omen? Were we being really stupid and crazy, just like our friends said? And after all, if people could just take months out of their lives and go off to play, wouldn't everyone be doing it?

Luckily, we had burned our bridges and there was no turning back. We had sold our house and furniture, and put the few things we wanted to keep in storage. We had worked out our budget and paid our bills ahead. With our last daughter graduating from college that very weekend, it was the perfect time for us to indulge our wander lust.

I have a naturally sunny and optimistic disposition, so Frank had put me in charge of "esprit de corps." It was my job to keep things on an even keel. He'd be doing most, if not all of the driving since I was just learning to drive the stick shift, so I said gamely, "Maybe we're just getting the most challenging experiences out of the way, and then it'll be smooth sailing from here on?"

When traffic finally started moving around 4 a.m., we drove to Orlando, checked into a hotel, took a nap, cleaned up and got to the University of Florida 80 miles north just in time to see our daughter Andrea accept her diploma. Following her graduation we got back on the road and headed for New York.

It was the week of my 44th birthday and we celebrated it in a round of parties and pleasant visits with my mother and our friends. I introduced Frank to my old stomping grounds in Nyack, West Point and Bear Mountain across the Tappan Zee Bridge, and we explored the museums and nightclubs in New York City. After about a week, we started itching to get back on the road, so we took off from our friend Dorrit's house in Yorktown Heights. Dorrit and I had been friends since we met in high school at age 12—and she was one of the few people who encouraged our adventure. ("Girl, you have to do what you want while you can," she said. "What's to stop you?")

Our first general destination was Acadia National Park in Maine. Neither Frank nor I had been in this part of the country before, so when we saw the first sign warning, "Watch for Moose in Roadway," we looked at each other in delight and burst out laughing.

"You're not in Kansas anymore, Dorothy," Frank said.

Our Great Adventure had begun. We drove 350 miles from upstate New York through rolling mountain scenery, stopping to explore whatever historic site caught our fancy. We had an uneventful lunch out of our cooler at a rest stop, but I got an unpleasant surprise at our next rest stop in Rockland. There were large wasp nests inside the bathroom, and some of the wasps were buzzing about. Frank says he saw me fly out of the toilet, holding my pants up with one hand. I didn't get stung, but I couldn't believe such conditions existed on the beautiful Maine seashore.

Not only were we not seeing any moose, but we weren't seeing any people. The towns were few and far between, and appeared to be completely deserted. We decided to take it easy our first night out and stay in a hotel as opposed to finding campgrounds and setting up camp. Near dusk, we pulled into a Super 8 motel in Freeport. As the person responsible for the family budget, I figured it was our least expensive choice.

The clerk said sure she had rooms, starting at $79.

"$79?" I blurted. "At Super 8? We just need a room because we don't feel like camping!"

"Well, how about if I give you one for $59?" she smiled.

I took it, and told her she was the most outgoing person we'd met since we got to Maine.

"Well, people here are—how shall I say this—reserved! But if you show them you're interested and want to talk, they'll talk you to death," she replied.

We woke up the next morning exhilarated, eager to explore the city and get some breakfast. The town was teeming with people. It looked like everyone we hadn't seen in those other Maine towns had congregated here. And they were all white. Our black faces were definitely in the minority.

We nodded and smiled at everyone that met our eyes, and they smiled and nodded back. Nobody tried to talk us to death, but it was early yet. Looking for breakfast, we could find no sign of the golden arches and finally had to ask someone if there was a McDonald's in town. He directed us to a building with a small, discrete M on the wall. Apparently the town restricts signage to a certain size, which does not include giant fast food arches. Inside, the furniture was made of wood, a big step up from the usual brightly colored plastic, and Frank said it was Duncan Fife furniture made by the famous American craftsman in the 18th century.

Later, we found out that the crowds were in town for the big end-of-season sale by sporting goods discount stores such as Reebok, Nautica and Ralph Lauren. Returning to our hotel to check out, I burst into laughter when I found myself standing in the parking lot studying a supermarket flyer. Sixteen hundred miles away from home on the wildest ride of my life, but we still had to shop and eat. We stocked our cooler with meat, fruits and vegetables, and just past lunchtime, hit the road again.

Our destination was Bar Harbor, the city just outside the boundaries of Acadia National Park. We drove through many small towns and villages that were the picture of tranquility. A sign in Wiscasset boasted, "The prettiest village in Maine," and a policewoman directed traffic at the major intersection. We didn't see one traffic light in town.

Just outside Bucksport, we turned a corner and there was the awesome panoramic scenery of mountains, river and ocean that I'd been anticipating since we left home. It was like driving into a painting. Only our second day out of New York, and already it felt as if we were in a different country.

In Ellesworth we stopped at a McDonald's that offered a lobster salad sandwich for $3.49. But we weren't the least bit tempted, since we'd seen restaurants offering fresh-caught lobster and complete lobster dinners for $7.99.

Coming into Bar Harbor, we saw another black person for the first time since leaving New York. His back was turned to us, and he was bending over a steaming cauldron outside the Chowder House. Instinctively, we thought about turning around and going back to talk with him, but our desire to see the park was greater and we decided to keep going.

Bar Harbor is undoubtedly one of the most beautiful cities in the country. The easternmost town in Maine, on the shores of the Atlantic, its one and two-story white buildings stood out sharply against the green mountain background. We took Route 3 into Acadia, sandwiched between the brilliant blue sea and the looming mountains, and caught a dramatic view around every corner. A panorama of colorful lobster traps bobbed in the water. Large gulls called and fished just beyond the tide pools. The deep green of the forest looked like a skirt around the bald-faced mountains.

We had just one dilemma—what should we explore first? We chose the scenic drive to the top of Cadillac Mountain, the highest peak on the eastern seaboard. To our amazement, we met bicyclists barreling down the steep, winding road, apparently oblivious to the danger. I sank deeper into the comfort of the truck, appreciating its substantial metal frame around my body. The road rose steadily and we emerged at last above the clouds, yet still the road led upward.

When we finally reached the top, it literally took our breath away. We were surrounded by a world so gorgeous and radiant, it could hardly be believed. On one side, the sunlit ocean merged with the infinite sky. On the other side, the sun glinted on a dozen leafy offshore islands, turning the water into gold. Everywhere we looked were large swaths of blue and green.

Among the visitors was a black woman from New York, who told us she had come on a bus tour, and that she definitely planned to come back. We chatted with her for a while and then drove back down the mountain to find a campsite.

Acadia has two campgrounds, Blackwoods and Seawall, and both were full that day. Bar Harbor caters to millions of tourists who visit Acadia every year and we could easily stay in a cottage in town for about $50 per night. But we were eager to start camping, so we headed back to town and chose campgrounds along US 1. We picked out a nice, secluded campsite, close enough to the bathroom in case we had to make a midnight run, but far enough not to be disturbed by others making the same trek.

I had never camped before and had no idea how to set up a tent. But Frank had carefully selected our small tent weighing only six pounds, and set it up and waterproofed it before we left home. He gave me instructions and I was able to follow them easily. It took even less effort than I expected. The bathroom had hot and cold water, and our site had a barbecue grill, a picnic table and room enough for the truck.

We had comfortable sleeping bags because Frank had done the research and bought the kind rated for 32 degrees and above. We put foam pads underneath to cushion them, and when we snuggled into the tent, it still left room for our shoes, clothes, a flashlight and the Bowie knife Frank had bought for the trip. We left the tent flap open and went to sleep with a sky full of stars imprinted on our minds, happy that we had realized part of our dream with so little effort. We were already experiencing more of the country in a more intimate and personal way than all the years we had traveled from city to city by plane.

Next morning, we woke up to a cacophony of wildness. Birds sang all around us in the trees, and we could identify the raucous calls of blue jays and crows. Squirrels raced up the pine trees and small animals scurried in the undergrowth. The smell of bacon and perking coffee melded with the smoky wood aromas wafting through the forest. Yes indeed, we had found paradise. I had never felt more carefree and at ease.

Chapter 2:
The Heavenly Realms
of Acadia National Park

Frank started a fire and we made a quick breakfast of bacon and eggs. We tried out our coffeepot and ate leisurely, savoring our first camping experience. To make certain we got a campsite in Acadia, we headed there as soon as we cleaned up. Our luck was holding and we got a site in Blackwoods for only $17. We set up our tent then took off on foot to explore the park.

At 40,000 acres, Acadia covers most of the Schoodic Peninsula and Mount Desert Island. Cadillac Mountain in any setting would be irresistible, so the addition of forest and the churning Atlantic Ocean makes it as close to heaven as I can imagine. We felt reverent as we walked along Eagle Lake, watching for beavers in the water and absorbing the sounds of the forest. Or maybe the forest absorbed us. A tension I didn't even know I had been carrying slipped away from me. I recognized it only by its departure. My nerves became calm. I sunk into the natural rhythm of the earth, breathing in the fresh air, feeling the breeze on my face.

Just before dusk, we drove to the top of Cadillac Mountain again to meet other photographers for a "sunset shoot." Frank brought out his Nikon 8008S and immediately fell in with the other photographers, all of whom were white. The sun descended from the heavens in a blaze of white light, once again turning the water into shimmering gold. Who wouldn't want to be here every day?

The park brochure described how the rich industrialists who owned the land had seen fit to put it into conservation in the early 1900s when they saw development creeping up. The Rockefellers, Vanderbilts and Carnegies all owned summer homes here, and John D. Rockefeller Jr. donated 11,000 acres of his estate to be preserved for the public's enjoyment. We strolled along the old carriage paths and soaked up the atmosphere favored by writers and artists since the 1800s. Late afternoon, we left the park to take a drive in the countryside.

When we came to the first roadside stand with fruit, vegetables, firewood and a jar with money on the table, we looked around in amazement. Where was the owner? A price list was pasted to the jar. We passed that one, thoroughly confused, and came upon another, and another, all of them unattended. We couldn't stop laughing as we thought about how something like this would play out where we came from. A minute in Miami and it'd be all over. But when in Rome, do as the Romans do... so we picked out fresh tomatoes and cucumbers, put our two quarters in the jar and left.

When we got back to our campsite, the family next door came by and introduced themselves. They were nearing the end of their stay and still had firewood, so they brought it all over and we built a huge campfire. We sat around it talking deep into the night, and no one would guess that we weren't old friends. Drinking wine, staring into the dancing flames under the vast starry canopy, I felt as if my body had plugged back into some elemental force. I felt as safe and serene as when I was growing up and still believed the adults around me could fix everything.

We spent two days exploring the park, hiking, sightseeing and taking photographs. Then, our senses calmed and satisfied, we headed out of town toward Canada. Suddenly, we saw that same black man again! It was 11:30 in the morning and he was outside the Chowder House raising the flags and getting ready for the day. Frank made a quick U-turn. As we got out of the truck, he came toward us, his face beaming. He introduced himself as James Raines.

"Are you related to Tim Raines in the major leagues?" Frank asked.

"My uncle," James smiled. "Why don't you guys come on in and I'll cook you up a couple of lobsters?"

Well, it was almost lunchtime, and how often would we get invited to eat fresh-caught lobster fixed by a brother who's a master of the art?

I winced when he threw two pound-and-a-half lobsters into the steaming cauldron, which he told us was "just the right combination" of fresh water and cooking water from the day before.

"They didn't feel a thing!" he laughed.

The atmosphere was casual and laid back. Our exuberant waiter/host kept us laughing with his stories. When we told James we had driven from Florida and were going around the country, he was excited and mentioned that his hometown was Fort Pierce, Florida. He said he came to Maine with his girlfriend, and now that they had a baby they had decided to stay close to her family.

"So what do you do in winter?" I asked, shivering at the thought of a snowbound Maine winter.

"You see that great big stove there?" he asked, pointing to a huge iron contraption in the middle of the room. "In winter, my butt doesn't get too far from it."

We gorged on two succulent lobsters, corn, coleslaw and rolls, and the check came to $17. We met some great people, laughed and shared stories, and we coasted out of there on a wave of positive energy, looking forward to the next adventure around the corner.

Invigorated for the trip across the country to the Pacific Coast, we decided to take a short detour up to Canada to visit my other childhood friend (also named Audrey) and her family. We reached the Canadian border around nightfall, and since we weren't in a hurry and didn't want to miss the views, we decided to stay overnight in Champlain.

We checked into the first motel we came to. They didn't take credit cards, which should have given us a clue, but we were tired and had cash, so we didn't see it as a problem. Next morning when we woke up and went outside, we could hardly believe our eyes. The motel was so dilapidated, we couldn't tell whether it was propping up the run-down building next door, or vice versa. Incongruously, both decrepit structures sat on the banks of Lake Champlain, which sparkled in the sunlight. We had spent the night in a version of the Bates Motel.

"God really does take care of dumb things and animals," I said to Frank. But we'd survived the night, and we were full of energy and enthusiasm, raring to go.

I popped into a convenience store to get some coffee. While I was making it, I remarked to the man making tea nearby that I had a sudden craving for a bagel. "Oh, but you'd have to get cream cheese and lox," he said. Then he called the attendant over to help him, explaining that he was trying to make tea for his traveling companion, who was still asleep. The attendant opened the microwave door and found the rotator broken. Immediately, she began speaking in French and he responded in the same language. Next thing I knew, they were having an animated conversation in French, and I'm thinking, wait a minute, we're still in New York!

I remarked on how odd I found it, and the woman told me she was originally from Montreal but she'd married an American 29 years earlier and they settled in the States.

"How did you meet?" I was curious.

She laughed. "My aunt did the same thing. She married an American, and she had a big party for all his American relatives, and that's how my husband and I met. History repeats itself," she chuckled.

When we arrived in Toronto and found that it looked like any major American city, I was a little disappointed. We had visited Frank's cousin Braddie and his family in Holland a few years earlier and gone on a tour of Europe, gaping in awe at the old town squares in London, Paris, Amsterdam and Antwerp. So I had been expecting Canada to look very different from America. Still, we spent a couple of happy days with Audrey, her Canadian husband Scott, and their two young children. Then we were off again, footloose and carefree, headed for Niagara Falls on the Canadian side.

I'm certain that if we'd seen Niagara before we saw Acadia, we'd have been awed by the power of the falls. But now it felt like a managed Disney experience, compared to the wild natural beauty we'd just discovered. Within hours, we were back in the faithful Ford, heading for Chicago and Frank's Aunt Eva's house.

We drove leisurely through the New York countryside, seeing mostly farmlands, talking about our childhood and the wonderful experiences we had had growing up. Both of us had been strongly influenced by our grandparents. Frank's mom and dad had grown up in Abbeville, a very rural part of Alabama, where Frank was born. When his parents decided to move to Fort Lauderdale, Frank's maternal grandparents would not hear of them taking the baby to that "alligator 'fested place," so he remained in Alabama for his first few years. At age four his parents were allowed to take him to Fort Lauderdale, but every summer after that he went back to Abbeville on vacation, spending his time with his grandfather and his uncles roaming the woods.

"My grandfather would collect roots and plants that he'd use to make medicines, and people in the village would come to him for help with whatever their ailments were," he recalled. "By the time I was 12, I had my own .22 caliber rifle, but the men in my family taught me that I shouldn't point a gun at anything I didn't plan to shoot, and I shouldn't shoot anything I didn't plan to eat. We used to shoot possums for dinner, and my Grandma cooked them with sweet potatoes. It was so good."

I grew up with my Grandma Ida in Summerfield, a small village in Jamaica so remote that when I took Frank there after we got married, he said to me, "Honey, you told me you were from the country, but I had no idea there was *this much country* in the world."

The 13-mile drive from the nearest major city, May Pen, took us almost an hour on a torturously winding highway. In some places there were potholes so deep that they had trees growing out of them, and vehicles coming from either direction had to negotiate the same narrow band of road.

"Even the potholes have potholes," he joked.

But he was astonished to see how close knit the community was. Although I had not been back to the village for almost 20 years since my grandmother died, it was like a great homecoming when I returned. From the village shopkeeper, Brother Cecil, and his wife, Sister Mulvena's store where my grandmother had bought our groceries every Saturday, everyone remembered me and the news traveled like wildfire.

"Ruby come home!" people I met exclaimed, calling me by my pet name.

When we went to my grandfather's property where I'd spent my formative years, nobody was home, so I took Frank down to the little stream that ran behind the property. As a child I used to bathe naked in the "gully" with all the other children. Mango and rose apple trees hanging over the water dropped their fruit liberally into the gully, and we would bob for them and come up eating the most succulent, fresh mango, with the juice running down our cheeks. As I led Frank along the riverbanks and into the orange grove, trying to find the property line so I could show him where my grandfather's property ended, I felt someone watching. I looked up and saw a man standing just above us. "Oh, excuse me," I began. "Are we trespassing?"

"I believe so," he said sternly.

"Well, I'm Mr. Butler's granddaughter…" I began.

Before I could finish, he said,

"Ruby? Ruby that went to Clarendon College then went to work at the Gleaner Company then went away to America and never came back?"

Got me! Just like that, he'd recited my entire history.

Frank was fascinated by this place I came from where everyone knew everyone else several generations back. We both agreed that our grandparents and the environment in which we were raised had indeed "given us wings."

Our leisurely reminiscence was interrupted by the sudden appearance of an angel by the side of the road. The exquisitely beautiful young Amish woman was selling vegetables from her horse and buggy. She wore no makeup and her face radiated health and wholesomeness. Frank wanted to take her picture, but when he asked her permission, she politely declined. We bought some fresh corn, not caring that we didn't need it, just because we wanted to be in her presence and support her.

When we arrived at Aunt Eva's, some of Frank's cousins came by to see us. Frank's mom had evidently told her sister about the foolhardy mission we were on, and everyone wanted to know what the heck we were doing. One cousin took Frank aside and offered him a pistol, but Frank reassured him that we weren't afraid and once again declined. After another round of parties and visits we were off, now truly headed for the Wild Wild West.

Passing through Green Bay, Wisconsin, the cheese capital of America, we stocked up on a variety of cheeses, got some fresh bread and restocked our cooler with fruit, vegetables, meats, wine and beer. Crossing the Mighty Mississippi into Minnesota, with dusk approaching, we found ourselves in a remote area where there were no signs of lodging. Finally, we came upon a sign that announced "O.L. Kipp State Park" coming up, with campsites four miles off the highway. Hallelujah! We turned onto the narrow dirt road and drove for what felt like 10 miles, with no sign of the park. My stomach started to tighten up a bit for the first time since we left home. Where the heck was this place? It was getting darker. We didn't know what lay ahead, and it would be a long drive back to the highway if we didn't find the campgrounds.

I looked over at Frank and knew he might be feeling the same thing, but both of us chatted away as if we were sitting in our living room. No one would have guessed that we were at all disturbed. We knew it was important not to give in to fear, and if one of us cracked, that would just put more of a burden on the other's shoulders. But we were incredibly relieved when we finally reached that park!

It was perched on a bluff overlooking the Mississippi River Valley. The park brochure said it included 3,000 acres of "half-dome bluffs with sheer rock cliffs and steep valley walls" on the banks of the Mississippi. We set up our tent, exchanged pleasantries with other campers who passed by, built a fire on the grill, fixed our meal and then sat outside with a glass of wine, gazing at the stars.

We'd turned in for the night and were just falling asleep when we heard a delicate sound, like tinkling crystal, passing over our tent. Huh? The sound dissipated into the air, and then it came again, starting subtly and then building into a crescendo before slowly fading away. Was it raining? It couldn't be rain… we had never heard any rain like this. After a few minutes we rolled out of the tent to witness a night that Frank described as "lifted from the pages of a Gothic romantic novel."

A full moon in a clear sky lit up the woods. Moonbeams danced off the gleaming white bark of the quaking aspen trees that surrounded our tent. As the wind passed through the leaves, it created the tinkling sound that had lured us from the tent. In the distance, a coyote (or a wolf?) howled. The sounds of the animal, the trees and the river joined in an unearthly concert. We sat outside for a long time enjoying the setting and each other's company. We wouldn't trade this experience for anything. This night would live in our minds forever.

Chapter 3:
Unearthly Formations
in Badlands National Park

After breakfast the next morning, we took a leisurely walk into the woods overlooking the river and saw that there was a marina on the other bank, with colorful riverboats tied up. The park has effigy mounds, graves resembling animals built by Native American cultures that lived in the area over thousands of years. By mid-morning we broke camp and were in the truck again, heading west. We measured the distance back to the highway and sure enough, it was four miles. I guess that proves "country miles" really are longer.

A third of the way across the country, we were plumbing not just the American heartland, but our own heart space as well. In the intimacy of the cab, with the long road undulating ahead of us, we had the time and opportunity to share everything. I have complete confidence in Frank, not just in his fidelity, but also in the caliber of his mind, so talking about my childhood and hearing his analysis broadened my perspective on my own life, and he said I did the same for him.

Shortly after we got married, he'd told me, "Honey, there are three of us in this relationship…"

"Stop right there," I'd said in alarm. "What do you mean three?"

"I mean there's you, there's me, and then there's the relationship," he finished. "The relationship is a living thing itself, and that means we have to be careful of the words we use to each other, how we talk to each other, and how we treat each other…"

Okay, that made sense. He also warned that each of us was likely to "get crazy" at one time or another, so when that happened, the other one had to make certain to remain perfectly calm. If we both flew off the handle at the same time, things may be said in the heat of the moment that couldn't be taken back.

Boy, was I lucky, I thought. This was my first marriage and I felt that I benefited a lot from Frank's experience in his two previous marriages. My parents had not married, and my grandparents got divorced shortly after I was born, so I had no examples of what a successful marriage would look like. At 20 I'd had my daughter Lisa, but her father and I hadn't gotten married either, and before Frank, I'd felt that there really was no need to get married. Who needs to wake up to the same person year after year?

Now I was more blissfully happy than I would have thought possible. Frank was happy, too. You really get to know if you like each other when you're stuck in the cab of a truck for weeks and weeks, even if it is by choice. This trip was paying dividends we couldn't have foreseen.

We had drunk in the heart-stopping beauty of mountains and ocean, raging waterfalls, vast acres of farmlands, green countryside and marveled at a series of small oval hills covered in golden grass that we passed in Wisconsin. But we had yet to see the dramatic "Wild, Wild, West" of buttes and mountains and plateaus immortalized in the movies. As we drove into South Dakota, we could hardly contain ourselves knowing that we'd soon be in the realm of the "Badlands."

Excitement turned to astonishment and then to annoyance when we started seeing the garish signs proclaiming "Wall Drugs" breaking up the placid scenery every couple of miles. Finally Frank said to me, "Honey, I don't care if I get gored by a bison, butted by bighorn sheep, run down by a pronghorn antelope or bit by a rabid black-footed ferret. I'd rather die than get drugs from that place."

And then we saw the sign for Badlands National Park. We turned a corner and drove off the road, and into an unearthly panorama. The effect was so powerful that it took our breath away. I'm sure I had my mouth hanging open for several minutes. When I recovered, I saw that Frank was lost in his own reverie. This, after all, was the vision that had drawn us all this way.

Were we on a different planet? Yes, this was Earth, but it was the most amazing color and shaped in more fantastic contours than I could ever have imagined. On one side of the valley, rainbow-colored mountains rose up in a solid wall, sculpted by nature into pyramids and temples. In the center of the valley, stretching away to infinity, a tableau of smaller monuments were connected at the base and reared up into individual spires. All around as far as we could see was an otherworldly landscape of beauty and wonder.

It closely resembled the pictures I'd seen of the Valley of the Kings in

Egypt. The Egyptians had built their enduring monuments more than 5,000 years ago, and the forces of nature had carved this scene over more than 75 million years. The action of continental plates and the eruption of the adjoining Rocky Mountains, receding water and climactic changes over eons had produced this solid, ever-changing phenomenon. But the explanation of "how" it happened is a crumb compared to the sensory smorgasbord of seeing it. And who could reveal how ancient civilizations that presumably never saw this place had replicated it in their culture?

"It reminds me of the Temples of Angkor Wat in Cambodia, or the pyramids in Egypt and Central America," Frank marveled.

The Badlands National Park covers more than a quarter of a million acres, and includes an extensive scenic driving trail. The park brochure said there were great places to hike and such, but we were so overcome by the sheer scale and enormity of this otherworldly view, that it was all we could do to rouse ourselves to take photographs. It was hard to reconcile this phenomenon as part of the same everyday world we inhabited. I knew I would never again be able to take the earth I walked on for granted.

Frank was glowing with the satisfaction of finally being in the place that had played such a prominent role in his childhood fantasies. Like most boys growing up in the' 40s, cowboy movies were his favorites and "cowboys and Indians" his favorite game.

"Oh yeah! I can see the cowboys thundering through these treacherous passages on their powerful horses, going after the bad guys," he grinned.

It was acutely satisfying to have fulfilled this part of his dream. What was a vague idea two years earlier in Belize was realized in the very fact of our being there, standing on that ground while our senses absorbed stimulation from sources we couldn't even define. It was as if the place had a life of its own, as if some ancient timeless spirit resided there.

Just seeing that view bolstered our conviction that we had done the right thing … there was no way to have an experience like this other than to go out there and see it. And all it cost us was a little bit of planning and frugality, and the confidence that we could do it.

The Badlands cover such an extensive area that as we drove miles into the spectacular Black Hills toward Mount Rushmore National Memorial, we could still see the bewitching panorama behind us. The sooty Black

Hills loomed high and craggy, looking like ancient Native American elders who had survived eons in the natural elements. We had read that the Black Hills was a sacred landscape to many Indian nations, and that some regard the Black Hills as the center of the world. The area was so remote, the peaks so towering and timeless, that we could practically absorb their spirituality by osmosis.

So it was quite shocking to round a corner and suddenly come upon the faces of four white men carved into the highest peak. The American presidents loomed from the top of the mountain, coldly elegant and supreme over all they surveyed. It really gave me a chill. I was struck by the skill and ingenuity that had erected the monuments, working in treacherous conditions hanging off the face of the mountain, using chisels to create such precise features. But I shuddered at the thought of the stark imperialism that the monument communicated, because the Native people had fought it with their entire beings. I knew the story of how the Lakotas had refused to sell their land to the American government, with Lakota chief Sitting Bull stating that he "would not sell so much as a pinch of dust." The U.S. had won the resulting Great Sioux War against a combined force of Lakota, Northern Cheyenne and Arapaho tribes, but the tribes held firmly to their ties to the land and considered the monument a desecration.

The very fact that a monument to Europeans could have been successfully erected in the heart of Indian country illustrated the balance of power, and the faces on the mountain reinforced it on a daily basis.

The sculptor Gutzon Borglum had envisioned the monument as a great American icon that would serve as a message from the culture that had built it, much like the Great Pyramid or the Sphinx. He wanted to store information about the four presidents—Washington, Jefferson, Lincoln, and Theodore Roosevelt—as well as the Declaration of Independence and the U.S. Constitution in a vault behind the presidents' heads. Between 1927 and 1941, approximately 400 people labored under his instruction to create the monument.

The monument was in the process of being repaired, with a network of scaffolding running up its sides, and the pleasure we'd had in the great outdoors was not to be had here. We were eager for the adventures that lay ahead of us in the Wild West, and after a brief visit to the Visitor

Center, we got back on the road. And that's when we came upon the wildlife "jam."

Rounding a blind curve, we ran into a crowd of people and vehicles partially blocking the road. Frank screeched to a halt, and we saw the reason for the commotion: A family of three mountain goats was feeding near the side of the road. Larger than the goats we're accustomed to, they had beautiful, thick white fur coats. There was a billy, a nanny goat and a kid. A dozen or more people were in the middle of the road, stopping traffic in both directions as they converged on the goats to get photos. The billy goat began to get agitated as people pressed closer, and he kept himself firmly between the crowd and his family. After a few minutes his patience wore out and he herded his family back up the mountain and disappeared in the forest. At long last we had seen our first large wild animals in their natural habitat.

The road into Wyoming led us past Devil's Tower National Monument, a tremendous rock formation shaped like a tower, standing with imperial grandeur in the middle of the valley floor. Legend holds that the tower reared up from the valley to save two children from a bear that was chasing them. The children scrambled up on the rock and it began to grow and kept growing, lifting the children out of harm's way. Devils Tower is a sacred setting of the Native Americans for prayers, vision quests and healing ceremonies. Even though we were miles away, we could see it clearly silhouetted, more than 1200 feet straight up. Such is the magic of the western countryside.

A little farther west, an enormous mountain face was being carved into a monument of Lakota Chief Crazy Horse, who defeated General Custer at Little Big Horn. The sculpture will be so huge that it will dwarf the Great Pyramid of Giza and the Statue of Liberty. Crazy Horse's head alone will be 87.5 feet tall, capable of holding all four of the presidents' heads on Mount Rushmore. We were tempted to detour to see it, but we really wanted to get to Yellowstone and promised ourselves that we'd come back to see the monument when it was complete.

Chapter 4:

Yellowstone – The American Serengeti

We finally stopped in Gillette, Wyoming for the night and stayed at the Ramada Inn, which was conveniently close to the highway. But after we registered, we discovered that it was hunting season and there were scores of hunters dressed in camouflage staying in the hotel, with guns and testosterone aplenty. This environment wouldn't have been our first choice if we'd known, but we didn't feel vulnerable and for one night, we could put up with just about anything.

Frank wanted a beer, so we walked out to the convenience store at the gas station. The friendly clerk told us they didn't sell beer, and we could only get it from the bar a little farther away. He gave us directions and we found the place with no trouble. We opened the door and stepped inside, and for a moment, everything froze. Time skipped a beat, and even the jukebox seemed to hiccup. I don't know who was more surprised – the people inside or Frank and me. Every head in the room swiveled to look at us.

For a second we stood frozen at the door. Then, almost like puppets on a string, Frank and I moved together and walked nonchalantly to the bar.

Just like that, the tension eased, and the eyes turned away. I guess it was as much a shock to the white patrons to see two black people walk in the door as it was for us to see their reaction. The perky barmaid restored normalcy, chatting with us in a friendly manner and asking where we were headed. When we told her, she said she was very jealous, because she hadn't had a chance to see much of the west, or even much of the area where she lived. We got our beer and got out of there.

Next morning we took off early, covering another 250 miles to reach Cody, Wyoming by evening. This charming town at the foot of the Yellowstone Mountains is a gateway to the very first national park established in the world. We checked into the campground closest to town, and went to set up our tent. When we found signs that, until very recently, the campground may have been used as a pasture, we couldn't stop laughing. But it wasn't offensive, and dozens of other families were camping in tents and trailers nearby.

It was as if we'd stepped into a cowboy movie when we went into town, except that this was the real thing. Cody was founded by Buffalo Bill Cody and was the hometown of his Buffalo Bill's Wild West Show and Exhibition. A new museum commemorating his legacy had just opened. We window-shopped and soaked up the western atmosphere, making sure to get back to our campsite and turn in early. We wanted to be well rested to tackle Yellowstone next morning.

We broke camp by 7 a.m. and drove up to McDonald's for breakfast. It was already crowded with tourists headed for Yellowstone, and the atmosphere was festive, as if we were all on a pilgrimage. We hadn't seen any other black people in the town, and the young man who served us was so nervous his hands trembled. It may have been his first day on the job or maybe he'd only seen black people on TV. The last time we'd seen any black people was in Wisconsin, and that was three days and three states ago.

Before we left Fort Lauderdale, I knew subconsciously that there were few black people in places like Maine and Montana, but it was a completely different thing to see that such large areas of the country had no visible racial diversity. With our coasts so racially diverse, and the middle so homogenous, it practically looked like two different countries. What influence did this have on our politics and culture, and how could we all get along if we didn't actually know each other?

With that bit of philosophizing on my mind, we pulled onto the road and joined the long line of adventurers heading up the mountain into the 2.2 million-acre park. The road ran through the Wapiti Valley along Buffalo Bill Cody's Scenic Byway. We drove through tunnels in the mountains and emerged beside a serene mountain lake. The road climbed higher and higher, seeming barely wide enough for two vehicles to pass, and there was a sheer drop down to the river. There was no guardrail. My palms began to sweat and my heart started to pound. I imagined that Frank must be feeling queasy too, and he was behind the wheel. I worked hard to control my anxiety, and we kept our voices pleasant and conversational. By the time we got to the top of the mountain, I was drained.

A park ranger was just getting ready to remove the barrier and open the gates when a large, red-faced man driving a big, white Cadillac barreled to the front of the line. He was gesticulating wildly and yelling at the ranger to move faster.

Frank looked at the short, red-haired ranger with a gun on his hip and said, "Oh, boy! This guy must be drunk."

The ranger calmly motioned the man out of line and made him park off the road. The line began moving and we passed them, the visitor still gesturing angrily.

As we drove into the park, we saw large areas of downed pine trees with roots still blackened from a fire. Frank recalled that the fire of 1988 had burned nearly one million acres in and around Yellowstone. A sign indicated we were entering the Lower Geyser Basin, and suddenly, we were in a different world.

While the Badlands had been hot and dry, the earth ahead of us was boiling. Columns of vapor curled over the tops of the trees. In places the ground was so brittle it had the consistency of potato chips, and boiling jets of water burst through. The towering forests sheltered a landscape that boiled and steamed as if stoked by the fires of hell.

"Old Faithful" was the only geyser I'd ever heard of, so I was stunned to see that there were scores of geysers all around. At Yellowstone, the superheated interior core of the earth is relatively close to the surface, and molten rock is just two miles underfoot. This "magma" superheats the underground water so that it bursts out in a geothermal wonderland of geysers, hot springs and mud pots. The world's largest collection of geysers and two-thirds of all the geysers in the entire world are in Yellowstone.

We parked in front of the famous Old Faithful Lodge, a graceful building of wood and stone built during the age of railroad travel to attract wealthy tourists. As Frank was getting his camera bag out of the trunk, a heavyset white man hurried over to talk to us. He said he was a reporter from Germany living in the U.S., and he wanted to hear all about our experiences on the road. Apparently, we were the first black people he had seen in the national parks. We chatted for a few minutes and told him we were really in a hurry to get to the geyser. We couldn't miss Old Faithful the first time it went off while we were in the park.

Dozens of people were sitting on benches in front of Old Faithful, waiting for the geyser to blow. Excitement tinged the air. The benches were close enough for us to get the full effect without being scalded by exploding water.

Adults and children alike keep asking, "When is the next show?" The park estimates that Old Faithful blows approximately every 81 minutes, up from about 60 minutes at the beginning of the 20th century. Frank found a spot away from the crowd to set up the tripod and camera so he could get good photos. Luckily, someone warned him he was right in the path of the steam and vapors.

"Trust me, I'd have no hesitation leaving my equipment behind," he said, moving to a safer spot.

Minutes later, we saw a young boy dangling his feet in the very same place. Frank passed on the warning and the child's mother got him out of the way.

Then it happened. First little spurts pumped from the geyser. It became a little more frenzied, followed by a pregnant pause that froze us in anticipation. Suddenly, like a rocket leaving a cloud of white vapor, there was steam and water shooting 80, 100, 150 feet into the clear blue sky! A collective "Aw-w-w!" rose from the crowd. Then, it was over.

A boy who looked like he was about 10, lying on one of the benches asked disappointedly, "Is that it?"

Frank and I looked at each other. We wanted to tell him that this was not a Disney show, but an awesome display of the earth's power and majesty. He'd probably seen movies and cartoons with more dramatic special effects on TV, and had no way of appreciating the difference between what was make-believe and what was real.

We walked along the boardwalk and gazed into a number of small pools in which the water was a dazzling aquamarine. We learned that microbes and bacteria harvested from these pools were proving useful in research for cancer treatments. Plentiful signs warned visitors to stay on the boardwalk because the ground was unstable. It was amazing to me how the huge buffalo and bears had survived in this environment.

Around noon we walked back to the Visitor Center. To our surprise, our German friend was waiting for us and came forward, beaming with pleasure. He said he'd been looking for us all morning. Apparently, in our hurry to see "Old Faithful" erupt, we had left our keys in the lock in back of the truck! Our Good Samaritan had taken them to the Visitor Center and wanted to let us know. We thanked him profusely. It was our only key, and we were a very long way from roadside service.

We were laughing about how it should have been easy to find us, since we were apparently the only two black people in the park, when we realized what that meant. Of several hundred visitors we'd seen so far, not one of them was black. Or Latino! Or Asian-American! And where were the Native Americans? It gave us a chill when we realized that in all this time, we hadn't seen any of America's sons and daughters who were "minorities." There were hundreds of Japanese tourists, and we heard many European accents in the sea of white faces, but essentially, we were the only two "chocolate chips" in this cookie.

No sooner had this fact dawned on us, than another startling realization followed right on its heels. We were standing outside the lodge when Frank, looking over at a scorched area on the hillside, mused out loud: "I bet that was burned in the fire of '88…"

An older man standing next to us chimed in, "Yes, it was." He introduced himself and said he was from Chicago and had just retired. "When my father brought me here," he continued, "they were building over there, and when I brought my son, they were building that."

I saw a shadow pass across Frank's face, and later he told me why.

"You know, I don't live my life with regrets, but when he said that, I really felt that I missed something by not taking my children to this place. That man and his son have a family tradition here; they feel a sense of ownership of this country. I didn't have that, and neither do my children."

"So now we'll take all our children and grandchildren," I said blithely. I completely understood the difference it would make to have the imprint of so much beauty of the spirit from a very young age, and a sense of ownership as a result of seeing these spectacular places.

Driving deeper into this wildlife preserve, I confess I screamed when I saw my first elk, a magnificent male with a huge rack of antlers, grazing near the road. He looked at us with interest, and went back to eating. We pulled off the road to watch him for a few minutes. Shortly after we got back into the truck, we came upon an entire herd of the sleek animals. A moose crossed the road in front of us, as large as a horse and dusky black, with legs that looked too thin to hold up its bulk.

A little farther down the road, we came upon a "bear jam"—a traffic jam caused when a bear is spotted and the cars stop practically in the middle of the road so everyone can watch it. The crowd was large and the road was narrow. It didn't look like the safest place to stop, and we decided we'd have to wait until later to see our first bear.

Rounding a curve, we passed a large wooden sign announcing we were in "Buffalo Ford." We did not have to wonder how the place got its name. All around us on both sides of the road were buffalo: little ones, big ones, dark ones, tawny ones, buffalo of every imaginable description. They were all on the road, in the road, blocking traffic and taking their leisurely time.

When we finally tore ourselves away from observing the buffalo we pulled into a picnic area and ate the last of our food. Large, raucous crows and bold gray jays let us know they were around and they were there for the food. But park rules forbid feeding wildlife, so we enjoyed their calls and antics without any guilt.

No wonder Yellowstone is known as the "American Serengeti." I had never in my life seen so much wildlife, and all together in one place!

The road between Cody and the park was under repair, and we'd been warned that the no one would be allowed down the mountain until 4 p.m. After a full day in this enchanted place, we drove back to the entrance 30 minutes early. There were only a few cars ahead of us. When the gates opened, the lead car slowly started down the mountain. The driver maintained the same slow pace, well below the speed limit, for the entire drive. I completely sympathized. We were driving on the very edge of the mountain, and it was a long, hard way down the side!

Rainforest and Marine Treasures in Olympic National Park

We bid goodbye to Wyoming and started through Idaho en route to Washington State. Before we left home, we'd agreed that we wouldn't drive more than 500 miles a day and that each of us had veto power. If one of us didn't feel comfortable with anything, we only had to say so, and there'd be no need for an explanation. We had covered more than 3,000 miles and neither of us had vetoed anything. But that changed when we got to Idaho.

Late afternoon we were driving through a heavily wooded area, and a sign advertised a campground on the banks of a river. It looked like a great place to camp, but the minute we turned in, I started feeling uncomfortable. I told Frank that I didn't think we should stay. He said he felt the same way, and we immediately turned around and drove back to the highway.

It may have had something to do with the fact that the O.J. Simpson trial was going on and Mark Fuhrman, a white detective in the controversial case, had taken refuge in Idaho among people who were reportedly biased against Blacks. I was a little embarrassed to feel this way, but "my mama didn't raise no fool," and neither did Frank's. Whatever the reason, discretion was the better part of valor. We were so spooked that we drove another 200 miles to Spokane, Washington and checked into a hotel.

Next morning, we went to gas up and saw an enticing array of food on hot trays at the gas-station/convenience store. It all looked so appetizing, I was suddenly ravenous and ordered some of everything. It tasted terrible! Even the coffee was so bad that I was relieved when I accidentally dropped my paper cup. That would be the last time I had any gas station food.

As we drove into Seattle, we got our first heart-stopping view of Mount Rainier. It looked like a giant snow cone, or a benevolent God looming over the city. We were headed to Olympic National Park on the farthest end of the Olympic Peninsula. We drove the truck onto a ferry that took us across Puget Sound. It had an enclosed deck so we could enjoy the breathtaking views of mountains and greenery sweeping down to the water. As the Seattle skyline receded behind us we basked in the satisfaction of having made it all the way from the Atlantic to the Pacific, and were now thoroughly familiar with what lay between. The land had proven to be so varied and exciting that we could hardly wait to see what lay ahead in this part of the country.

Straight off the ferry we took Highway 101, meandering for miles through the forest. About nightfall we reached the town of Forks, and pulled into the Towne Motel, attracted by the lavish flowers growing all around it. We got a nice efficiency and a warm welcome for less than $40. After a restful night, we woke up early next morning and continued north, eventually arriving at the Hoh Rainforest. I never even knew that there was a rainforest in America! We drove between large trees that seemed to reach the sky. Sunlight filtered through the branches, gleaming off the leaves and lighting up the forest floor. Garlands of moss decorated the branches. The undergrowth was lush with the largest ferns I'd ever seen. It felt as if we'd wandered into a fairy tale.

At the Visitor Center we learned that the Olympic peninsula gets more rainfall annually than almost any other place in the U.S., which explains the Hoh and two other temperate rainforests in the park. Many of the large wild animals that lived on the North American continent before the Europeans arrived still reign in Olympic, including black, brown and grizzly bears; cougar, bobcat, elk and black-tailed deer. When we saw warning instructions about what to do if we encountered a bear, (make yourself look smaller and non-threatening, or fall into the fetal position and lock your hands behind your neck) or if you see a cougar, (make yourself look larger, indomitable) we laughed. What if we got our signals crossed and treated the bear like we should treat the cougar? As urban people to whom these large wild animals are completely foreign, we felt no fear, but we resolved to take sensible precautions such as not wandering off the trail or going into the woods by ourselves.

For lodging, we had our choice of the Kalaloch Lodge or Kalaloch campgrounds above the beach. We had lunch at the lodge, overlooking a wide stretch of the Pacific, with hummingbirds feeding at the window outside. But once we saw the campground, it won hands down.

The campgrounds sit on prime beachfront property, about 30 feet above a wide crescent of the Pacific beach. All the campsites overlooking the beach were already taken, so we chose one among the trees. We walked the couple of hundred feet to the beachside to watch the sunset, and Frank struck up a conversation with one of the lucky people who had a spot on that side. The young man told him he'd be leaving next morning, and offered to hold the spot for us until we got there.

At the edge of the beach, we were shocked to find warnings announcing, "Trees Kill!" Huh? They looked pretty friendly to me. It turned out that soil erosion wipes out the earth beneath some of the huge trees and they fall into the ocean. When the tide hurls them back to shore, they land on the beach with tremendous force. When we saw the size of the driftwood, we really appreciated the warning.

When the tide went out, we could walk almost a quarter of a mile out and the ocean barely came up to our knees. There were lots of rocks and tide pools filled with marine life that we could see up close. Scores of starfish, bigger than my hand, in bright pink and yellow, and emerald sea anemones, with their tentacles gently sweeping the water, were so close that it was all I could do not to touch them. Sea otters frolicked in the waves, eyeing the humans as we delighted in their antics.

Later, as the sun descended into an ocean of dazzling gold and innumerable stars stood out in the sky and the woodsy scent from a score of campfires wafted through the air while people and their dogs sat staring into the flickering flames, I felt a deep contentment. It was as if we had fallen back into an ancient ritual of community. The sense of Oneness was palpable.

Next morning Frank picked up our tent and walked it over to where our new friend was waiting until we arrived, literally holding the campsite for us. We passed a campsite with a large RV, sporting lots of protruding antennae. While a woman sitting outside applied her makeup, the man sitting next to her pointed to the tent Frank was carrying and said,

"See, honey? That's what I meant when I said 'Let's go camping.' "

The lady barely looked up from her mirror.

We set up our tent and went off to explore. First, we drove up to the Makah Indian Reservation at Neah Bay, at the farthest northwestern tip of the peninsula. We anticipated a robust and thriving Indian culture, but instead found signs of hard times. Many of the buildings were shuttered and an air of depression hung over the town. We didn't linger, driving instead to Ozette, where there was a three-mile boardwalk leading down to the Pacific on the other side of the peninsula. I was alone in the car for a moment when I spotted movement out of the corner of my eye. A bird unlike any I'd ever seen before was sitting on a post in front of me. It looked like a miniature peacock, with a striking crest of intense indigo. It was the size of a blue jay, and its color ranged through several shades of brilliant blue from its face to the tip of its tail. What a jewel! I watched in fascination until it took off with a loud squawk. It turned out that the bird was a Stellar's Jay, described in our Audubon Field guide as "the common crested jay west of the Rockies." It's hard to understand how anyone could describe any part of this bird as "common."

The trail down to the beach ran between berry bushes that were at their peak of ripeness. I wanted so badly to sample them, but Frank warned against it, because we didn't know which ones were edible. The trail eventually opened out on a wide sweep of beach where a colony of sea lions basked on the rocks just offshore. Campers were setting up tents in the woods at the edge of the beach, being careful to hang their food on lines up in the trees. There are a lot of bears in Olympic, and food draws them like a magnet.

Walking back to the parking lot later, we fell in with a group of Boy Scouts and started talking with the scoutmaster. He joked that this was as good a time as any to come upon a bear, because there were so many berries around that the bears would be too full to be interested in people. When he said that the wild blackberries and huckleberries were edible, I lost all restraint. Frank said later that I was stuffing small branches into one side of my mouth and disgorging sticks and seeds on the other. It's not a flattering picture, but it was probably accurate.

That evening, we watched Native American men casting for grunion, wading into the ocean to scoop up the small silver fish. An older man cast his shimmering net into the ocean, and a child who may have been his granddaughter watched in fascination from the shore, and then joined him in the water. The Olympic landscape felt like the real Jurassic Park, and its power was mystical and magical.

By now it had become routine to make our meals on a campground grill or on the little hibachi we set up on the tailgate. In no time, Frank could grill a steak marinated in plastic containers in our cooler or fresh fish that we had on ice. And I could whip up rice or potatoes in our single pot. The longer we stayed in the parks, the more we saw how little we really need the things that seem indispensable in our everyday lives. The experience was becoming more and more liberating.

At the end of a completely relaxing couple of days, our feelings had become so calm that we could truly appreciate the slogan for Olympic National Park, "a place for the soul to expand and for the mind to be refreshed with the beauty of life—a place of serendipitous discoveries..."

We took the ferry back to Seattle and picked up I-5 South to Portland, where we planned to visit some former neighbors from Florida, Beat and Myla Stauber. We'd met them in our apartment complex the year before, just as they were preparing to move to Portland. With boxes stacked to the ceiling and their pre-arranged help a "no-show," Frank and I'd pitched in and helped them load their U-Haul.

We crossed over to Pacific Highway 101, enjoying the view of the glittering ocean on one side and majestic green mountains on the other. We kept telling each other that it was OK to push on just a few more miles and by the time it started getting dark and we were ready to stop, there were no accommodations in sight.

Once again our luck held as we came to a sign announcing "Cape Blanco State Park, prime whale watching site." It had the symbol for campgrounds, so we were quite relieved. Maybe we'd even see our first whale in the wild!

We turned off the highway in the direction indicated, and here again we were traveling miles in the dark, with no park in sight. When I felt that tightening creeping into my stomach, I reminded myself how well things had turned out at O.L. Kipp State Park under similar circumstances. Still, it was a great comfort when we finally reached the campgrounds.

It was late, and the volunteers who run the site had turned in for the night. Envelopes were provided for latecomers like us, and we stuck the required $14 dollar fee in and dropped it into the slot. We set up our tent and went to sleep right away.

Next morning we discovered that the thickly wooded park was perched on a long, curving stretch of the Pacific. Frank immediately got out his camera and tripod and set off down the deserted crescent beach. I followed with binoculars, scanning the water for any sign of whales. After we picked up shells on the beach and drank in the view to our hearts' content, we returned to the campgrounds to find that we'd become minor celebrities.

There were no other African Americans in the campgrounds, and several of the other campers came by to talk with us. When they found that we had come from Florida and were traveling around the country, everyone wanted to share stories of their favorite experiences. A young American serviceman told us he was stationed in Hawaii and had planned his vacation so he could camp his way around the Northwest. He also confided that he had recently sustained a very serious injury and attributed his recovery to his devoted practice of Zen Buddhism.

We didn't see any whales, but we made a lot of new friends and shared a lot of stories. The volunteers told us that they spend their entire year moving from park to park as volunteers, as it allows them stay in some of the most beautiful places in the country practically for free!

Over and over again it struck us that nature is the great equalizer. In the supernatural beauty, among the multitude of natural processes all going on simultaneously, people seem to identify with each other as human beings, stripped of the masks of race, color or social status. This is how people really should be living, I thought.

Chapter 6:

Awesome Natural Monuments in Yosemite and Zion National Parks

We left Cape Blanco feeling very satisfied and drove to Portland, where we had a joyful reunion with our friends. Next day, we hit the road to California. The highway through Oregon is so thick with pine forests that the smell was as strong as if we'd accidentally set off a can of pine spray in the truck.

For almost the entire day's drive through Oregon and into California, we could see a great, snow-capped mountain towering ahead of us. At dusk, we stopped in Yreka for gas and decided to spend the night. We checked into the first motel we came to and went to sleep. Next morning when I woke up, Frank was just coming back into the room, his eyes bulging.

"Babe, just wait till you go outside… you're not going to believe it," he said. "Just look to your right."

The mountain that had been tantalizing us all day was right there in the center of town! We had unknowingly chosen a town built on the base of the great Mount Shasta. The effect was like being face to face with a cosmic being.

I was practically babbling when I went into the office, where the owner told me that at 14,179-feet, the mountain is the fifth highest peak in California. Moreover, it's volcanic, and the town is actually built on its base. It last erupted in 1786.

"I bet it keeps you guys humble," I said.

He chuckled and said, "Without a doubt. No matter how big your accomplishment or how big your problem seems, you take one look at that mountain and your ego falls right back in place."

We got as close as we could to the mountain to absorb its energy before getting back on the road. This time we were heading to Oakland to visit our friend Monica. Another day's drive and San Francisco, the gleaming white city on a hill, came into view.

San Francisco sprawled down to the Bay, and the Golden Gate Bridge looked like a giant adornment. This was my first time seeing the city, and I was entranced from the first moment. Of course, Frank the cosmopolitan traveler knew just where to go, and we promptly headed for Fisherman's Wharf to sample the famous seafood. We watched scores of seals basking on their wooden floats at Pier 39, and explored the shops and "watering holes" on the wharf.

We had a joyful reunion with Monica, her new husband and two-year old daughter. Several years before, Monica had moved into my house in Fort Lauderdale after her young nephew drowned in the pool at her house. My daughter Lisa had just gone off to college, and I understood when Monica said she couldn't bear to stay at the house where the accident happened. We had become close friends and she used to tease Frank and me about how blind we were to the fact that we were perfect for each other. She had left the state before we finally got together, so the reunion was a lot of fun.

By Monday we took off again, this time headed to Yosemite National Park. Driving across the Mojave Desert, we came upon what seemed like a mirage, a lake in the middle of the desert at Lone Pine, with wood storks perched at its edge and a pelican serenely bobbing in the center.

"How do you get your wife to go camping with you, man?" I heard a Hispanic man ask Frank when we stopped for gas. "My wife will never go camping with me. She grew up poor in Mexico and she says camping reminds her too much of that."

"I just got lucky, man," Frank laughed.

We arrived in Yosemite at dusk after a long drive up the steep, winding mountain. It was our third anniversary and we were looking forward to a romantic night at the lodge. We didn't have reservations, but our luck had been phenomenal so far, and we had no doubt there'd be a place for us at Yosemite Lodge.

Imagine my surprise when I heard instead, "Sorry, we are completely booked."

As we digested that information, the young woman behind the desk continued, "Oh, don't worry. It's your forest. Just pitch your tent anywhere." Then, on our way out the door, she called, "Just remember to hang your food in the trees. There are a lot of bears around!"

Frank and I exchanged the look that says, "We've really done it this time. Now what? "

We drove to the nearest campsite, which was bustling with light and activity. It was more crowded than anything we'd seen on the entire trip. We drove around to find another campground, and eventually got tired and decided just to pull over by the side of the road. We had everything we needed in the truck, and we could certainly survive one night in the cab.

With typical aplomb, we adjusted to the idea, anniversary or not. Our only concern was whether a bear might come too close. There was food in the cooler in the back. Would that attract them? Soon we started thinking how to get some of that food for ourselves. We had the bright idea that Frank would get out first with the machete he kept behind the seat, and follow me while I scooted into the back. This feat was soon accomplished, and we got back into the cab with a loaf of crusty bread, cheese and a bottle of merlot.

How effective a machete would have been against a hungry bear, I don't know, but I do know that the wine forced us to go outside several times during the night to pee. We napped with the key in the ignition, in case we needed to take off fast. Every now and then one of us would wake up with a start and ask, "You OK?" Reassured, we'd fall back to sleep.

We couldn't have been more relieved when morning came and we found we had survived. It struck me during the night that a bear wouldn't have any difficulty smashing the window where my head lay. But in the freshness of dawn, with the land exhaling a gentle mist and the first rays of the sun rousing the valley, I was caught in a sublime moment. It was as if the world was just being born again and me along with it.

We drove through the park in a state of ecstasy, agog at the truly spectacular views around every corner. Towering granite domes of unfathomable bulk gently enfolded the valley, thick with wildflowers and exotic grasses. Time was suspended in this place, and it felt like everything was proceeding in the same natural rhythm that had been going on for millions of years.

"How great thou art ...," was all my heart could murmur.

We were coming around a blind corner when the sound of rocks tumbling down the mountain broke my reverie. A large deer that seemed to have lost its footing tumbled down the hillside, coming to a stop directly in front of the truck. I braced myself for the collision. I couldn't see how Frank could possibly avoid hitting it. There was a steep drop on the other side, and he had no room to maneuver.

But without even skidding, he brought the big truck to a gentle stop inches away from the deer. He didn't even swerve. The animal looked him straight in the eye and then turned and bounded down the hill.

"Wow! How did you do that?" I asked incredulously.

"For some reason, I just had a feeling that I needed to be extra careful around that corner," he said. A sixth sense? Whatever it was, it had undoubtedly saved our lives.

That same day, we drove down the mountain, heading across the Mojave Desert to Las Vegas. Once again, we came upon an entirely foreign ecosystem, the arid, flat landscape rising into bulging, grey mountains. After more than 100 miles in this ashen landscape, we were suddenly deposited in a scene that was its perfect opposite in appearance. Compared to the desert, Las Vegas had the glittering intensity of a thousand suns concentrated in one small valley.

We drove down the Strip, ogling the exotic buildings, the flashing lights and opulent fountains among which a constant stream of humanity moved. Near the end of the Strip, we pulled into Circus Circus and got a nice room. When Frank looked through the window next morning, he saw people lying on cardboard in the parking lot next door. The juxtaposition of money, poverty and the artificiality of Vegas made us un-inclined to linger. After trying our luck at the hotel slot machines, we left town only slightly lighter in the wallet, heading for Zion National Park in Utah.

Twenty miles outside Las Vegas, we were back in the country. The city is such an anomaly in the desert that until you come to it, you can't imagine it's there. And once you leave, it's hard to believe that it was anything but a mirage.

I-15 wound us through rocky mountains that made me feel small, and each time we turned a corner, another dimension opened up. It made me appreciate the ingenuity that had gone into building a road through these very dense rocks. For the first time, I thought that geometry, trigonometry, geology and all those science subjects I had deemed irrelevant in high school might be good for something after all.

The sight of our first big horn sheep was riveting. A large male stood on a rocky outcropping as if he was surveying his domain. An imposing pair of horns set off his muscular body, and our excitement knew no bounds. What else were we likely to see in this part of the world?

A little over 90 minutes from Vegas, we drove into another unworldly scene where the mountains had been transformed into golden mesas and buttes as far as we could see. An hour or so more and we arrived in Springdale, the town just outside Zion National Park. Millions of tourists pass through Springdale on their way to the park each year, yet it retained the feel of a cozy small-town community.

The cliffs literally enfolded the valley, streaked with rainbow colors ranging from purple to gold, pink and blue. When I dragged my eyes down from the cliffs, I saw a sign for "Bumbleberry's Restaurant," offering something called "bumbleberry pie." Since I had never had anything called a bumbleberry, we had to sample some right away. The restaurant staff was friendly and welcoming, the food was great, and we topped off our meal with hefty slices of bumbleberry pie. It turns out that there's actually no "bumbleberry" fruit, and the pie's name referred to the concoction of multiple kinds of berries it contained. It was so good!

Our first act was to get a campsite in Watchman Campground ($8) and set up our tent. The ground was packed so tight that Frank had a hard time driving in the tent spikes.

"You can almost feel the energy rising up from the earth," he grunted.

The campground was on the bank of the Virgin River, the life force and principal architect of the canyons. Once we got the tent up, we walked down to the river, passing a herd of mule deer wandering between the campsites. The combination of flowing water and large wild animals sheltered among the towering cliffs has to be experienced to be believed.

Afternoon passed into evening and then came the most dramatic sundown we had ever witnessed. The sun passed over the western cliffs, and just like that, the day was over. The cliffs were so high that they completely blotted out every sign of the sun's presence beyond.

Cozy in our tent that night, watching the glittering stars, we felt utterly content. We had spent six weeks on the road, and our passion for our country had deepened exponentially from the sheer number and variety of sensationally beautiful places we had seen. We could never have gotten the same effect from parachuting into a city and going into a nearby park. Seeing them in one continuous loop made us feel like we were building up to a crescendo. But each time we thought we had peaked, the next place took us to higher heights. Zion had to be the highest pinnacle of all.

"First you feel Zion, and then you see it," Frank said in wonder.

Early next morning, we watched the sun make its sudden appearance over the eastern cliffs, its rays instantly transforming the cliffs and the valley into vividly brilliant colors. Wow! If the entrance to the park was so amazing, what would it look like inside? We were too excited to make breakfast, and hopped into the truck for the ride of our lives.

The Scenic Highway ran through a mind-boggling array of gigantic, multi-colored cliffs, each with its own unique shape. They looked like tremendous sculptures, each one more spectacular than the next, with names equally exotic: *"The Great White Throne." "The Temple of Sinawava." "Angels Landing," "Weeping Rock"* and *"The Court of the Patriarchs: Isaac, Abraham and Joseph."* For the first time, I understood what the word "monolith" means, because it was the only one that came close to describing these towering formations.

Feeling completely humbled and at the same time very, very special to be part of such creation, we turned around to drive back to the campsite. The last thing we expected to see was the young white woman on the side of the road, thumbing a ride. Frank and I looked at each other, momentarily disconcerted. Would she appreciate two black Samaritans? But without hesitation, we pulled over.

She hopped into the truck as if we were the most natural sight in the world, although we were quite likely the only two black people in the park.

"Thanks for stopping," she said cheerfully. "I'm meeting my boyfriend at the trailhead down the road. We're going camping in the backcountry, so he went ahead with our gear and I came to park the car. Where are you folks from?"

"Florida," we said in unison.

"I've never been to the South," she said, excited for us that we had come so far.

She was a California girl, and Zion was one of her favorite national parks to camp.

"We usually come in September because school's in session by then, so there are fewer people in the park," she said.

We hadn't even known that, yet we had managed to choose the best possible time to be in the parks.

We dropped her off in a few minutes, with "Good Luck" wishes all around.

Frank and I looked at each other in amazement. How awesome was that? All three of us had acted just like normal human beings. This was definitely not how it would have turned out on TV.

Back at the campgrounds, we made breakfast and then took off on a hike up the Watchman Trail. Across the river the trail rose gradually, and most people were taking it slow. We reached a point where two people could barely pass, when an older man came running down the trail. He stopped politely to give us room, but I couldn't contain myself, I burst out,

"Would you do that again... what I just saw you doing?"

He smiled, took off his cap, shook out his long, gray hair and said,

"What, running down the mountain?"

To my delight, he told us that he runs regularly through the mountains, "for sport, just to keep in shape."

I didn't want to be forward, but I felt compelled to ask how old he was.

"I'm 72," he laughed. "But this is easy. It gets a little harder when I'm running a 100-mile marathon!"

It turned out that he'd spent the better part of his life training cross-country runners, and now that he'd retired, he spent most of his time outdoors in his favorite wild places. His incredible physique and obvious great health dispelled the myth about how feeble we become past age 50.

We made it to the top of the trail and stood at eye-level with the white-topped cliffs across the valley. The climate was hot and dry, the foliage sparse. Everything else seemed like a supporting cast for the grand configuration of Nature that dominated the valley. Just thinking about the time it had taken these monoliths to develop and the energy that had shaped them blotted every other thought from my mind.

"It's like a giant, open air Cathedral, with all creatures in it giving praise," Frank said reverently. "You can see and feel the presence of a Higher Power."

We spent two days exploring and enjoying the park before heading off to the North Rim of the Grand Canyon. For many, many miles we could still see the unbelievable bulk of Zion's cliffs behind us.

Chapter 7:

The Grand Canyon:
A Natural Wonder of the World

The Grand Canyon is the centerpiece among the parks known as America's "Crown Jewels." It is one of the Seven Natural Wonders of the World and the only one on American soil. I was breathless to find out how it could possibly top all the spectacular places we'd already seen.

The road from Zion ran approximately 125 miles to the North Rim, which our map showed was 69 miles from the nearest town. There were pine forests on either side and we finally came to the sign announcing Grand Canyon National Park. In a meadow on our right, a coyote was trying to sneak up on two vultures. I had never seen a coyote before.

We were planning to camp until we came to the sign, "Campground Full." We drove the remaining few miles to where the road emptied into the parking lot at the Grand Canyon Lodge. To Frank's dismay, the lot was full and teeming with activity, including several tour buses disgorging passengers. It was late evening and he wisely observed that, with no reservation, we weren't likely to get a room at the lodge. If we had to make it back down the mountain, it'd be best if we started now and came back next day.

I wouldn't hear of it. We were at the Grand Canyon!! No way were we leaving! I was certain we'd get a room. Veto power went out the door. I hopped out of the truck and walked into the lodge.

At the desk, people were standing three deep. I heard the clerk telling the people ahead of me that they were full. They had no more rooms. I have no idea what made me continue to stand in the line, but when it came my turn, the clerk was interrupted by a phone call. When he came back to me, I told him we wanted a room and he said:

"You must be the luckiest person in the world. They just told me on the phone that we have a room open because a guest fell ill and they had to airlift him out of the park."

Once again Providence, fate or whatever power was working on our behalf had come through for us. I bounced out of the lodge with a key to a cabin, and to this day, Frank says I must have worked some voodoo. He was even more astonished when he found out that it only cost $50 per night.

We walked to the edge of the canyon and looked out. I remembered reading that when President Teddy Roosevelt first saw the Grand Canyon in 1903, he said, *"Do nothing to mar its grandeur. Keep it as the one great sight which every American should see."*

"Thank God!" I breathed.

"A smorgasbord for the senses," Frank said.

As far as we could see, for more than 11 miles, a mind-boggling world of rainbow colored rocks gathered into every conceivable shape, formed temples and cities suspended in the air. Extending to the horizon and for more than a mile down was a treasure-trove of the most beautiful creations that only God could have wrought. Tears sprang to my eyes and joy flooded my heart.

So this was the Grand Canyon! Never again could I spend moment thinking about what is wrong with the world, or "making the world a better place." I understood intuitively the magnitude of the power that could sculpt this creation from the earth, using fire, water and air. It had been made perfect in every way, and no human genius had been involved. The thought flew into my mind that the Earth was whole when humans arrived here, and humans have created every problem that we have today.

The power of the Canyon acts upon you on so many levels. It dominated my vision, tugged at my heartstrings and flooded my mind with lofty thoughts. Except for the calls of birds and rustling sounds of small animals, the silence was palpable. I could almost imagine what it might sound like in one of the formations way down at the bottom. I understood why it was one of the wonders of the world.

We went for a short hike on the Bright Angel Trail, but mostly, we just strolled around the rim, mesmerized by the views. It was amazing how little effort we needed to expend to enjoy so much beauty. Frank met a woman who told him that she had been coming to the Canyon every year for the past 25 years, and planned to continue visiting every year for the rest of her life.

Our cabin turned out to be a small, cozy room with a huge stove for heating, a comfortable bed and windows that looked out over the forest. We spent two blissful days exploring the canyon. At night we ate in the historic Grand dining room, which hung out over the edge of the canyon. While the dining room was brightly lit, behind us the canyon was a dark, impenetrable void. But when we walked outside, we could see the Milky Way so vividly outlined, it felt like we could reach up and pluck our very own stars. It brought out the poet in Frank.

"If colors were music, the Grand Canyon would outshine Handel's 'Messiah,' " he said. "It is a visual natural extravaganza engorging the eye with color, hues, shapes, tones, forms and the play of light and shadows. Standing next to someone seeing it for the first time is a singular experience. There is a reverent stillness as they look in awe and appreciation. No words need to be spoken."

(He told our sons and sons-in-law later that if they ever seriously messed up with their wives, the North Rim of the Grand Canyon was the place to take them to reconcile.)

We tore ourselves away from the canyon at last, heading for Flagstaff and the Petrified Forest National Park. Not far outside the park, we stopped at a Native American outdoor market and rest stop. A car pulled in beside us, covered with bumper stickers advertising the National Rifle Association and the North American Hunting Club. Frank and I exchanged looks, silently telegraphing, "We want to steer clear of this guy."

But he made a beeline for us.

He told us he was from Switzerland and addicted to traveling. He was on the last leg of a long trip through the Caribbean and the U.S. With his money dwindling, he had bought the Ford LTD in Philadelphia for $700, took out the right front seat and converted the space into a bed. Then he'd driven cross-country up to the national parks in Alaska, and he was just leaving the Grand Canyon.

"I think I have to go home now and do something sensible," he moaned, "like get married and have children."

I suggested that if he considered it such a chore, maybe he wasn't quite ready.

"Did you put those on your car?" Frank asked gently, pointing to the stickers.

"Oh, no!" he replied, laughing. "They were on when I bought it. But I think they protect me."

I was puzzled.

"I've been sleeping in my car in all kinds of places," he went on. "And the cops look at me — one policeman even shined a light into the car, but then he told me not to look at him and went away. I figure it must be the stickers. People must think I have big guns in here or something!"

When we left him, I reminded myself that it was a bad habit to make judgments on the basis of assumptions. Our peers thought we needed guns to protect ourselves in the woods, and it turned out we didn't. We assumed that a car with NRA stickers meant a scary, gun-crazy owner. And this guileless traveler believed that signs hinting at the presence of guns might have protected him from who knew what fate? Go figure!

As we continued down the mountain to Flagstaff, we were amazed to drive for miles through areas that looked like miniature Grand Canyons, with the walls such a deep pink that the even the sky picked up the color. Just as I'd thought there was only one geyser at Yellowstone, I thought the Grand Canyon was just one large hole. It hadn't occurred to me it was part of an ecosystem and shares characteristics with the surrounding lands. We even saw cowboys on their horses riding the range behind long, barbed wire fences.

We stopped at Meteor Crater, which is featured in the movie "Starman." A private company preserves the site where a meteor fell to earth approximately 50,000 years ago. It left a hole deep enough to swallow the Washington Monument, the size of 20 football fields. Described as the planet's "most penetrating attraction," the crater is 570 feet deep, nearly a mile wide and three miles around.

We ogled the 1,406-pound piece of the meteorite on display. It was hard to imagine that the errant meteor had shot to earth at more than 45,000 miles per hour and hit with the force of 15 million tons of dynamite. What an explosion that must have been!

We peered into the chasm to locate the statue that the brochure said had been erected at the bottom. It was a six-foot statue of an Astronaut holding an American flag, but from the rim, we could barely see it as a speck.

Our final stop was at the Petrified Forest National Park. I hadn't even known that such a place existed. For miles before we got to the entrance, we saw hand lettered signs offering petrified wood for sale.

As soon as we turned onto the short drive into the park, we saw the glint of jewels in the grass. There were small pieces that were maybe a couple of inches, and gigantic pieces that were literally tree trunks. We were surrounded in a dazzling display of jewels without price, that no one had ever had to mint or polish. The trees were more than 225 million years old, and scientists have proven that they washed down from a grove higher up, got stuck in a logjam, and were buried for millions of years under ash and silt. With their oxygen cut off, the process of decay had slowed down. Then, mineral-rich water seeped into the wood, and slowly, the organic fiber of the trees was gradually displaced by multicolored quartz!

The park also bears the relics of an ancient Native American civilization, which apparently left the area around the 1400s. But their accomplishments are indelibly written in petroglyphs that they drew on the rocks and the brick remnants of their community structures. Intricately positioned boulders form solar calendars that they used to chart the passage of the sun across the sky.

The park covers 50,000 acres, and we learned that it contains more than 500 archaeological sites that reveal the bones of ancient amphibians and reptiles, including some of the earliest dinosaurs. We promised ourselves that one day we would go back and join an archaeological dig.

Park rules strictly forbid visitors from removing any petrified wood — or anything else — and park rangers question everyone leaving to assure themselves that nothing has been taken.

Frank and I had been traveling for more than seven weeks now and we were eager to continue our journey. But word had reached us that a letter had come from the Immigration and Naturalization Service (INS) informing me that I had an appointment to take my citizenship exam in mid-October. So, it was time to start back home. Our entire adventure had cost approximately $3,000, in gas, food and lodging. Frank had bought a National Parks Pass at Acadia for $50, good for one year, and it covered our entry fee into every national park we'd visited.

I called Dorrit from our motel, practically tripping over my words to convey the incredible beauty and majesty of the places we'd seen. As I rattled off the names, she kept saying, "Where? Where's that?" and I gradually realized that she had no idea what I was talking about. I wasn't that surprised, since it was only because of Frank that I knew about the national parks. Reading about them or seeing them in pictures could not compare with actually being there.

That's when it dawned on us that we were honor bound to do something to share the wonders we had found with everyone, especially the people whom we felt were most clearly alienated from the parks—African Americans and other people of color. The idea to publish a newsletter promoting the parks was born at that moment.

Not only had we been thrilled and stimulated, but we had also got quite an education. Now we knew what the land looked like where dinosaurs had roamed. We had observed the artifacts that ancient Native American cultures used to plumb the mysteries of the heavens. We had seen the vast gleaming heart of America that survived the coming of Europeans and the development of cities. And we appreciated the uniquely American conservation ethic that had assured us the opportunity to enjoy these experiences.

The adventure expanded our vision of ourselves, making us feel like links in a chain from antiquity to the future. It gave us history and also responsibility, and we would fulfill that by providing what was most needed—information and invitation to America's children of color: Don't be an absentee landlord! Discover and take ownership of the incredible natural treasury that is our heritage!

The stately Great Blue Heron is among the exotic wading birds that can be seen from the Anhinga Trail in Everglades National Park. (Frank Peterman photo)

The Hoh Rainforest and intimate marine life make Olympic National Park an incredible treat. [NPS photo]

There are more geysers in Yellowstone than anywhere else in the world. Frank snapped this view of Old Faithful from a distant trail. [Frank Peterman photo]

Stunning views abound from the heights of Cadillac Mountain in Acadia National Park. [Photo: Eric Metzler - United States]

Petrified Forest National Park protects a treasury of trees that have turned to stone. [Audrey Peterman photo]

Biscayne is the largest marine park in the park system, and was the home of the Jones family featured in the 2009 documentary, "The National Parks: America's Best Idea." [NPS photo]

Enslaved Africans labored to build Fort Jefferson on the Dry Tortugas National Park, FL, in the mid-19th Century as part of America's coastal defense system. (NPS photo, ©Mike Theiss)

The Grand Canyon stunned and delighted our grandsons, Yero and Taffrey. [Frank Peterman, Jr. photo]

The grandeur of Zion National Park exerts a powerful pull on the senses. [Audrey Peterman photo]

The carvings atop Mount Rushmore National Memorial remain a source of controversy. [NPS photo]

Yosemite National Park is home to stunning natural vistas and the Ahwahnee Hotel, patronized by presidents and royalty. [Ken Karst photo]

The Giant Sequoias in Sequoia National Park are among the largest living things on earth, and were protected by the Buffalo Soldiers in 1903. [From the Peterman family album]

Unearthly formations are the norm in Badlands National Park. [Photo: Peterm from Germany]

Part Two:

The Making of a
Black Environmentalist

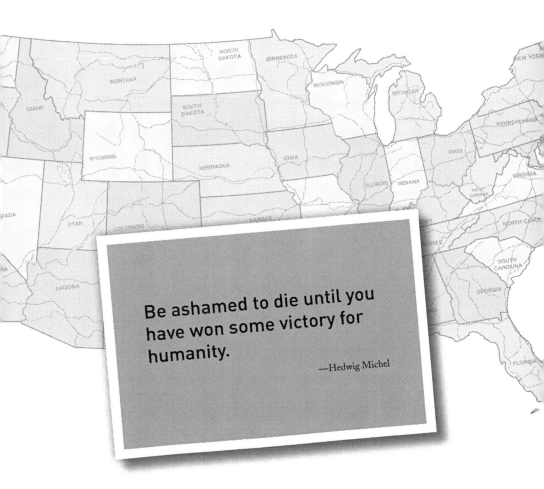

Be ashamed to die until you
have won some victory for
humanity.

—Hedwig Michel

Chapter 8:

Ambassadors for Our Newly-Discovered Park System

We returned to Fort Lauderdale flushed with excitement and feeling the pride of ownership in our country. We had traveled through 40 states, covered 12,000 miles, and visited 14 national and state parks. In the entire time we had seen less than a handful of black people, Latinos, Asians or Native Americans among the hundreds of thousands of white visitors enjoying the natural treasures. I understood that in many social and economic ways, black and white Americans live in two different worlds, but I didn't know that was physically the case as well! By some unwritten, unspoken rule, the most beautiful and inspiring public places in our country remain the playgrounds of white people, almost as if there is an invisible barrier separating them from Americans of other races.

I learned later that Stephen Mather, the first director of the National Park System fervently believed: *"He is a better citizen with a keener appreciation of the privilege of living here who has toured the national parks."* He could have been describing Frank and me. I'd lived in America for 17 years and had become eligible for citizenship after five years, but I hadn't felt any urgency about becoming an American and participating in public life. Now, however, I felt compelled to do something that let others like me know about the parallel world that exists just beyond their city borders. I wanted them to know that it was not only desirable to explore, but also safe; that it was the best thing they could do for their children, offering the greatest opportunities for young people to develop their self confidence and pride, and pursue an incredible range of exciting careers including ecology, archaeology and multiple aspects of management. They should know that the parks are public property and they literally own them, since they are part of every American's heritage, maintained with our tax dollars.

Since we'd sold our house and hadn't decided our next move, we happily accepted the invitation from our friends Cathy and Neil Ritter to stay with them on the seven-acre ranch in Plantation Acres where they lived. The ranch was near the edge of the Everglades, and was owned by Midge

Hainline, a longtime friend of Neil's family. Midge's husband Joe, a well-known international journalist, had died not long before, and Midge said that so many people around the world had been hospitable to her and her husband during their travels that she tried to return the favor.

Living on the ranch was just like a continuation of our adventure. We pitched our tent at the top of the long driveway, sheltered between a macadamia nut tree and a large eucalyptus. We had at least three acres of open land between us and the nearest neighbors, and Cathy and Neil left their door open at night so we could answer the call of nature.

My big challenge on the ranch was Midge's fierce-looking Rottweiler, Rocky, who practically came up to my waist. I was terrified of him. I grew up thinking that you had to be very careful around dogs or they'd bite you, and the size of this dog was very intimidating. He had the run of the ranch and the neighborhood, but I wouldn't even come out of our truck if Rocky was anywhere in sight, unless someone was with him.

Frank patiently explained that the dog was friendly, and I was creating a problem where there was none. He said if I sent out fear vibes to the dog, he would sense that something was wrong and might feel the need to defend himself against me, thereby bringing on just the response I was so afraid of. He told me to try to relax and treat the dog like everyone else treated him—as part of the family. Well this took effort! But I couldn't live in fear of Rocky, or my world would become very limited. I began training myself to relax around him, and it worked! We became the best of friends, and soon I was the one person on the ranch that he obeyed immediately. It opened a new world of self-awareness to me to discover that I had created a problem for myself, and that I could fix it by disciplining my own feelings and actions.

Frank and I had set up Earthwise Productions, Inc., a year earlier, intending to publish a magazine that would address social and political issues from a black perspective. A keen observer of society, Frank's experience as an American born into a segregated society, who got his education at Morehouse College and Howard University, practiced law in the 1960s, ran for state office, worked for a major industrial defense corporation, and was actively involved in the Civil Rights Movement, gave him an ample lens on American history and society. My training in journalism and my love of writing made publishing a natural fit for us.

And now we knew what we had to publish: a magazine that focused on the outdoors and showed Americans of all races enjoying the parks and forests that are part of their inheritance. In the newspapers and magazines that we subscribed to, only white people were ever shown in the outdoors or speaking about the environment. We would change that by writing about our fantastic experiences in the national parks and using photographs showing how much fun we were having, thereby encouraging other people like us to visit the parks. We would also reach out to the managers of the National Park System and offer to partner with them to bring more information about the parks to Americans in urban communities. After all, I wouldn't even have known about them if it wasn't for Frank dreaming up our adventure.

Cathy is a magazine editor, and our close friends included a graphic designer, Keith Conzett and another writer Eloise Davis. So we had a ready-made team. We developed our company's logo as a globe with the words – *People > Information > Action.*

The ease with which it all came together convinced me of the rightness of our decision. We designed the newsletter and named it *Pickup & Go!* to symbolize the freedom that comes from traveling to the national parks, some of which are among the Top Ten tourist spots in the world. We emphasized that visiting national parks is the ideal way for families to get away and have new experiences without spending a lot of money. National parks are in every state except Delaware, and many of them don't even have entrance fees.

The first issue came off the press in November 2005, extolling the virtues of the national parks and encouraging Americans of color to get to know and enjoy them, as well as to get involved with the environmental movement. The cover story read:

America! Go See It!
How much of this country have you seen?

More than 700 million acres of American land, from the gleaming Atlantic to the Pacific, belong to you. Brilliant, beautiful land filled with awesome, mysterious treasures, direct from the creator. From Florida's wild, mystic Everglades to awesome Cadillac Mountain, towering above the Atlantic on Maine's shores; from the rainforests of Washington state to the supernatural beauty of the Grand Canyon in Arizona; from the bubbling caverns of Yellowstone National Park in Wyoming where you can see the earth still being formed; to the ethereal shapes and colors of South Dakota's vast Badlands, this country is liberally endowed with luscious sights that stir powerful emotions.

Burned out from the hectic pace of life in the cities? If you really want to get away from it all, America's famous public landmarks in the national and state parks and forests provide an affordable alternative for adventure, recreation and spiritual revitalization.

Whether you seek the excitement of breathtaking views that make your heart pound, or you crave the solitary serenity of nature, these places stir your heart with sheer joy..."

Realizing that safety was a concern, we addressed that issue as well, using our experience to allay fears.

"Travels give lie to 'growing racial divide'"

Who would believe there are places in America where you can drive for days and never see an African American or other minority? When we traveled around the country this fall, across 40 states and through countless cities, we realized we had a lot of misconceptions. The America we see on TV is only a narrow view of reality. Not only is the country more varied and vividly beautiful, but there is far more diversity in the culture of individual states and the people are much more generous-spirited than the media portrays.

Frank provided practical information such as how to select a tent and campsite, what was needed and what steps should be taken to ensure a pleasant experience.

Tenting: Here's What You Need to Get Started

Camping allows you to enjoy the outdoors at whatever price you choose to pay and in whatever style you prefer - from luxurious land-yacht RVs with the noisy generators, TV dishes and vibrating beds, to tents with a bucket and shovel for nature's call, and a campfire for food and warmth.

If camping in a tent is the experience for you, here's what you must start with:
- Tent
- Sleeping bag
- Cooking equipment
- Footwear
- Lighting

Just like everything else that had fallen so easily into place, Frank's long-time friend Charles Fulwood agreed to contribute a monthly column. As Communications Director for the Natural Resources Defense Council (NRDC), a major environmental non-profit in New York, he understood the national environmental scene even better than we did. While Frank and I wrote from our personal experience, Charles wrote from the unique perspective of a black man at the height of the mainstream conservation movement.

Environment—It's Time to Join 'The Big Cleanup'
By Charles Fulwood

Traditionally, environmentalists have been viewed as a bunch of glassy-eyed, sandal-wearing, tree-hugging eccentrics with too much time and money on their hands. To be sure, people of color looked upon them as escapists from the gritty and unpleasant political issues of the urban centers where most of us live. While grains of truth could be found in both stereotypes, people of color have been tardy in recognizing the inextricable link between quality of life and environment. Worse, we now discover that air and water pollution, pesticide and other chemical exposures wield a disproportionate impact on our communities. Today, 70 percent of all Americans call themselves environmentalists. I don't know what the percentage is among people of color, but I doubt it is that high. It needs to be, and more. There is a direct connection between our health and happiness and the answers to the questions of whether we are breathing clean air or diesel fumes, drinking clean water or polluted water, and living in places with or without green parks, trees and blue sky.

Communities of color bear the toxic blight of industrial-ization and chemical agriculture in this country, and for the sake of our children, we must throw our weight into efforts for The Big Cleanup.

But it creates a false dichotomy to imagine that people of color—even those who live in urban areas—should care only about our cities and not about the wild places, forests and national parks now under threat by the same Congress, with its stealth attacks on environmental protection, that is also trying to demolish economic and social programs.

Many of us who live on the coasts rarely visit the great public parks and national forests of the interior, and whether the reasons are lack of money or wariness about venturing into unfamiliar territory (if you know what I mean), they are certainly rational. But by staying away, we and our children are missing out. For Native Americans, Latinos, African Americans, and all the rest of us, natural beauty is deep in our spirituality and our art. Go back and visit the forests, the lakes, the wilds and pristine areas and you will hear the mur-mur of nature at its undisturbed best.

Like all citizens, we own the natural heritage of this country, in spirit and in letter. If Congress sells it to the highest bidder, we lose a birthright. This is one issue that all Americans have a vested interest in, no matter where we live or who we are.

We printed 3,000 copies, and mailed them to our family, friends and public libraries around the country. Each included a subscription box, and we waited for subscriptions to pour in while we got the next issue ready for press.

Imagine my disappointment when, from that first mailing, we got two subscriptions, at $25 each for 12 issues, and we had spent more than $3,000 putting the publication together and mailing it, not counting our own time in writing and production. I was stunned, but then we reasoned that it took time for people to embrace new things, and in time, subscrip-tions would pick up.

Meanwhile, the *Miami Herald* ran a feature story about our trip and the fact that we had started the newsletter to promote the national parks. They included our phone number, and about a dozen people called to congratulate us. We couldn't believe how many people said we were so "brave." One day I heard Frank telling someone on the phone, "Don't cry, man. It's OK." He said the Hispanic caller told him that he had long dreamed of exploring America, but he was too afraid of what might happen to him "out there."

Native born and immigrant Americans of color who would seem to be living the American dream were telling us that they were extremely fearful and nervous about winding up in places "where we don't belong" or may not be wanted. We became even more determined to use our experience to show that, as Franklin Delano Roosevelt said, "The only thing to fear is fear itself." My experience with Rocky had reinforced that lesson.

Months later, I found out that no matter what you're marketing, a one-percent return was standard in the direct mail business, and a 10-percent return meant you'd hit a homerun. That meant that of 3,000 copies we mailed, we could expect 30 to 300 subscribers at maximum.

By then, we had sunk close to $15,000 into the newsletter and had fewer than 100 subscribers. It was a scary place to be, but we were convinced that we would eventually be successful. After all, how could anyone possibly not want to experience the fantastic world we had discovered?

Frank's cousin, Margie, who owned a marketing company in Chicago, gave us a clue:

"Honey, when I go on vacation I'm looking to enjoy myself. I don't want to have to worry about somebody giving me attitude because of my race. I have to deal with that every day in America, so I spend my free time where I don't have to deal with that."

But we hadn't had any negative experiences in the parks. That's what we were trying to show. When I thought how many foreign tourists were enjoying the pristine air and the natural treasures in our backyard, it made me more resolute than ever to make black people aware that these treasures are owned by the American people, and as such, they belong to us. Ignoring them makes as much sense as staying away from your mansion while living in a hovel.

The Everglades – Imperiled Treasure in Our Backyard

Now that we had started on a life of exploration, adventures readily presented themselves. One night we saw a TV show about a group of people called the Koreshans who believed that we live inside the Earth, and aligned their lifestyle and religion with the planets and stars. How exciting! Then Frank mentioned that the Koreshan settlement was on the west coast of Florida, just north of Naples. The settlement was preserved as a Florida State Park. Of course we had to see it, and it would make a good story for the newsletter.

We left home around 7 a.m. on a Saturday to catch the early morning animal activity, since we knew that animals are more active early in the morning and late afternoon. Interstate 75 links east and west Florida and cuts through the heart of the Everglades. For miles and miles we were surrounded by the "River of Grass" as the Everglades is known, stretching off into the distance on either side. The branches of the cypress trees were covered with large, exotic, graceful white birds, including the wood stork, their wings more than five feet wide. Great herons and egrets sported their breeding plumage, with an extra group of long, delicate feathers hanging from their throat. In the late 1800s, the trade in bird feathers to adorn ladies attire almost led to the decimation of these species, until the Audubon Society intervened on their behalf, actually employing guards to protect the birds from indiscriminate slaughter. Ospreys perched high above the canals, their stately white head and breast flashing in the sunlight.

I counted more than 100 alligators sunning themselves on the canal banks. Tractor trailers whizzed by on the highway at more than 75 miles per hour, but we tuned them out and thoroughly enjoyed the fact that we were in a wildlife preserve 88 miles long.

We followed the sign for Koreshan State Historic Site and turned off the highway just below Fort Myers. Two miles later, we stepped through a time warp.

From the parking lot, the white-sand trail ran through overgrowth and ended in a clearing where a number of wooden buildings stood, shaded by graceful stands of trees. There were few people around, and it felt as if we had walked into a well-ordered community whose members had all gone out together, and would return together at any moment. A pamphlet we picked up said that 10 buildings remained of the original 50 developed by the Koreshan sect in 1894, as part of their vision to build "A New Jerusalem."

The first building we came to was the Art Hall, where an orchestra dominated the large stage, just as if the Koreshans might come out any moment and play, though the last member of the sect had died in 1982. A huge painting of "The New Jerusalem" showed leader Cyrus Teed's plans to build the perfect city. It included streets that were 400 feet wide, the bottom level being for heavy traffic such as trains, the second for lighter-weight loads and the top level for pedestrians. Utilities lines were to be laid underground, and sewage would be carted away underground for 30 miles, composted and brought back to the site as fertilizer.

Over the course of the morning we learned how Teed, a New York doctor, said he had changed his name to Koresh, Hebrew for "Cyrus," after he had a vision one night of an entity who gave him the answers to life's great mysteries. He became so captivated by the vision that he devoted himself to practicing it, and won a number of converts from among his friends, including doctors, lawyers, artists and musicians.

Teed and his converts gathered first in Chicago, and in 1894 a devotee gave them the first 300 acres on the banks of the Estero River in Florida. They were looking to establish a community of 10,000 or more people that would live by the Golden Rule, practice equality between men and women, own the land equally and live in peace, harmony and love.

They also believed we live inside the earth, and we saw the instrument described as a rectilineator that Koresh said proved his theory that the Earth's surface is concave, and all the planets and stars and galaxies are contained inside it. Koresh reportedly offered a $10,000 prize to anyone who could prove him wrong. There were no takers.

Besides the fact that they were a highly cultured and industrious people who practiced racial and gender equality and held concerts and theatrical events on the banks of the Estero River, they also built a power plant, a printery and other industries that supplied the surrounding community. Thomas Edison lived nearby in Fort Myers and visited them regularly, using tools in their workshop that he didn't have at home.

But there was one vital factor that would doom their undertaking:

The Koreshans believed that their leaders should be celibate. Without sexual activity, they didn't procreate, their numbers dwindled and the community eventually faded away.

Still, they had a profound effect on us when we came to the grave of Hedwig Michel, the last of the Koreshans, who died in 1982. A member of the Hollow Earth Society in her native Germany, she was so excited when she learned about the Koreshans that she came to America to join them, and spent the rest of her life at the settlement. She died still convinced that we live inside the Earth, and her legacy was the 300 acres of the settlement that she'd succeeded in getting preserved as a Florida State Park. This was particularly admirable since we learned that Estero is the only remaining site where you can experience the relics of their society relatively intact although sites had also been established in Washington, Oregon and California.

A statement, carved on the headstone of her grave, held us riveted:

"Be ashamed to die until you have won some victory for humanity."

We felt as if she was challenging us from beyond the grave to develop the fortitude necessary to complete what we had started. Frank and I left the park feeling more confident than ever that we had been given an opportunity to win some victory for humanity—to bridge the physical and psychological gap between the great outdoors and African Americans in particular, thereby contributing to the improvement of each. By reminding all Americans of our symbiotic relationship with nature, we would win "some victory for humanity."

Our chance came sooner than we anticipated. It was a regular monthly meeting of the Broward County Chapter of the Audubon Society Chapter, and Frank and I were the only black people in the room of around 40. Members had been surprised when we showed up a couple of years earlier, one woman going so far as to ask Frank, in a friendly way,

"So, what brought you here?"

"Our truck," he replied disingenuously.

We had become regulars and took bird-watching classes that helped us identify a large variety of resident and migratory birds.

But this night, something miraculous happened: The guest speaker, Lisa Bock from the Miami office of the Audubon Society's Everglades Conservation Office, made a presentation about a massive, upcoming project to restore the Florida Everglades. She said it was a priority for both the state and federal governments as it involved the survival of Everglades National Park. It would transform South Florida over the next 20 years and was vital to ensure that South Florida had an adequate supply of water for its large and growing population. She said that the project was so huge and complex that it could be compared to building a space station. Countries as far away as Egypt and Brazil would be watching it closely as an example of how to do their own ecological restoration. The project's success would depend on local citizens' involvement and support and it would bring in tons of jobs and pour more than $5 billion into the local economy.

The entire time she was talking, Frank and I kept looking at each other, our eyes getting bigger and bigger. Surely this was manna from heaven! With African Americans and Hispanics making up almost 50 percent of South Florida's population, it was a Godsend that we had all this experience with the national parks and the environment, and had developed a vehicle to get the information out to this audience.

We could hardly wait for the meeting to end to talk with the speaker. We told her about our trip, some of the fantastic discoveries we had made and how we had channeled that into a company and publication. She was very excited and invited us down to Miami to meet with her Executive Director, Stuart Strahl.

The Audubon Society had set up its Everglades office on Brickell Avenue, in the heart of the financial district. It had a suite on the eighth floor of a building on the Miami River, with views of Biscayne Bay on one side and the river on the other. Dr. Strahl was a big man, over 6 feet tall weighing more than 200 pounds, and very friendly. He had just returned from a stint in South America working with a native tribe, and he immediately recognized that we could fill a valuable niche in the restoration project. He gave us more details, including the fact that Congress had ordered the Army Corps of Engineers to devise a plan to restore the Everglades and present it to the Congress by July 1, 1999. (The Corps originally built the canals in the 1940s, draining water from the Everglades out to sea to prevent flooding and promote development.) The restoration project would affect the 16 counties south from Orlando to Key West, an area in which the South Florida Water Management District was responsible for all issues related to water. Funding for the project would be split 50-50 between Congress and the State of Florida.

Since federal money was involved, it triggered Title VI laws against discrimination on the basis of race, color or national origin in their programs and activities, so South Florida's very large "minority" population would have to be included. Stuart suggested that we become partners with the Audubon Society and apply for funding to inform the region's African American population about the restoration.

We envisioned a campaign that used *Pickup & GO!*, as well as radio and TV spots to bring information about the restoration and what it would mean for everyone in South Florida. We wanted to emphasize the opportunities for jobs as well as introduce people to the recreational opportunities at Everglades National Park. The possibilities seemed endless, and to me, it seemed like the fulfillment of our destiny.

But first, we had to get to know Everglades National Park that would be the focus of all this activity. Neither Frank nor I had ever been to the park. So on a perfect December day, we drove down the Florida Turnpike to the park's main entrance in Homestead, south of Miami. The turnpike empties into U.S. 1, where a sign indicated the turnoff to Biscayne National Park on the left and Everglades National Park on the right. We had a hearty lunch at a seafood restaurant near the turnoff since we didn't know what might be available inside the park.

A couple of miles off the highway we came to a large, colorful fruit stand proclaiming, "Robert is here!" It was bulging with exotic tropical fruit including papayas, guavas and the *mame sapote*, which I'd never seen outside Jamaica. We stopped and sampled a few, then got back in the truck and drove past acres of farmlands where workers bent low picking beans and tomatoes. There were rows of avocado trees and lychee nut trees beside the road, laden with fruit.

After a 12-mile ride, we reached a sign set in a large coral rock announcing Everglades National Park. As we drove the last half-mile to the

Visitor Center, we saw another sign, "Watch for Panthers!" It brought back the feeling we'd gotten in Maine when we saw our first "Watch for Moose" sign, except that we were practically in our backyard, not 1500 miles from home.

The first people we saw in the park were a black family standing outside the Visitor Center. I leapt out of the truck, ran over to them and introduced myself to John G. and Barbara Brown, and their children Emmanuelle, Cheryl and Chakeyna. They were visiting the park for the first time to do research for Cheryl's college project.

"There's so much to see," Barbara marveled. "I can't believe we never did this before. Just being out here, I feel more in tune with nature."

"I'm definitely a nature person," she continued. "I tell my friends that when I get upset, all I have to do is go out into my garden, look at the flowers and the trees, get my hands in the dirt, and I start feeling better right away. People think I'm strange, but I believe everything has feelings, and when I work around plants, it really lifts me up."

We checked out the multi-media exhibits in the Visitor Center describing the plants and animals of the Everglades ecosystem, looked into the bookstore and gift shop, and then set off to explore the park. At the entrance station the ranger checked Frank's Golden Age Pass and gave us a map and color brochure of the park. About a mile in, we saw a sign pointing to Royal Palm and the Anhinga Trail. We turned off and drove through the saw grass spreading away to infinity on either side. Dozens of wood storks, egrets and herons paraded gracefully through the grass. Great Blue Herons and hawks flew overhead. The million-and-a-half acres of Everglades comprising the national park have been these birds' breeding grounds for eons, and they thrive here more than any other place in the country.

The road deposited us in a parking lot with restrooms, a bookstore and an archway that led us into a natural wonderland as exciting as we'd seen in Yellowstone. A concrete trail led up to a low coral wall on the edge of a gently-flowing canal. On the bank closest to us, five large alligators were sunning. A giant alligator swam serenely in the middle of the canal, its eyes and the length of its back the only things visible above water. The far side of the canal was lined with pond apple trees with their roots in the water. Among their branches glossy black cormorants and anhinga preened and dried their wings. Stately herons and egrets stood motionless at the water's edge as they waited for a meal to swim by. The saw grass marsh spread out beyond the trees.

The canal was teeming with fish, including the sleek gar and sunfish. Walking along the mile-long trail and boardwalk over the marsh, we saw a turtle laying its eggs on the bank and covering them with her flippers. A Purple Gallinule popped out of the reeds, dazzling us with its purple and green body, red bill and yellow legs. At the end of the boardwalk, dozens of alligators hung out, some actually on top of each other. Large birds picked their way nonchalantly among them.

We could happily have spent the day there, but we wanted to see as much of the park as we could. We drove on to Flamingo, 38 miles further south, having the road practically to ourselves. Our traveling companions were Ospreys, Anhinga, Ravens, Grackles, Great Blue Herons, Wood Storks, hawks, and even a rare Snail Kite that lives only in the Everglades. Everywhere we looked, there were birds soaring over the vast saw grass prairie, perching, stalking fish, and occasionally feeding on road kill.

The two-lane highway led us into the small settlement of Flamingo on the edge of Florida Bay. Signs pointed to a marina as well as the Flamingo Lodge, which offered accommodations and a restaurant. We went straight to the campgrounds right beside the water. Breathtaking views of blue water extended to the east, and to the south were mangrove islands where birds fished at the water's edge.

The campsites were set among tall palms and hardwood trees, and there was a restroom with running water. We drank in the restful beauty and promised ourselves we'd come back, and then we sauntered over to the wildlife watching area at Eco Pond. We were just in time to see a flock of red-winged blackbirds rising dramatically from the cattails, their red and yellow wing markings flashing in the sunlight. Across the pond, the biggest American Coots I'd ever seen bobbed and dipped under water for food.

We finally tore ourselves away from the park. Driving home that evening, we could hardly contain our glee. This treasure on our doorstep was comparable to any of the other national parks we'd gone so much further to see. It proved the point that wherever you live in America, you're only a short drive away from adventure once you know about the national parks.

Chapter 10:

"Restoration" Means Urban Removal?!

Compared to the elegant simplicity of nature, the entities assembled to work through the details of Everglades restoration seemed incredibly fragmented and territorial. As excited as we were and eager to get involved, it was only through our friends at the Audubon Society that we found out about the intense meetings that were being held at the West Palm Beach offices of the South Florida Water Management District. The District represented the interests of the State of Florida, while the U.S. Army Corps of Engineers represented the federal government. A third group, the 42-member Governor's Commission for a Sustainable South Florida created by Gov. Lawton Chiles, comprised leaders from business and agriculture, developers, the Miccosukee Tribe and environmental organizations such as the Audubon Society and the Sierra Club. The Commission worked with both the District and the Corps, and had no one representing the largely African American and Hispanic communities in the urban area. It baffled me how so many of the entities that had reduced the Everglades to its present condition could be put in charge of restoring it.

Both the Governor's Commission and the Water Management District's Governing Board held day-long meetings at the District's headquarters once per month, while most people were at work. This cut down significantly on the number of working class people that could participate. At the first meeting we attended, we listened to detailed scientific information presented by members of the Corps and the District about the hydrology of the Everglades and all the pieces of the "River of Grass" that would need to be reconnected. The environmental, business and tribal groups countered with how those proposals would affect the natural system and their business interests, and argued for how they'd need to be adjusted. But we heard no mention of how these changes would affect the people in the urban area, particularly people who had been historically disadvantaged.

This was curious since we were also hearing from the dais how the restoration would affect *everyone* in South Florida and could not be achieved without the involvement of "all parties." Yet I could ask any black person on the streets of Fort Lauderdale or Miami, and they had no clue what I meant by Everglades restoration. Many of our friends and colleagues, including journalists, college presidents, business people and ministers, only knew about the project because we couldn't stop talking about it. For that matter, white people didn't seem to know about it either, except for the few who were directly involved with the project in some way.

Frank researched the definition of the term "sustainability" and found that according to the United Nations Brundtland Commission Report of the World Commission on Environment and Development (1987), where the term originated, achieving sustainability demands that over-riding priority must be given to the needs of the world's poor. So for the Everglades to be "restored" and to be "sustainable," attention would obviously have to be paid to the needs of the people at the lowest end of the socio-economic spectrum who were the predominant surrounding population.

By default, since there seemed no one else to speak up for the voiceless people, Frank and I decided that it was up to us to place the interests of these communities on the table. We took every opportunity to ask point-ed questions at the meetings and when it was time for "public comment," we stated for the record that specific steps must be taken to integrate the interests of people in the urban area into the plan. We pointed out that this could be best accomplished through a public information campaign specifically targeted to these communities, developed by people who had expertise in these markets. It should obviously include the images and voices of black and Hispanic people and should address the issue in a way that showed its relevance to their lives. We pointed out that if the restora-tion was to be sustainable, we'd have to start by improving conditions for the most vulnerable people.

The one African American among nine members of the District's Governing Board, Attorney Eugene Pettis had known Frank practically his entire life. From the dais, he proposed that the Board make outreach to minorities a high priority so that these communities could help de-velop the plan rather than have it imposed upon them. But his was the sole voice of support. The leaders of the District's Governing Board, the Corps, the Commission, and the other all-white groups treated us cordially and made it clear we were irrelevant. The subtle message we got was that we had to be either really stupid or blind not to see that we didn't belong there. We heard repeatedly how "people of color have no interest in the environment" because "they have so many other 'survival' issues to contend with." If it were not for Stuart and the Audubon Society, we might have thought we were invisible.

Having only recently come to know the glories of the National Park System, and realizing that many of our peers did not have that background nor the opportunity to be present, we accepted it as our duty to attend the meetings religiously and report what had transpired. I could not escape the burning desire to see a change, when the entire community would know the glories of our country and embrace the opportunity to care for such a magnificent place as the Everglades. The fire in my breast was relentless, and it made me creative and tireless in finding ways to get the information out to the public. Frank was equally committed, and having been involved in the Civil Rights Movement, he knew it would be a long haul.

As a journalist, I had collegial relationships with publishers of six weekly newspapers serving the African American community, and Frank had a long-standing friendship with the Henry family that publishes the oldest black newspaper in Fort Lauderdale, the *Westside Gazette*. When we sat down with the Gazette's publisher, Bobby Henry, who loved the outdoors and fished regularly in the Everglades, and explained the project to him, he was enthused. He published every article we wrote almost verbatim. For the first time in history, the black community of South Florida was being regularly addressed on environmental issues that affected them and the Everglades in particular.

Then the other shoe dropped.

While we had been rhapsodizing about the beauty of the Everglades and the importance of the restoration to the ecosystem, our water supply and future quality of life, we got the shock of our lives when the Commission introduced "Eastward Ho!" an initiative they described as "the urban arm" of the restoration. In order to restore the 'Glades, they said it was obviously necessary to stop developing farther into the swamp. However, an anticipated five million new people were projected to move to South Florida by the year 2020. In order to accommodate that growth, federal, state and local governments had developed "Eastward Ho!" to focus comprehensively on redeveloping the urban corridor. This corridor was defined as lying between the CSX and FEC railroad tracks in the tri-county area from Palm Beach County south to Monroe County.

A chill literally ran up my spine. That corridor was uniquely African American, the historic domain of Blacks who came south to Florida and north from the Bahamas to help build Henry Flagler's Florida East Coast Railway in the final years of the 19th century. The railroad tracks divided the black side on the west from the white side east to the Atlantic Ocean. Over time, the black community was concentrated between the CSX and the FEC railroad tracks built parallel on the west. The homes, churches, schools, parks and institutions of black culture were almost exclusively rooted in that corridor. The majority of the residents were black, and there was significant poverty in some areas.

Having grown up on the black side of the tracks in Dania, just south of Fort Lauderdale, Frank knew this story intimately. During his childhood, African Americans knew that to be caught on the "white" side of the tracks after sundown was to risk life and limb, sometimes at the hand of the law. The demographic group that the restoration leaders had ignored despite our pleas was now squarely in the sights of developers. To add insult to injury, "Ho!" is considered a derogatory reference to black women. So the restoration leaders either meant to be blatantly disrespectful to the community, or were clueless and hadn't cared enough to do even the standard research that precedes any basic marketing campaign. In either case, it was an ominous sign.

As they explained it, Eastward Ho! would transform the downtowns along a 90-mile corridor from single family neighborhoods and low income housing interspersing the business district, into an upscale environment comprising mixed-use development, with retail business and offices on the ground floor and living space on top. The profile of residents in the redeveloped downtowns was white, hip, affluent.

"But... but..." I practically sputtered.

The difference between the community that was living in the area and the projected future residents was so glaring that you'd have to be blind not to see that mass displacement would occur. If planners did not take this into account and institute measures to help existing residents hold on to their place, it could only be interpreted as a deliberate act of urban removal.

Ominously, the news media was full of stories about the redevelopment of downtown areas around the country that resulted in gentrifying the neighborhoods where black and poor people lived for generations. Often, those people were dispersed to the winds, unable to find affordable housing. Cash-poor people had been dazzled by the price offered for their homes, only to find that they could not find affordable or comparable housing elsewhere. As expensive new developments came downtown, taxes went up and low-income homeowners were driven out.

In order to facilitate Eastward Ho! Federal, state and local government authorities had created a "Brownfields remediation" program which provided government funding and tax rebates to clean up and rehabilitate potentially contaminated sites and put them back into productive use. Former gas stations and industrial premises could be designated by cities as a "Brownfield," which would trigger government incentives for developers to clean up and redevelop them.

In this case, it meant that some of the same developers who had built up the beaches of South Florida in the '70s and '80s, then skipped over the urban areas and built gated-developments in the Everglades, would now get tax-payer dollars to develop the urban areas. The process was heavily skewered to favor a development boom which would increase the cities' tax base. Unless there were definite strategies put in place to counter balance the scales, the resident communities would be more vulnerable than ever.

We drew the Commission's attention to the state's history of forcing minorities off their land, from the Indian Removal Act of 1830 which sent Native American Indians from Florida on a forced march 1400 miles west to Oklahoma (commonly known as the Trail of Tears), to the more recent dispersal of black communities in Overtown and Liberty City when Interstate 95 was routed through their center. There was still bitterness in some of those communities that had never recovered their cultural or economic integrity. Now they were targeted in Eastward Ho!

And what about those Title VI laws? If the interests of minority communities had to be taken into account, the obvious solution was to use the initiative to raise the standard of living for people in those neighborhoods. The restoration project would involve a lot of simple earth-moving, which was a perfect match for the low-skilled laborers that comprised a high percentage of the Eastward Ho! neighborhoods. The Brownfields remediation program would require low-tech help and the Eastward Ho! brochure showed that the local population was well suited for such work. The brochure quoted the 1990 Census stating that one third of the population 25 years or older did not have a high school diploma, and residents had significantly higher poverty rates than the region as a whole.

The restoration would also include real estate negotiations to buy land for conservation, and would require the services of people who worked in business management, administration, marketing and other industries. We envisioned communications companies such as ours, as well as black and Hispanic newspapers and urban radio stations to be in the forefront of the public information mix to get the people involved. Since the program was projected to continue over 10 years it would make sense to work with South Florida's colleges and universities to develop a steady stream of scientists, and increase the numbers of young people of color entering scientific fields. We raised all these issues before the multiple layers of leadership, and it all seemed to fall on deaf ears.

Frank and I poured our hearts out in the newspapers, informing the community about the plans that were in the works and urging them to contact their state and federal representatives. But the specter of mass urban removal in downtown Fort Lauderdale and throughout the corridor left some of our friends unnaturally resigned as if it was somehow inevitable.

"Where they gonna move us now, honey?" one influential woman asked me when I told her about the plans.

"They gonna do what they want to do, honey," others said, referring to the white power structure.

Obviously, there was need for education and change on both sides. But since the restoration involved the weight of the federal and state governments and the expenditure of our tax dollars, it was the leaders' responsibility to reach out and provide the information to the communities they were supposed to serve.

When Stuart Strahl invited us to share space in the Audubon office on Brickell Ave., we jumped at the chance. Many of the movers and shakers in the restoration visited the Audubon office at one time or another, so Frank would be closer to the decision makers. Being in the office would also make it convenient for him to work with the Audubon grant writers and potentially get a contract for our company. We had been working tenaciously to stay informed and to bring information to the community, but we had yet to earn a penny from the restoration and we were operating completely off our savings. It was a Godsend that our living costs were low and we could focus all our resources on what we were trying to accomplish.

Frank made the hour-long trip each way from Fort Lauderdale to Miami every day. The stakes were much higher, so we were convinced that something would materialize. Now it wasn't just a question of whether black and Hispanic people got a chance to benefit from the national parks. It was whether or not the 800,000 African Americans and two million Latinos in the restoration area had an equal opportunity to participate and benefit from the project that would transform their backyards.

Chapter 11:

Deadly Environmental Disaster in Our Own Community

Then we found out about the environmental justice movement and President Clinton's Executive Order on Environmental Justice, which seemed tailor-made to rectify the situation. It came with a call from Leola McCoy, a community activist and Frank's longtime friend. She had read our stories in the *Gazette* about the restoration and wanted to draw our attention to the Superfund site that was literally in her backyard.

The Wingate Landfill and Incinerator, approximately 10 miles across town from the ranch where we lived, lay between the same major cross streets, Sunrise and Oakland Park Boulevards. But in terms of environmental conditions, it was light years away. It sat in the middle of an older neighborhood of homes owned by black families since the 1950s. Between 1954 and 1978, all the solid waste generated in Fort Lauderdale had been processed at Wingate. The landfill covered 40 acres, and the incinerator occupied another 20 acres. Rock Pit Lake bordered Wingate and the black neighborhoods on the east. Many people in the neighborhood used the water from Rock Pit Lake to irrigate their gardens, and young people from the neighborhood swam in the lake.

Residents said they had suffered from the smoke and fumes from the incinerator for many years, with ash raining down on their houses, covering their cars and making it impossible for them to enjoy being outdoors. They breathed a sigh of relief when Wingate closed down in 1978 after failing to meet the standards set by the Environmental Protection Agency. They thought their long night of suffering was over. Until people in the community, young and old, began to die of cancer.

In 1989, the Environmental Protection Agency designated Wingate as a Superfund site, one of the most toxic and polluted in the country. In 1984, the Florida State Department of Health mailed letters to people in Leola's zip code, informing them that there were five different kinds of cancers occurring as much as four times more frequently in their neighborhood than in other neighborhoods around the state.

Leola said she wasn't surprised when she got the letter, since she was going to so many funerals of her friends and neighbors every week that she had amassed a collection of black dresses. Leola and her husband "Mac" said that when they bought their middle-class home in the 1960s, they did not know the landfill was nearby. It wasn't until later that they realized they had been *redlined* into that area - the banks had deliberately steered them to buy in the "Negro District." When the incinerator first began raining down ash on their home and assaulting them with the stench from the landfill, their "American Dream" became a nightmare.

The diminutive grandmother became indefatigable in her quest to find out the truth and to get accountability from those responsible. She organized the neighborhood into Bass-Dillard Neighborhood Issues and Prevention, Inc., and called a summit where she brought in Professor Robert Bullard, Chair of the Environmental Justice Resource Center at Clark Atlanta University (the foremost expert on the subject) and his team to educate the community. The information they provided was a dose of reality more horrible than anything we could have imagined.

Dr. Bullard cited prodigious research showing that America's industrial progress in the 20th century had come at the expense of the poor, who in many cases were black and Latino. The number of cancers in these communities was so far off the charts, particularly in the South, that a "Cancer Belt" had been identified from Florida all the way through Louisiana to Texas. A 1992 *National Law Journal* study had uncovered glaring racial inequities in the way the Environmental Protection Agency cleaned up Superfund sites. Not only did white communities receive a higher level of clean up assistance once an environmental problem was identified, but they got it sooner than other communities and had their properties bought out, or became relocated, at a much higher and faster rate.

Dr. Bullard introduced us to the President's Executive Order 12898 on Environmental Justice signed by President Clinton in 1994. The Order, (*On Federal Action to Address Environmental Justice in Minority Populations and Low-Income Populations,*) issued on February 11, 1994, specifically required

> ...the fair treatment and meaningful involvement of all people regardless of race, color, national origin or income with respect to the development, implementation, and enforce-

ment of environmental laws, regulations and policies. Fair treatment means that no group of people, including racial, ethnic or socio-economic group should bear a disproportionate share of the negative environmental consequences resulting from industrial, municipal and commercial operations or the execution of federal, state, local and tribal programs and policies.

The Executive Order reinforced existing environmental laws and built upon the 1964 Civil Rights Act prohibiting discriminatory practices in programs that received federal financial assistance. The Order called for the creation of a Working Group comprising the heads of 15 federal agencies, including the departments of Defense, Health and Human Services, Agriculture, Transportation, Justice, Energy, Interior, Commerce, and Environmental Protection Policy and charged them to develop an agency-wide environmental justice strategy that:

> ...identifies and addresses disproportionately high and adverse human health or environmental effects of its programs, policies, and activities on minority populations and low-income populations. The environmental justice strategy shall list programs, policies, planning and public participation processes, enforcement, and/or rulemakings related to human health or the environment that should be revised to, at a minimum: (1) promote enforcement of all health and environmental statutes in areas with minority populations and low-income populations: (2) ensure greater public participation; (3) improve research and data collection relating to the health of and environment of minority populations and low-income populations; and (4) identify differential patterns of consumption of natural resources among minority populations and low-income populations. In addition, the environmental justice strategy shall include, where appropriate, a timetable for undertaking identified revisions and consideration of economic and social implications of the revisions...

What a perfect fit, we thought. Bass-Dillard was a minority group that wanted the Superfund site to be cleaned up to levels that would protect their health and the environment. They wanted health studies done on the local population, looking at carcinogens produced by the incinerators and the occurrence of disease in specific organs of the body that those pollutants are known to affect, and a research and treatment facility developed in their community. The restoration and Eastward Ho! required *greater public participation*. The lack of diversity among users of Everglades National Park, as well as the higher percentage of people of color who fished in the canals to supplement their diet constituted a different pattern of consumption.

From our point of view, the circumstances in South Florida had conspired to create the perfect opportunity for a new model of environmental inclusiveness, if the Environmental Justice Order was applied in the restoration. Many of the agencies charged with implementing the Order were already involved in the restoration.

We visualized the Department of Health conducting the health studies that the Wingate community was calling for, and the departments of Community Affairs, Labor, Housing and Commerce coordinating to solve problems in the urban area. We expected them to develop the labor pool that was there so they could participate in the economic benefits, provide opportunities for small businesses to participate in the funding that would be spent, and generally help stabilize the community. We envisioned the Department of the Interior, which governs the national parks, developing programs to expose the recreational, career and contracting opportunities in the four units of the National Park System in South Florida.

Since Wingate was within the Eastward Ho! Corridor and the landfill sat on top of the Biscayne Aquifer, the vast underground "sponge" from which South Florida draws its drinking water, it seemed a no-brainer that it would naturally become a centerpiece of the restoration whose principal mission was to assure our drinking water supply.

We became staunch allies with Leola who called regular meetings that brought representatives of the government agencies to meet with community members in a place and time that was convenient for the community. She made it clear that environmental justice required that the community's needs take priority, and that the agencies were there to serve the community.

But at meeting after meeting, representatives from the Environmental Protection Agency, the Florida Department of Health, the Department of Community Affairs, and the Broward County Department of Natural Resources, every one of whom was white, provided reams of information showing why there was no connection between the health effects the people were experiencing and the pollution of their environment. Of course, since no studies had been done, that meant nothing. And the State Department of Health insisted that they did not have the money to carry out a study.

We brought the issue of Wingate and the whole concept of environmental justice before the Governor's Commission and the District's Governing Board, and received mystified looks. They seemed not to have a clue what we were talking about, although many people in the room represented the agencies charged under the Environmental Justice Order. We pointed out all the opportunities, and especially how this presented the chance to change the minds of many people in the community who thought that white environmentalists care more about birds and alligators than about suffering black people.

Even Leola's formidable skills and the support of Legal Aid of Broward County could not overcome the government's unwillingness to clean up the site to the standard the community desired, which would either involve excavating and removing the buried material, or chemically freezing it in place. Instead, they were determined to cover it with plastic that was a little thicker than tarpaulin, and which the EPA's studies around the country had already showed would leak. Given Florida's propensity for hurricanes, this would seem like the least desirable option to environmentalists.

But when Bass-Dillard went before Broward County to implore them not to sign the Consent Decree that was being forced upon them by the Potential Responsible Parties, (including the City of Fort Lauderdale and Waste Management Corporation) only the Sierra Club and the Audubon Society sent letters supporting the community's position. No other members of the white environmental sector showed up. The decision was taken to accept the Consent Decree over the community's passionate objections.

When Secretary of the Interior Bruce Babbitt came to Florida to address the Everglades Coalition Conference (comprising representatives of more than 40 environmental groups), he painted a rosy picture of the transformation of Florida and the benefits that restoration would bring. The room was filled with white people except for me and Frank and a handful of black people. When Secretary Babbitt finished speaking, I asked him what would be done to inform and involve the minorities of South Florida, who were not represented in the room.

"I don't know," he said vaguely. "I just thought they would get involved."

I persisted - the Brundtland Commission said you couldn't have sustainability without first addressing the needs of the poorest, so that should go to the top of the list. There had to be a plan, or it wouldn't happen. Then how sustainable would the restoration be?

Frank describes the kind of silence that followed as akin to a loud expulsion of stomach gas in a house of worship.

Initially, the restoration leaders emphasized the need to get racial minorities involved. Then they segued into "the challenge" of getting "those people" interested. When we brought our expertise to the table, the conversation shifted to the lack of money available for outreach.

So, we had come from the exalted heights of the Great American Outdoors into the trench warfare of systemic racial inequality. We could see how it worked, and the devastating effects it had on the affected communities.

A highly placed official actually said to me once, "Well, we know you can't be discouraged…"

Huh?!

I didn't know anyone was trying to discourage me. I might have guessed that since, despite all the talk of inclusion, nothing had materialized in the way of a business opportunity, and I didn't know of any outreach that was being funded or conducted in surrounding communities. But hey, if Harriet Tubman, John Brown, Frederick Douglass or any one of millions of abolitionists of every color had been easily discouraged, what would America be like today? Our resolve was even stronger to "win some victory for humanity" in the arena where we had, fortuitously or cosmically been placed.

Chapter 12:

"Many of Us Look to the Parks as an Escape from... Minorities"

I was leafing through the *Broward Times*, one of the black newspapers that carried our reports, when I saw the ad for the National Parks and Conservation Association, (NPCA) describing the group as "an advocate for America's National Parks." I did a double take. This was the first time ever that I had seen anything about the national parks in any black publication. The ad listed an 800 number, so I called right away.

I introduced myself to the woman who answered the phone, told her our story, and that our company was seeking to become partners with organizations or groups that were interested in helping us get word out about the parks.

"Oh, you want our Cultural Diversity Manger," she said.

They had a diversity manager? I was shocked. None of the other environmental organizations we were dealing with had done much more than talk about diversity.

I got voicemail and a cheerful voice inviting me to leave a message for Iantha Gantt. Her message ended with the statement, "Choose to make this the greatest day of your life."

A woman after my own heart! I left her information including our phone number, and closed with, "You are going to be so happy to know me."

She called back within the hour, and we immediately hit it off. She'd recently joined the organization and was working to identify individuals and community based groups around the country that were focused on parks, public lands and the environment, and organizations that serve youth. She planned to create a nucleus of national park supporters, and connect them with public land managers.

The census projected that "minorities" were the fastest-growing demographic groups in the country and the combination of African Americans, Latinos, Asians and Native Americans was set to become the majority in America. The National Park Service and its allies accepted that they had to reach out and engage those communities that did not have a relationship with the parks, since the parks' survival depend upon public support. As advocates for the park system, the NPCA wanted to help develop this new constituency.

Our relationship grew with lightning speed, and gave us a taste of what it was like when a mainstream organization really wants to work with a community group. Within a few months, Iantha arranged for Frank and me to fly up to D.C. and meet with her and the president of the organization, Paul Pritchard. The NPCA awarded us a $3,000 grant to help publish the newsletter, and agreed to sponsor an ad for *Pickup & GO!* in their monthly magazine, *National Parks*. In September 1996, they paid our way up to D.C. to lobby our representatives in Congress in support of a bill to create the "Selma to Montgomery National Historic Trail" as part of the National Park System. The designation was proposed for the 54-mile route along Highway 80 in Alabama, where thousands of people from many races and nations marched in solidarity March 21, 1965, for African Americans' right to vote. Two weeks earlier, on March 7, scores of black people had been beaten bloody by Alabama state troopers as they tried to cross the Edmund Pettus Bridge, an event that lives in infamy as "Bloody Sunday." The resulting outrage across the nation culminated in an even bigger march on the 21st, and eventually to the passing of the Voting Rights Act August 6, 1965.

Our representative, Congressman Alcee Hastings, is Frank's longtime friend since they both attended Howard University School of Law in Washington, D.C. Visiting his office was like old home week. We found that Congressman Hastings, a Democrat, had an 81-percent record of voting for the environment. According to the League of Conservation Voters, some Republican congressmen weighed in with a 6 percent record. We learned that members of the Congressional Black Caucus have an unequivocally high pro-environmental record, but like us, their constituents at home are clueless to this fact.

Our desire to experience America had taken us from the back of our pickup truck to the halls of Congress, talking with senators and congressmen and their staff. Many of them were surprised to discover the extent of our experience with the national parks. We met many other black and white Americans from around the country who support the parks and were lobbying to get the bill passed. When the law authorizing the Selma to Montgomery National Historic Trail was signed that same year, it gave us a taste of sweet success and showed what a powerful combination it could be when environmental organizations and community groups work together. They had the knowledge, expertise and resources, and we had the interest and passion to see that these things are accomplished.

I was beginning to feel that we had finally found our niche when, leafing through some back issues of *National Parks* magazine we'd taken home, I came upon an article in the May/June 1994 issue, *"Designing for Diversity: Ethnic minorities are largely absent from most major national parks, a problem the Park Service is working to correct."* Written by Jack Goldsmith, it stated:

> The National Park Service (NPS) has a proud history of welcoming special groups to the parks. Visitors older than 61 carry Golden Age Passports that remove entrance fees. People with disabilities have benefited from enormous improvements in access, and foreign tourists are likely to find brochures written in their native languages. Our national parks host Sunday services for several religious denominations, as well as programs that draw equestrians, bicycles, shutterbugs, even wine tasters.
>
> But one segment of U.S. Society is still largely unseen at the national treasures their tax dollars help to maintain: ethnic minorities.
>
> Studies show overwhelmingly that America's fast-growing black and Latino populations are effectively absent from major parks. In a nation that is 12 percent African American, Texas A&M researchers found in 1992 that only 0.4 percent of Yosemite's visitors arriving by car and 3.8 percent of those arriving by bus were black.
>
> At Grand Canyon National Park in Arizona, African Americans accounted for 1.5 percent of those who arrived by car and 2 percent by bus, and the representation of Latinos was not much better. In a state with a large Latino population, this ethnic group accounted for 4.7 percent of visitors traveling by car and 1.4 percent of those traveling by bus. The Bureau of Land Management (BLM) stated u

buts Recreation 2000 Report on California that Asians and Latinos had a lower average rate of participation in wildland outdoor recreation activities.

Although an accelerating movement for ethnic diversity in the park system has begun with some encouraging plans and programs, much more is needed.

We are not achieving the goals of the National Park Service (NPS) if the treasures of the park system are not being enjoyed by all elements of society...

Wow! I thought. Somebody really got it! And it's been out there for three years in the voice of a highly respected national organization whose founding mission is to advocate for the parks' welfare. So if this wasn't news to the powers that be, why was there still no information about the parks targeted to these communities? We'd been looking so hard for partners and doing what we felt needed to be done on our own dime, it was incomprehensible that a major government agency and the powerful environmental organizations had evidently accomplished so little.

Then I started reading the September/October 1994 issue of *National Parks,* and my jaw hit the floor.

In the *Letters* section, five of seven were in response to Goldman's article. They included the following statements:

Your recent article by Jack Goldsmith, "Designing for Diversity" (Forum, May/June 1994) is way off target. To modify the National park System to lure ethnic minorities would be a disaster and one more facet of our country that would be changed to please a few, ignoring the desires of the majority.

Bringing more minorities into the parks would probably raise the crime rate when the rangers are being forced to spend more of their time in law enforcement than ever before.

If minorities do not like going to the parks, it is their loss. But please, don't let us be duped into thinking it is our loss. Many of us look to the parks as an escape from the problems ethnic minorities create. Please don't modify our parks to destroy our oasis.

Another read:

All ethnic groups are free to visit any national park without discrimination of any kind. It is obvious that the activities and environment in the National Park System, which many of us deeply appreciate, are not of great interest to most blacks and Latinos. They prefer other activities. Goldsmith's own studies confirm that. Our parks are overcrowded now. Whether Goldsmith wishes to be realistic or not, bringing in blacks and Latinos from the ghettos will only contribute disproportionately to vandalism and other criminal activities, including robbery, murder, drug trafficking, and gang activity.

Ideas such as this, although, 'politically correct,' are intellectually bankrupt. By publishing the article, 'Designing for Diversity, 'National Parks' does current visitors a disservice.

Wow!!

I was stunned. It hadn't occurred to me that people felt that way. But it helped explain why, with all the rhetoric we had heard about "outreach" and "inclusion," so little action was being taken. Subconsciously, I believed that people who had the privilege of enjoying the natural beauty of God's creation would also have a higher consciousness about our common origins as human beings and of brotherhood. The joy of the outdoors is how it breaks down barriers, as all realize that these natural wonders are part of our heritage as human beings and as Americans. But obviously they had a different effect on others who could see the same lofty sights and want to restrict others from enjoying them. I felt angry and compassionate at the same time.

Thank goodness, the January/February issue of the magazine carried several letters from other NPCA members who had a different view on the issue:

When the May/June issue of National Parks included the well-researched and timely article by Jack Goldsmith entitled, "Designing for Diversity," we were glad to see that such an important topic was featured. Unfortunately, it took the shock of the 'Debate on Diversity' letters, (September/October 1994) to activate our voices. We had not realized that there were members of NPCA, an organization to which we have belonged for many years, who hold such strong anti-minority views. We have been under the impression, as our mixed-racial family has enjoyed the beauty, serenity, and recreational opportunities that the parks have to offer, that these are our parks to enjoy. We are prepared to fight to protect this right for all Americans and to preserve these parks for many generations to come.

But what would happen if those of us from mixed-racial and ethnic minority families should begin to feel that the parks are only for an elite group and not for us? What would happen if nothing is done to encourage those who have not yet had the opportunity to visit the parks to do so? What will happen if, by the year 2000, when one-third of the nation's school-age children are ethnic minorities, these children do not have the opportunity to experience the parks first hand? Is there any guarantee that when they grow up they will want to continue to safeguard them from exploitation? How can we expect people to respect and protect something they know very little about?

We are both teachers. The majority of our students are fine young people who belong to the ethnic minority populations that are underrepresented in the parks. We feel that more outreach work must be done to encourage ethnic minorities not only to visit the parks but to choose park related careers.

Is there any evidence that encouraging ethnic minorities to come to the parks would have disastrous consequences such as increased crime? On the contrary, it seems likely that if more young people from the inner cities had the opportunity to work in and enjoy the parks, overall crime would drop.

And:

As the historian at Lowell National Historical Park, I am writing to thank you for the excellent article by Jack Goldsmith, "Designing for Diversity," and to let you know how troubling I find the response letters.

The United States is becoming a more racially and ethnically diverse nation. The National Park Service welcomes these changes and is striving to make the system accessible and meaningful for all people. According to the NPS report, 'Humanities and the National Parks – Adapting to Change,' to serve today's public, the Park Service 'must develop an array of educational presentations that reflect the many voices, needs, and traditions of America's diverse population.' Alternatively, NPS could adopt the racist arguments reflected in the response letters. However, under the leadership of director Roger Kennedy, NPS is committed to moving aggressively in the direction of inclusion, rather than exclusion.

Wow! There were obviously many perspectives on the issue, and Frank and I knew which one we wanted to prevail. After the way in which the parks had propelled our lives into new dimensions of service, we knew the heights of enjoyment and citizenship that others were missing. We provided consulting services that assisted in creating change and we had become role models for people of color and the parks.

Chapter 13:

"African Americans and the environment? This I have to see!"

In 1997, we signed a contract with the Audubon Society to provide information and build support for Everglades restoration in the African American communities from Broward and Miami-Dade Counties. It included a plan to develop and conduct informational meetings with black leaders from the business, political, civic, religious and academic sectors. In addition, there would be public information meetings, and stories written for South Florida's black newspapers and radio. We were already doing most of those things, but the contract gave us breathing room and allowed us to finally show the community that there was some support for our issues within the environmental sector. We credited the Audubon Society in all our materials for helping us bridge the gap between the white environmental segment and the black community. It was a win-win situation.

But the resources invested in outreach were very limited compared to the scope of the task. Given how important the restoration was supposed to be, we expected stories about the process to be on TV and especially on urban radio. We expected that black businesses would be embraced by the environmental sector and included in the contracting opportunities. We thought that the manpower in the surrounding community would be trained and prepared to participate in the restoration and Brownfields remediation jobs. But where we expected to find inclusion, instead we found barriers and defensiveness.

The predominantly white participants at the meetings discussed how to attract developers, financial incentives and legislation that would make it easier to develop the corridor. But there was no mention of the actual people who live in the corridor.

In partnership with Audubon, we wrote position papers and "white papers" about the impact of the restoration on the black, Hispanic and poor communities. We presented them to the Commission and had them published in the black newspapers. We urged the Eastward Ho! planners to involve community development agencies and job training institutions to prepare the work force. We tried to influence the environmental organizations to use their clout with the government agencies to implement the Environmental Justice Order. We lobbied Congress and emphasized the importance of making sure the law authorizing the restoration spelled out how the interests of low-income and minority communities would be addressed. We briefed black elected officials from the state and local government about the restoration and the implications.

Business people from the minority community, particularly in communications and marketing, showed up at the meetings to get involved and to do business, but soon found that there were no opportunities for them. The discussions were complex and scientific, so if you missed one or two meetings, it was unlikely you'd be able to follow the proceedings next time.

The Environmental Justice Order created the opportunity for a new paradigm—one that included the community instead of displacing it. At our urging, the Governor's Commission finally agreed to invite Prof. Bullard to address their meeting and tell them what the Environmental Justice Order required. A number of black business owners, environmentalists and civil rights leaders turned out to hear Prof. Bullard and to let the Commission know the services they could offer. To our amazement, the very people who were supposed to "engage" people of color dismissed the skills, knowledge and abilities that the black participants brought to the table. In the face of our eagerness, they continued to emphasize how "difficult" it was to get the public to participate.

Then we learned that deals were being cut behind the scenes, and they did not include the "affected" communities.

When Frank was appointed to the Miami-Dade Brownfields Task Force in 1997, he found that there was only one other black person on the team. This was indefensible in Miami-Dade which has a high concentration of African Americans who had lived there 30 years or more. Moreover, it soon turned out that the area being targeted was Liberty City, a historically black community to which Frank was personally connected.

We brought this inequity to the attention of the Eastward Ho! leaders, and when Frank was interviewed by the *Miami Times*, he emphasized that the project had been chosen before the black community even knew about the opportunity. His statement drew a rebuke from the regional director of Eastward Ho! who pointed to the small contract we had been awarded as proof of the program's community involvement. From our perspective, the amount was a pittance compared to the extensive job that needed to be done. It barely allowed us to continue the work we'd been doing for free.

A fabulous opportunity to connect urban communities with the Everglades environment presented itself in the form of the North Fork of the New River in Fort Lauderdale. A stone's throw from downtown Fort Lauderdale, this remnant of the original Everglades system remained nestled in the heart of a black community. It remained a riotous over-growth of trees and foliage, providing habitat for exotic birds and wildlife just as you might find deep in the Everglades. The North Fork was one of the few projects in the urban area that was included in the Everglades restoration plan.

Residents charged that it was the effects of racism that had cut off the North Fork from the South Fork, which allowed access to the main channel of the New River, leading to the Intracoastal and the Atlantic Ocean. To enter or exit the North Fork, boats had to go under the Broward Boulevard Bridge. But the bridge had been built so low that only small john boats could go up the North Fork or south from it.

Frank remembered that, as a young boy, he often rode with his father to a nightclub on the North Fork. His dad worked as a foreman in the orange groves in Davie, southwest of Fort Lauderdale, and every Saturday afternoon they drove to the nightclub in Fort Lauderdale where the orange pickers hung out so he could pay them.

"It was called *The Two Spot*," Frank recalled. "It was set in the middle of cypress and pond apple trees and streams spanned by old bridges. There were lanterns strung around the area, giving it a permanently festive look. It was such a natural setting. I wasn't old enough to go in, but it was a magical place to me. I had a powerful urge to find a way to show the public the difference between the North Fork and the sections of the New River that had been developed."

Frank conceptualized the project as a daylong photo and video shoot along the North Fork, with photographers of color from the community. We interviewed a wide spectrum of people from the community as well as their representatives about their memories, their experiences and their hopes for the North Fork. We involved students at nearby North Fork Elementary Marine Environmental Science Magnet School and gave them cameras to document their impressions of the river.

We wrote up the concept and raised funds from inside the community as well as from environmental groups and government agencies. We chose three photographers along with Frank and videographer Howard Moss. Elisabeth Cascalheira was a fashion photographer; Sule Johnson specialized in wedding photographer and Denis Williams was a news photographer.

From sun-up to sundown, August 12, 1997, the group roamed the banks of the North Fork in small john boats and followed the river as far south as the Intracoastal. To the north it was bounded by water control structures that wouldn't allow our small boats to pass through even at high tide.

Later, we interviewed the government representatives whose influence could help spur the restoration. On the federal, state and city levels, the representatives were black men who had either grown up in the area or had a long-standing relationship with the river: Congressman Alcee Hastings; State Representative Josephus Eggeletion, and Fort Lauderdale City Commissioner Carlton Moore. We also attended the regular monthly meetings and interviewed leaders of two neighborhood groups, the Dorsey River Bend Community Association and the Franklin Park Homeowners Association. Many of these people had poignant memories of the North Fork and expressed their desire for it to be cleaned up.

One hundred fifty people came to the reception at the community center on the banks of the North Fork, including many white people who would almost certainly never have visited the area otherwise. The North Fork worked its magic as people saw how lush and beautiful it was. Driving into downtown Fort Lauderdale, they had only seen the developed South Fork, and many had no idea there was so much of the Everglades practically in the city.

The most beautiful part of the evening was when the residents spoke about how much they appreciated what we had done. As we watched people from the environmental organizations, government agencies, and city and state offices connecting with people from the community, we thought, "Ah, now! This is the start of something big."

Within a year, the County's Department of Environmental Protection issued a contract to dredge the bottom of the North Fork and remove some of the accumulated sludge. Muck on the bottom may have built up from the fecal matter that the City of Fort Lauderdale used to pump into this part of the river in the Jim Crow era. The Wingate Landfill and Incinerator was just a mile or so upwind from the river, so it was likely that ash had blown into the river for years.

The Waste Management Corporation had administered the facility. Now, Waste Management was awarded the contract to dredge the river. The company benefited from both the creation and the clean up, all at taxpayers' expense.

We became aware of another major environmental justice issue affecting the predominantly black communities around Lake Okeechobee, the headwaters of the Everglades, located in Palm Beach County. The largest freshwater lake entirely within America's borders was the heart of the Everglades system, but it had been degraded by agricultural run-off and pollution from the surrounding sugar cane farmlands. Residents of the adjacent neighborhoods including Belle Glade, Pahokee, South Bay, Chosen and Canal got their drinking water from the polluted lake. Environmental justice advocate Cynthia Laramore, who lived in Belle Glade, was a counterpart to Leola in seeking to get justice for her community. She cited a public health crisis in the high incidence of liver, kidney and respiratory diseases among people in the area.

Palm Beach is one of the richest counties in the country. In winter, the Intracoastal-Atlantic side of Palm Beach is the playground of some of the richest people in the world. Yet 40 miles in the opposite direction, people had all the challenges of a Third World country. Residents complained that the sugar industry only burned the cane for harvesting when the wind was blowing west, AWAY from the affluent east side.

So we were almost apoplectic when, as part of the restoration plan, the Corps floated a proposal to pump millions of gallons of water deep underground at selected spots around the lake, with the expectation that the water would sit in a "bubble" between two aquifers. The Biscayne aquifer, a shallow underground "sponge" which stored rainwater and the spill-over from Lake Okeechobee, was the one from which most of Florida's drinking water was pumped. Much deeper underground was the Floridan aquifer, but the water from this aquifer is so laden with minerals it is too expensive to treat. The Corps proposed to drill through the Biscayne aquifer and pump millions of gallons of water down between the two aquifers to be stored and withdrawn as needed. The water would then be treated with chemicals for human use.

Since this technology had never been tried anywhere before, the consequences of failure were too grim to imagine. The National Academy of Sciences Committee on the Restoration of the Greater Everglades raised serious issues about the feasibility in its report, but the Corps ploughed on, ignoring the pleas of the predominantly black and poor communities. Cynthia Laramore told us that the Corps had actually indicated in their report that there were no people in the area that needed to be considered!

Now we were beginning to appreciate the full dimensions of the mendacity of institutional racism. It is the responsibility of the federal, state and local governments to protect the health and well being of its citizens equally. They have not only dropped the ball when it comes to protecting people of color and poor people, but they refuse to use the full extent of the law on behalf of these citizens.

Similarly, the federal government has a responsibility to educate the American public about our national parks and public lands as part of their mission to "preserve the national park system for the enjoyment, education, and inspiration of this and future generations." But it doesn't happen. The continuing growth of the environmental field involves the expenditure of billions of dollars in careers, consulting and other business opportunities, yet African Americans, Latinos and other people of color are practically locked out of this revenue stream. As the great abolitionist Frederick Douglass said in 1857, "Power concedes nothing without a demand. It never did and it never will." That obviously remained true. For things to change, a "demand" would have to be made, and the most logical place to do this was at the Congressional Black Caucus' Annual Legislative Weekend in Washington, D.C. in September.

We approached Congressman Hastings, whose district includes a large area in the restoration zone, as well as the Wingate Superfund site. He agreed to sponsor a session on *"African Americans and the Environment"* at the 27th Annual CBC Legislative Weekend in September 1997.

Congresswoman Carrie Meek, whose Miami district included part of the Everglades, served on the House Appropriations Committee and became our most stalwart ally. When we first visited her office, she said with characteristic frankness:

"I never even knew there was such a thing as a black environmentalist."

Congressman John Lewis and Congressman Elijah Cummings co-sponsored the session. The panel included Frank and me, speaking about the opportunities available in the national parks, and Prof. Bullard, speaking about the burden of industrial pollution borne by minority communities, and the resultant impacts on their health and quality of life. The Keynote Speaker was the director of the EPA, Carole Browner. The majority of the people in the audience were environmental justice advocates. Some knew people who had cancer as a result of the placement of toxic facilities in their neighborhood, and they were quite uninterested in our presentation about the outdoors, which seemed so far removed from their world. It didn't help that a Louisiana branch of the NAACP had recently supported a Japanese company in its bid to open a plastics factory near a black community that was already suffering health problems from airborne toxins released by multiple industrial plants.

The people wanted answers from the NAACP, the polluting companies, their elected leadership and the Environmental Protection Agency. But few answers were forthcoming. Ms. Browner only reiterated the EPA's "commitment to protect the environment for all," and challenged the people to "hold her feet to the fire."

We followed up with a reception that evening at the Grand Hyatt Hotel, sponsored by the Audubon Society and Earthwise, for which Audubon provided the money and we did the leg-work. We had invited the congressional representatives who sponsored the session as well as other members of the Congressional Black Caucus and the participants at the session who were working on Everglades restoration. Iantha had invited her contacts from D.C.— we anticipated a good turnout.

For a few anxious moments, all the hosts stood together, anxiously watching the door. Who wants to throw a party and have nobody come?

We needn't have worried. Our friend Bobby Henry soon arrived with a group of his friends. Then he went to the door and started inviting people in. Before long we had a party going, as well as spirited conversations between people from the "green" segments and those from the "environmental justice" segment.

But the most unforgettable part of the evening for Frank and me was when we went to greet General Joe Ballard, the Chief of the Army Corps of Engineers and the top-ranking African American in the restoration. We were thanking him for coming when he laughed and said,

"Are you kidding me? When I got the invitation to *"African Americans and the Environment,"* I said, 'This I've got to see.' "

Chief Ballard had been in the Corps for many years dealing with water and engineering issues, and he was still amazed to see African Americans involved in that environment. We knew from experience that there were a much larger number of people of color involved in a life- and-death struggle around the environment than were portrayed in the mass media and the environmental debate. It seemed past time for the issue to take center stage, and now there were lots of us zealously working to awaken our communities to the fact that the environment is relevant to all our lives. We were more determined than ever to be an effective force at bridging this chasm.

Chapter 14:

Global Warming and Climate Change – The Stakes Get Higher

We got our first inkling about global warming and climate change in

a call from the group "Ozone Action" in Washington, D.C. in the late 1990s, asking us to help get African Americans from the community to an environmental briefing they were holding at the Anne Kolb Nature Center in Dania Beach, Florida. The recently-opened nature center was one street over from Dania Beach Boulevard where Frank grew up on the other side of the tracks.

A canal ran along the southern side of the boulevard bordering a mangrove forest connected to the nature center on the south. The interwoven roots of the mangroves, the gently flowing water and the profusion of large wading birds among them made for a very scenic and pleasant environment. Frank and I loved that walk down to the ocean for all its esthetic beauty and wildness, but it had become even more special to me because that's where I felt the first thrill of romantic interest in Frank on a Sunday morning walk.

To get to the beach meant crossing the railroad tracks that had delineated the division between the black community and the white side of town when Frank was growing up. He pointed out the places that had been covered in tomato fields during his childhood, earning Dania the reputation as "Tomato Capital of the World." He saw the tomato industry die and a way of life disappear when the Corps dug canals that drained the Everglades to create more land for development. The canals promptly created salt water intrusion, allowing salt water to seep into the fields. Now, fifty years later, we were getting ready to spend billions of tax-payer dollars to take out the canals and restore the Everglades. It was ironic that we had to pass this area that Frank had experienced as an example of unintended negative and costly consequences of upsetting the natural balance.

The representatives from Ozone Action outlined how the decimation of Amazonian rainforests and wooded areas all over the world, combined with the exploding human population and the increasing amounts of pollution was upsetting the balance of the entire planet. The heat was already melting glaciers and raising sea levels, and changing atmospheric currents circling the globe. They said the logical and urgent thing for America to do was to create a policy to reduce our effect on the planet. That should include the development of clean and renewable sources of energy that don't pollute the environment.

Ozone Action stated that while Americans make up only four percent of the world's population, we contribute more than 25 percent of the pollution. We'd have to shift to a new way of life that included greater availability and use of mass transportation, less "sprawl" and more "planned" communities, and greater attention to conservation.

The visiting Prime Minister of the island nation of St Kitts and Nevis described the effects that his country was already seeing. He said they were losing as much as a foot of beach every year. With a country only one-and-a-half times the size of Washington, D.C., that was ominous indeed.

I was chilled and exhilarated at the same time. I was baffled that people as privileged as we are in America show so little respect for the earth. Seeing the graceful herons and egrets fishing in canals laden with garbage made me embarrassed for my compatriots and my species. I saw a big connection between our disrespect for nature and the disrespect we show to ourselves and for each other. If nothing else, our humanity should make us care for each other, and a cursory glance at our society shows a desperate need for us to see that *"There, but for the Grace of God, Go I."*

If our entire planet was threatened, we had no choice but to bond together to repair it. I visualized a depth of healing where we would begin to look at the earth with new eyes of appreciation and love, and it would be a small step from there to love and heal ourselves. The national parks were the perfect place to start.

Once again, I expected to see a big publicity campaign informing the American people about the brewing crisis. And once again, I was way off base. The issue barely appeared as a blink on the environmental, media and political radar. When global warming and climate change were mentioned on TV, it was almost in the same tones that people talked about UFOs. The reports produced by climate scientists corroborating global warming were followed by a host of disclaimers by the station saying scientists were divided over the issue.

We noticed that there was little dissent about whether global warming was taking place. The controversy centered on whether it was caused by human activity. A small minority of scientists held to the view that perceptible changes in the earth's temperature and an increase in violent weather events were just part of recurring weather cycles.

Our colleagues' response to the problem was to do more studies and issue press releases about global warming. But the press releases routinely went to the mainstream media and seldom made it to the radio and TV stations from which most urban people get their news. Since all the people speaking about the issue were white, there was a tremendous disconnection between the importance of the message and how it was received. The response from many of our friends was that white people caused the problem, and they were the ones with time and money on their hands to find solutions to the problem. I didn't entirely disagree with the idea that the problem was being caused by people who had gotten rich from exploiting our natural resources. But I realized that on-going environmental degradation put life on Earth at risk, so every human being should have an interest in correcting it. A depleted, arid, bleak planet that can barely sustain life should not be our bequest to the future.

The Great Outdoors was our salvation and our inspiration. Being able to get back into the woods kept us from going mad over the glaring inequality and downright hostility to people of color and poor people, and the apathetic response to the critical environmental problems facing our planet. I told Frank that the term "environmental community" was a misnomer, and we should call it the environmental "segment," instead because I saw no sense of "community" at all.

We went camping at Flamingo Campground in the Everglades frequently, and wrote about our experiences in *Pickup & GO!* and the black press. Soon, we had a group of regulars camping with us, and we decided to form a club to cater to people across the country who might want this experience. In 1998 we formed Earthtones Camping & Travel, Inc., with Larry Frazier, a long-time Boy Scout leader who had been camping in the Everglades since the 1950s, Valentina Langley, who regularly organized camping trips for 50 or more people, her cousin, Anthony Danzine, and

Charles and Maria Sherrer, who had recently moved to Miami from their property in the woods of Maine.

Our first trip out of state was to Denver, Colorado. We had been invited to the conference, *"Justice for All: Racial Equity and Environmental Well-Being,"* organized by the University of Colorado, Center of the American West. The director and co-founder of the Center, Patti Limerick, organizes an annual conference every year to bring people of different backgrounds together to explore issues of importance to American life. The topic that year was how the full inclusion of people of color in environmental policies and activities would change the terms by which people in the American West, and Americans in general, approach environmental issues.

The Director of the National Park Service, Robert Stanton, appointed by President Clinton as the first African American to serve in that capacity, was scheduled to give the keynote address. The park service would host the second day of the conference in the outdoor splendor of Rocky Mountain National Park.

Six of the founding members of Earthtones signed up for the conference. Afterwards, we'd explore the Rocky Mountains and meet up with members of the James P. Beckwourth Mountain Club, a group of black outdoor adventurers in Denver. The Club was named in honor of the black mountain man James P. Beckwourth who was also an Army Scout in the Seminole War that raged in Florida between 1835 and 1842. The Club honors his legacy by providing programs that expose young black people to the great outdoors, taking inner city youth hiking, camping, fishing, horseback riding, river rafting, rock climbing, and giving them wilderness training.

When we reached the Mile High City, we picked up a 16-passenger van for the week, checked into the conference hotel and went looking for the "black" side of town. We found an inviting barbecue restaurant plastered with photos of black celebrities who had eaten there. The menu rated dishes from "Hot" to "Hell Hot." As a Jamaican woman worth my salt, I figured that nothing in Colorado could be too hot for me. I ordered "Hell Hot" and when I bit into the ribs, my face almost exploded. I had never tasted anything that hot in my life. I had no qualms about asking them to replace it with the next level down.

At the conference next morning, I was thrilled to find that one of the speakers, Dr. Dorceta Taylor, was from Jamaica. As part of a panel, she opened a new window into the historical reasons that people of color have a different relationship with the land than white people do:

> If you are a person of color in this country, you would have been enslaved; land would have been taken away from you; you would have lived on a reservation; you would have worked as an indentured servant. Those experiences basically influence how you view the environment. You don't see it as this free place you can run off to ... You see it as the place that you have worked and labored in, in very different ways from the person who has the absolute freedom to decide whether they're going to work or not, where they're going to work, and where they're going to play.

The separation of people of color from present land conservation issues was reinforced by another speaker. Denver attorney Hubert Farbes, Jr., an African American and former president of the Board of Water Commissioners for Denver, said that before the conference, he received many calls from reporters, asking, *"Could you explain why people of color should be having a seminar about American resource preservation and environmental issues?"*

At the end of the session, I almost leapt over the chairs and tables to get to Dr. Taylor. The first thing each of us wanted to know was what part of Jamaica the other was from. When I found out that she was born in Beckford Kraal, just 13 miles away from where I grew up in Summerfield, we were both in shock. Jamaica is a very small country, but it's not that small. She was the first black woman to graduate from Yale School of Forestry and said, "Some of my professors told me that forestry was no place for a black woman."

On the second day, all the participants were shuttled up to Rocky Mountain National Park on tour buses. Snow-capped mountains loomed against the horizon as far as our eyes could see. Above 14,000 feet, the plants stay low to the ground for protection against the elements. It looked like a scene from the Arctic tundra.

Our host, Chief Park Interpreter Bill Gwaltney, had assembled a team of racially diverse rangers who had come from all over the country for the conference.

The most fascinating person we met was Ranger Shelton Johnson who had come in from Yosemite National Park. Born in Detroit, this young African American found that he was more comfortable in the great outdoors than in the city, and had spent most of his career working in Yellowstone and Yosemite National Parks. Shelton played haunting melodies on his clarinet as the bus climbed up the mountain, and as we sat on the grass in an alpine meadow. The setting was so magnificent, the comradeship so deep, that my heart felt as if it would burst.

At the end of the conference, Earthtones had arranged to go on a hike with the Beckwourth Club. Our meeting place was the base of the trail to Ouzel Falls, just a few miles from our cabins in Estes Park. Nine very athletic members of the club greeted us, including Cheryl's pre-teen daughter, Jasmine. We were joined by Ranger Gillian Bowser, a young African American biologist from the Director's office, who was working on her doctorate. Gillian is an avid outdoors woman, and our Beckwourth friends knew the Colorado Mountains intimately.

They warned us that we might find it harder to breathe because we were at a much higher altitude than we were accustomed to, so we should maintain a comfortable pace and drink lots of water. The trail rose a thousand feet within just three miles up to the falls at 11,000 feet.

Before we took off, Gillian gave us the once over to make sure we were properly clothed and shod.

"In an emergency it would take eight of us to bring someone Audrey's size down the trail, so we want to make sure to prevent emergencies," she warned.

There were at least a couple of people in our group heavier than my 130 pounds, so that was a sobering thought.

It was suggested that we split into three groups; Frank went into the fast group, I chose moderate, and others chose the slow group. But soon after we got started, Frank found his mettle tested by some of the accomplished hikers in the fast group, as he described later in *Pickup & GO!:*

> Sandy is about 5-feet, 3-inches tall and races motorcycles,
> breaks bones skiing off the side of mountains, and is taking

up boxing. 'The Goat' is cute, 11-year-old Jasmine. Jasmine's mother, Cheryl Armstrong, Executive Director of the Club, said by the time she was seven years old Jasmine had already climbed her first 14,000 foot mountain. She'd climbed two others since, and was preparing for her fourth.

Everyone in the Club conceded that Sandy would set the pace. In less than 15 minutes, there were three groups. In my effort to keep up with Sandy, Gillian and the Goat, the four of us had separated from everyone else. Up the trail we raced. Thankfully, Gillian would stop every so often to sample wild berries, speculate on the age of a stand of trees or just look at the ever-changing vistas of snow-capped mountains, tree-covered valleys or granite-faced cliffs.

In the background was the primeval rumble of Ouzel Falls. Almost imperceptible at first, but growing more insistent with each step we took. And then, there it was! Gushing out of a crevasse in the face of a granite wall some 200 feet up.

Of course, Sandy and the Goat were not content to stand in awe at the foot of the falls, but hiked above it, and I obligingly followed. What a view, with the falls, the river below, and the mountains in the distance, as clouds rolled above. Sandy patted me on the back and said, 'Not bad for a man.'

The last group had just made it to the top of the mountain and sat down to lunch when Ranger Gillian looked at the gray clouds gathering over a distant mountain and politely but firmly insisted that everyone start back down the trail. She said the clouds were a harbinger of snow. By the time we got back to the base of the trail, it was raining, the temperature had noticeably dropped, and a couple that had been camping up in the mountains told us they got caught in a snowstorm.

We spent the next several days exploring wild Colorado. We'd heard that the road up the mountain to Pike's Peak was dangerously steep and curving, so everyone agreed that the only person we'd trust to drive was Frank. Following the map, we turned off the highway onto a country road. It didn't look like the way to a major tourist attraction, and we thought we might have made a mistake. We saw a woman walking down the road and Frank started to pull over so we could ask her for directions. The woman took one look into the car and ran away as if the hounds of hell were after her. We looked at each other in shock, and then we burst out laughing. A van full of black people was definitely not a familiar sight in this neck of the woods.

Frank's entire attention had to be focused on the road. One miscalculation, or a bad move by a driver coming from the opposite direction, could unite us with the Rocky Mountains permanently. There were no guardrails between us and the valley thousands of feet below. It was the most white-knuckled ride I've ever taken.

Fortunately, the worst corner was the last, and we finally reached the top. We tumbled out of the van and drank in the very same view that Katherine Bates was looking at when she wrote the words to "*America the Beautiful.*" The "purple mountains' majesty" was all around, and far below us fluffy clouds hung motionless above the valley. We spent a rapturous couple of hours at the top of the mountain.

Then it was time to make the return trip down the mountain. The drive is so steep that halfway down, park rangers stopped every vehicle to check our brakes and make sure they were not overheated and we could get safely to the bottom of the mountain. They told us that sometimes they have to drive people down who made it to the top but refuse to drive back.

Earlier at the gift shop, a female employee told me, "Sure, we drive up the mountain and back down every day." That was mind boggling. We found out later that you can also take a train up to the top of Pike's Peak, but even if we'd known that, we'd still have opted to take the drive as a once-in-a-lifetime adventure.

We visited the Garden of the Gods, a valley filled with mysterious red-rock formations where the Ute Indians, known as the "Blue Sky People," had their winter encampments. At the incredible Royal Gorge, some of the more adventurous members of our group went whitewater rafting. We explored the Cave of the Winds and returned to Florida thoroughly refreshed and excited about the outdoors and the movement that we were part of.

Chapter 15:
Communities Discover, Embrace National Parks

Partnering with Iantha and the NPCA gave us ample opportunities to explore and advocate for the national parks. Iantha was literally "the fulcrum that turned the wheel" to diversify the parks. With the backing of NPCA she had brought together a small group of individuals from across the country in 1996, and polled us about the idea of convening a national conference on the issue of race and the environment. The group included Frank and me, Ira Hutchison, PhD, head of the Roundtable Associates, Roger Rivera, head of the National Hispanic Environmental Council, and Flip Hagood , Executive Vice President of The Student Conservation Association. All agreed that a gathering was desperately needed to bring all interested parties together if we were going to be able to change things.

Director Stanton had a keen appreciation of the racial disparities, having served his entire career in the park system and worked his way up. He bought into the concept of the conference immediately, and provided funds through the National Park Service to help support it. He also provided scholarships so that young people working with conservation organizations could attend at minimal cost. Our planning committee worked for more than a year, talking regularly by phone and broadening our connections with community groups around the country. As the conference date drew closer, we gathered at the secluded Algonquin Center on the banks of the Potomac River in Virginia. The fall foliage was in riotous color, gently enfolding our wooden cabins with vaulted ceilings and fireplace. Many people in our core were familiar with places of such natural beauty. In fact, it was what had brought many of us into the service of the environment. So we were jolted when David Nieto, a young Latino man from East Los Angeles representing a Youth Corps, blurted:

"I hear you talking about 'environment,' but you have to understand, I have never even seen a place like this before. In my neighborhood, the only park is run down and dirty, and the only people who hang out there are the druggies."

I could relate to his shock. I'd felt the same way when I first saw the expanse of fall foliage from Bear Mountain State Park in New York, having just come from Jamaica. I'd seen postcards of fall leaves, but I thought they were art. I had no idea that such variety of colors and vastness of space existed in real life until I saw it for myself. It was a whole different world. David's comments made us appreciate the urgency of our efforts to connect the parks to people who sorely needed their peace and inspiration.

Director Stanton came to Algonquin to address our group. He told us how he had come up through the ranks of the park system in the 1960s and done most of his service at The Grand Tetons National Park in Jackson, Wyoming, one of the whitest areas in the country.

The young black and Latino men and women listened in amazement and were impressed to have access to someone of the Director's stature. It made them feel that they could aspire to lofty heights, too. The adults were no less awed and inspired by his example.

For four day in January of 1998, approximately 650 Americans of Asian, Native, Latino and white backgrounds traveled to Fort Mason, part of Golden Gate National Parks on San Francisco Bay. It was a display of diversity and animation, and it was the first time many of us were seeing that we had peers from many different racial backgrounds, and we were all in one place. The interaction was magnetic. We took pleasure in the realization that "We are not alone! There are many, many of us, doing so many incredible things!"

Among the groups represented were Lakota, Sioux, Red Horse and Navajo; Vietnamese, Japanese, Chinese, South and Central Americans, Mexicans and black people from urban and rural areas. The discussion revealed that contrary to the popular stereotype that "people of color have too many survival issues to be concerned about the environment," absolutely the opposite was true.

There were many questions raised by this diverse gathering: How could urban communities benefit economically from the parks? Why are they locked out of the concession business? Why aren't indigenous people awarded contracts so that they can tell their authentic stories and earn money? When land is made into a national park, why are Native Americans removed and denied access to their traditional resources and sacred sites?

At the end of the conference, NPCA presented Frank and me with their "Marjory Stoneman Douglas Citizen Conservationist of the Year" award. We felt incredibly honored and humble to be linked in any way to the redoubtable Marjory Stoneman Douglas who had awakened the world to the natural treasure that is the Everglades, and pressed relentlessly for its protection.

As a result of the conference, NPCA decided to establish "Community Partners" groups in five cities around the country—Miami, Boston, Washington, D.C., Los Angeles and San Francisco. The Community Partners' focus would be to bridge the gap between the parks and local communities. I became the Coordinator of the Miami Community Partners Program at its inception. My first act was to reach out to Nadine Patrice, founder and Executive Director of Operation Green Leaves, who had been a strong environmental force on behalf of her native Haiti and the Haitian community in Miami since 1994. She enthusiastically joined in to help develop the group.

The Mosaic conference had exposed us to a wide range of people of color around the country who were involved with the environment. In Florida, we were involved with the environmental justice community and the environmental groups at the forefront of the Everglades restoration, so working with the Community Partners created a gestalt effect. We were virtually channeling the environment 24/7. With NPCA's support, the program grew rapidly. We cast a wide net in recruiting members and attracted representatives from other environmental groups, Miami-Dade Transit Authority, the public school system and other organizations geared to serving youth.

Our first meeting was at Everglades National Park. Iantha flew down from D.C. and, like many of the people who showed up, she had never been to the park before. The newcomers were surprised and delighted to find that the Everglades was so different from what they had imagined.

"When I read about the Everglades in the paper, I thought it was all swamp and snakes and mosquitoes, so I never paid any attention. Then I come here and find it's beauty, it's history and culture," first-time visitor Anne Humphrey expressed with wonder.

There are four units of the National Park System in South Florida—Biscayne, Everglades and Dry Tortugas National Parks, and the Big

Cypress National Preserve. Interpretative Ranger Alan Scott (whose job was to tell the stories of human history in the park) and Superintendent Maureen Finnerty were really excited about the program. They saw it as one solution to their responsibility to make the racial mix of visitors and employees more reflective of South Florida's diversity. The Community Partners program was very useful in bringing people of color to the park.

Even at the Visitor Center, away from the trails, wildlife was abundant. We gaped at baby alligators lying in the saw grass, and fish darted under the watchful eyes of a Great Blue Heron and many egrets and herons. Ranger Scott took us on a guided tour of the Anhinga Trail, where wildlife was in full profusion. There were scores of alligators in the water around the boardwalk, and anhinga, cormorants, Great Blue Herons, Egrets, Wood storks and warblers were everywhere. It was a thrilling introduction for people who were seeing the park for the first time, and it never got old to me.

Because we were focused on exploring the outdoors environment, we made contact with other groups that operated city and state parks and historic sites, so our monthly meetings were held in some of the most beautiful and salubrious settings in South Florida. We became tourists in our own backyard, meeting at exotic Fairchild Tropical Gardens, Dearing Estate on the bay, the Black Archives History and Research Foundation of South Florida in Liberty City, Diaspora Vibe Gallery in Miami, and at the Biscayne Bay Nature Center. In a short time, our group included representatives from six community-based organizations, two government agencies, one federal program, the four national parks and the Audubon Society.

In 1999 the Community Partners pulled off our most ambitious event, a "March for Parks" to celebrate Earth Day. We contacted people across neighborhoods in Miami-Dade and Broward Counties, and our partners at Miami-Dade Transit provided buses and drivers that picked them up at pre-arranged spots. More than four hundred people arrived at Everglades National Park for a day of discovery, nature walks and food to celebrate Earth Day.

The celebration included ranger-led tours of Long Pine and the Anhinga Trail, a huge barbecue that Frank and some of the other men and boys presided over, and presentations from park officials, elected officials and Community Partners. The event was so successful that Partners organized Earth Day "March for Parks" every year since, introducing thousands of people to Everglades and Biscayne National Parks, and the Big Cypress National Preserve.

In December 1999, the Community Partners organized a trip to introduce residents of Liberty City to Everglades National Park. The historically black community was 10 minutes from downtown Miami and an hour from the park, but no one on this trip had ever been there before. By then it had become heartbreakingly common to find that whenever I visited a predominantly white school and asked, "Who has been to a national park?" almost every hand shot up, and we got into an animated discussion about everyone's favorite park. But when I asked the same question in a predominantly black audience, the children stared back at me blankly. Then an arm or two would go up tentatively, and almost invariably they cited a small local park.

Shortly afterward, the U.S. Air Force proposed to expand Homestead Air Force Base on the edge of Biscayne National Park into an international airport. The idea was to take the pressure off Miami International, but it was hard to imagine a worse location than in the heart of 3.5 million acres of protected lands. The noise from flights taking off and landing every few minutes would wreak havoc on the wildlife, and a "quiet getaway" to the Everglades would turn into the unending sounds of airplane traffic.

This was a frightening possibility for people in the conservation community, who knew what was at stake. A year ago it would have meant nothing to the people of Liberty City. But now that they had experienced it, they valued what it had to offer. So when the U.S. Air Force came to town to hold public hearings about the proposal, not only did members of the Community Partners speak out against it, but so did residents of Liberty City. Community Partner members Joy and her daughter Rufaro attended, and Joy went on record, expressing her love and passion for the Everglades.

It was a proud moment for the Community Partners. Joy was not a woman of means. She'd told me about a government training program she was enrolled in that required her to take two buses to Homestead from downtown Miami, arriving by 6 a.m., with lateness punishable by fines or expulsion. The education and nurturing of her daughter was her chief priority. It was amazing to watch this ordinary woman from the community overcome her nervousness and stand in front of the highly-decorated Air Force brass to defend a piece of the Earth that had touched her. It was the fulfillment of what we had envisioned in our motto: Give the people information, show them what there is to protect and they will value it and be motivated to guard it for the future.

The proposal was soundly defeated.

Chapter 16:
The Exotic Dry Tortugas National Park

In 2000 the Partners went on a retreat to one of the most exotic units of the National Park System—the Dry Tortugas National Park, 70 miles off the coast of Florida. The park spreads over seven small coral islands at the point where the Atlantic, the Gulf of Mexico and the Caribbean Sea intersect. Its chief feature is Fort Jefferson, a massive brick fortification built in the 1800s to protect America from incursion by enemy ships. The fort practically covers Garden Key, an island where we'd be spending the weekend as guests.

In Key West, we boarded the commercial catamaran, the Yankee Freedom. For $120 per person, the boat provides transportation to Fort Jefferson and back, and provides lunch and snorkeling gear. Our little group was entranced by the beauty of the environment as we skimmed across the blue waters, under a cloudless sky, with the greenery of land receding behind us. After about two hours when we had lost sight of land, a mirage appeared before us: a massive, shimmering structure of red brick, seeming to be rooted in the ocean even as it towered up into the sky. It glowed with an ethereal beauty that literally made our jaws drop.

As we drew closer, we heard a cacophony of bird calls, and saw thousands of birds soaring, perching and fishing on the island nearby. The captain told us it was Bird Key, an official bird sanctuary that was legally off limits to humans during the birds' breeding season. He told us that this was one of the places where the world famous ornithologist, John J. Audubon, had come to study birds (unfortunately for the birds, he shot them in order to study them). As we pulled up to the dock, we saw dozens of large black birds soaring overhead, and recognized them as the rare Magnificent Frigate birds, with wingspans as much as ninety inches across. The males had their blazing red throat pouches extended, looking like they had an inflated balloon beneath their beaks, and the females, differentiated by the white under their throat, soared serenely.

We trooped off the boat and found that we actually had to walk over a drawbridge and cross a moat, just as if we were entering a medieval castle. Schools of fish swam in the moat, which had openings into the ocean.

We could watch the marine environment without getting our feet wet and there was no entrance fee. There are also no public accommodations or facilities in the park, so we had the privilege of staying in the section of the fort that is generally used by park rangers.

First, we went snorkeling on the reef, one of the richest and most diverse in the world, comparable to the Greater Barrier Reef and the reefs in Belize. With a little help from my friends, I got to see the fascinating underwater life, with schools of silver, yellow and other brightly colored fish darting and resting among the coral and sea fans.

Later, Ranger Scott took us on a tour of the fort and showed us the dark cell in which Dr. Samuel Mudd had spent years of confinement, after being convicted as an accessory in the murder of President Abraham Lincoln. I barely looked in, unwilling to face the agony of confinement and isolation he must have endured. I bet the islands that were so entrancing to us may have seemed like purgatory to Dr. Mudd who was so far away from the life he knew. We walked across the parade grounds where soldiers mustered when the fort was functioning, and through narrow passageways to the top where a number of big, black, forbidding-looking canons still pointed out to sea.

It was truly surreal to look down from the rooftop at the picture post-card scene—ocean stretching into the distance, barely bordered on one side by tree-covered islands filled with birds—and to remember that this structure was built for war.

The history of the fort is as exotic as its appearance. Midway through the 1830s, the United States decided to build a series of strategically placed forts that would protect the country from being attacked by foreign ships. This spot at the mouth of the Gulf, the Atlantic and the Caribbean was ideal, and work began on the fort in 1846. Among the laborers were enslaved Africans, many of whom were leased to the government by their "owners," and who were skilled in masonry and brickwork. The workforce included members of the U.S. Army Corps of Engineers and prisoners at the fort.

The islands of the Dry Tortugas have no fresh water at all. The workers who built the fort ingeniously rigged up a water cistern system that caught rainwater, stored it and distributed it as needed.

But the fort's usefulness as part of our coastal defense was short lived.

In 1862, the British developed ammunition that could pierce eight-foot walls, thereby making masonry forts obsolete.

However, life and work continued at Fort Jefferson until 1875. In 1908, President Theodore Roosevelt declared the area a wildlife refuge. In 1935, President Franklin D. Roosevelt declared it a national monument to protect Fort Jefferson, and in 1992, Congress designated the area as a national park.

That afternoon, as we skimmed across the water to visit Loggerhead Key, another of the seven islands in the park, a huge, green-speckled loggerhead turtle popped up close to our boat. It looked at us in panic and swiftly submerged. This prompted Ranger Scott to tell us how relieved Ponce de Leon and his men were when they landed on the island in 1513, and found loggerhead turtles in abundance. They had been running short of meat on their trip, and they killed and ate many of the turtles, as well as curing the meat to take on their voyage. Ponce de Leon named the islands for the turtles that saved him.

The dominant feature of Loggerhead Key was an old lighthouse that survived from the days when the island was a Coast Guard base. As we trooped up the trail we came to a gravesite with a memorial for a dog named "Wally." Apparently, Wally considered himself one of the team of Coast Guardsmen, so he did not appreciate it whenever they went over to Fort Jefferson for frivolities and left him behind. Legend has it that once he jumped into the water and braved the currents, the sharks and other threats, arriving at Fort Jefferson tired but satisfied.

Back at Fort Jefferson, we went for a tour under the full moon. Walking on the ledge of the moat, we saw sea anemones and a huge Queen Conch on the bottom, moving very slowly. Blue-and-green-streaked parrotfish slept in a slimy cocoon they had spun around themselves. We even saw a baby octopus turn itself inside out!

Frank and I set up our tent on the beach, and went to sleep with the flap open to the sky. The sound of the waves lapping gently nearby, and occasional peals of laughter from the boats anchored nearby, lulled us into a peaceful sleep. When Frank came out of the tent next morning, he saw large animal tracks passing right by the tent. We told the young researcher who was on the island studying the loggerhead turtle, and when she measured the tracks, she told us they were made by a loggerhead turtle weighing between 200 and 250 pounds. Everything was so wild and natural that the line seemed to blur between humans and animals, the past and the present. Everything was in harmony.

By the end of our weekend retreat, the Community Partners had come up with our Mission Statement,

"To increase community awareness and participation in South Florida's National Parks and Preserves among underrepresented and culturally diverse segments of the population, particularly in regard to park accessibility, park use, park programs, park protection, employment and decision making."

We'd also outlined our goals and strategies to accomplish them. But most favorably, we had fallen deeply in love with the Dry Tortugas and knew it as a special, mystical place to which we could return at any time.

Later, we learned that there was a proposal to create a Dry Tortugas marine eco-reserve, which the Community Partners enthusiastically supported. The reserve would extend 185 nautical square miles and prohibit fishing, collection or other "taking" of marine life, " so as to provide a place where fish can feed, grow, spawn and export larvae, juveniles, and adults across its boundaries to enhance fish population elsewhere..."

When I gave public comment in support of the Eco-reserve to the Florida Fish and Wildlife Conservation Commission, I was encouraged to see two African Americans, Quentin Hedgepeth and Tony Moss, among the eight faces staring back at me. At least the state recognized the need for diversity on this commission. Community partners submitted written testimony supporting the creation of the reserve, and a story in *Pickup & GO!* gave readers across the country a web address where they could join the discussion. The Commission voted 8-0 in favor of the reserve, and the Dry Tortugas Ecological Reserve was authorized in 2000.

By now we were fully aware of the multiple challenges that could pop up which, if not addressed by the community, could cause irreparable damage to cultural, historic and natural places. But a 1999 proposal to change the formerly segregated Virginia Key Beach in Miami into an upscale, $250 per night eco-destination was the trigger for a large number of African Americans to get involved. Virginia Key, also known as the "Colored Beach" had been the only place in Miami where African Americans were allowed to use the public beach and recreational facilities, and it came at a price.

Fed up with the abrogation of their human and civil rights, members of the black community staged a protest at Baker's Haulover County Park, wading in among white bathers. In response, Miami County leaders grudgingly designated Virginia Beach for "Colored Only" and the beach was dedicated in 1945.

It was close to a garbage treatment plant, and the currents were known to be very treacherous. But the black population of South Florida turned Virginia Key Beach into a paradise. The small island, covered with greenery including sea grape and coconut trees, looked out over the glittering bay. It became the central meeting place for people from all over Miami and Broward County, with picnics and dances and Easter Morning Sunrise Services that continue today. There was a carousel and a bandstand and cabins were available for people to stay overnight. It became the entertainment and spiritual hub of South Florida's black community.

So when word came that the City of Miami was planning to turn the property over to a developer to build high-end campgrounds and rustic lodging, community leaders and elders sprang into action. Recalling the courtships, the marriages, the fun and enjoyment that took place at Virginia Key, they speedily organized to get the beach preserved as a unique part of American history.

Together with Mrs. M. Athalie Range, one of the leaders of the historic "wade in," Professor Gene Tinnie and Garth Reeves, publisher of the 75-year-old *Miami Times* newspaper, formed the Virginia Key Task Force. In January 2000, the task force convened a three-day Design Charette at the University of Miami Rosenstiel School of Marine and Atmospheric Sciences on the Rickenbacker Causeway. Frank, who had played at Virginia Key Beach as a boy, was the facilitator. For three days, a steady procession of people poured into the charette, contributing their memories and commenting on **the draft plan to identify which features of the site they wanted to be most emphasized.** The group agreed that the highest and best use would be for Virginia Key Beach to be included in the National Park System, completing a "blue necklace" linking Virginia Key Beach, Biscayne Bay and Biscayne National Park in the South. Congresswoman Carrie Meek introduced the Virginia Key Beach Resource Study Hill, H.B. 2109, highlighting the beach's value to the nation and Florida, based not only on its natural beauty, "but also as a symbol of the ongoing struggle of African Americans for equal rights and social justice."

In a tremendous environmental victory, the National Park Service began working with the community to get the site included in the park system.

Chapter 17:

At Last – A Breakthrough
at Everglades Conference

Not only did the black publishers give us access to their pages, but they also gave us a platform to speak at their events. In September 1998 Keith Clayborne, publisher of the *Broward Times*, and the Florida Black Newspaper Publishers Association (FBNPA) held a Black Publishers Summit and Rock the Vote event at the Sheraton Hotel in Dania, just south of Fort Lauderdale. They gave us the opportunity to put on a workshop addressing critical environmental issues facing the black community. We emphasized that power and money seemed to be stacked on the side of the developers and entrepreneurs, while the community seemed barely aware of the tide preparing to engulf them. Ironically, the Governor's Commission for a Sustainable South Florida had created a sub-committee to develop a "communications strategy." To head it up they chose Roy Rogers, a senior VP of Arvida, the development corporation which built the exclusive Weston subdivision in the heart of the Everglades. But two years later, the committee was still working on "the message…"

Despite this incomprehensible turn of events, the community responded to our call and when the Everglades Coalition held their Annual Conference in Miami, January 21-24, 1999, for the first time in the Coalition's 14-year history participants included a dozen African American environmentalists. We felt as if our dream was finally coming true.

Florida's new Governor Jeb Bush kicked off the conference in Miami by stating his unequivocal commitment to Everglades restoration, stating that the problem of the urban core must be addressed because the urban area is a 'mirror image' of the Everglades. Congressman Peter Deutsch closed the conference by declaring that national support for the Everglades was so high and opposition to drilling off the coast of Florida was so great, that any politician who wants to have a future knows they must support restoration and oppose drilling.

The three days of meetings, panel discussions, updates from state and local officials that included international scientists, and presidents of some of the world's leading environmental organizations were attended by a plethora of influential African Americans including: a young Harvard-educated environmentalist, Nicole Maywah; Environmental Atty. Patrick Scott, and Irby McKnight, Chairman, City of Miami Community Development Block Grant Advisory Board; Al Calloway, Chairman and founder of the Ft. Lauderdale branch NAACP Environmental Justice Committee, and publisher Bobby Henry.

Illustrating the community's eagerness to participate in the restoration, panelist Irby McKnight told the audience that his Overtown community had the spirit, vision and plans to change their community and were at the stage where they could use partnership with professionals and members of the development community, many of whom were in the room.

We were riding a wave of such enthusiasm that Al Calloway of the Fort Lauderdale Branch NAACP concluded: "This weekend I saw that we now have the Civil Rights movement of the 21st century. If all the community leaders, the Civil Rights leaders and our politicians from across the country were present, they would have witnessed that the new movement is underway. And the leadership is coming out of Florida."

At the close of the conference, the coalition presented us with the George Barley Award in recognition of our leadership efforts. The *Miami Herald*'s environmental reporter Cy Zaneski brought the issue to the mainstream media in his eco-column the following week:

Inner cities vital to saving Glades

The crowd that gathered at the Everglades Coalition conference in Miami last week had reason to feel good.

Everglades restoration had risen to the top of the nation's environmental agenda. President Clinton had just mentioned the Everglades in his State of the Union address and was proposing a whopping 35 percent hike in funding for the project next year.

But Wayne Rawlings knocked the wind out of the 250 or so conservationists in the ballroom of the Sheraton Biscayne Bay.

Within just a few block of the hotel were children who had never seen the Everglades or the Atlantic Ocean, said

Rawlins, the executive director of Weed & Seed, a government program aimed at fighting crime and spurring economic development in Miami-Dade's poor neighborhoods. There were longtime Miamians, he added, who had no clue about the restoration or any of the other bold environmental initiatives on the coalition's agenda.

The room went silent. The realization hit every one: There was no way a restoration initiative that could cost almost 8 billion dollars was going anywhere unless people from Overtown and Liberty City, in Northwest Fort Lauderdale, in Little Havana and Hialeah bought in.

"'Let's make the Everglades restoration work for everybody,' " Rawlins said.

The message hit home for a coalition that includes more than forty national, state and local organizations committed to Everglades restoration. Its membership is overwhelmingly white.

The coalition's lack of diversity was not much of an issue until its meeting last year in Key Largo, when Broward conservationist Frank Peterman, who is black, stood in an open session and lectured everyone on how they should start broadening their constituency.

Peterman's message hit the mark.

So this year's conference, which was organized by National Audubon Society, was different. It convened with Rawlins' panel on how to forge partnerships in the black community and was followed by another group discussing Hispanic interests in the restoration. It closed with the coalition presenting Peterman and his wife, Audrey, with an award for their activism.

Though people of color made up a tiny minority in the conference—about a dozen African Americans attended all the sessions—those numbers were dramatically better than the last two years, when the Petermans stood alone...

In March 1999, we got a letter from the George Wright Society, an influential organization of public land managers, informing us that an anonymous benefactor had sponsored Frank and me to attend the Society's 10th Annual Conference on Resource Management in Public Lands in Asheville, North Carolina. The donor would pay our registration fees, which was several hundred dollars, and our hotel bill. We eagerly accepted.

The drive into Asheville through the Great Smoky Mountains was a study in deep green and blue. Range after range of forested mountains were stacked one behind the other and the hazy blue skies above them spread far into the far distance. It was a dramatic difference from the mountains we had seen in the west, most of which are rugged and rocky.

When we arrived at the conference, we saw fewer black people than we could count on one hand. But for the first time, I heard a white person on stage draw attention to the parks' neglect of communities of color, even the ones just outside their borders.

The keynote speaker, Don Barry, was Assistant Secretary in the Department of the Interior, which governs the Park Service. In the question and answer period following his presentation, I asked him how the Park Service intended to engage America's increasingly diverse population.

He agreed that the parks definitely needed to make a better effort inviting non-white people and those populations that did not have a history of visiting the national parks. To illustrate, he told the audience how surprised he'd been to visit Everglades National Park and find that the signs and information was printed in English and German, even though there was a huge Spanish-speaking population less than 12 miles from their doorstep.

I was so excited to finally hear someone in power talk about the disparities in the parks with real concern. He apologized to the group for having to leave immediately after his presentation, because he had an engagement in D.C. that evening.

A crowd gathered around him when he came offstage and I couldn't get through, so I practically chased him to his car. I introduced myself and told him what Frank and I did. He was surprised and enthusiastic and we exchanged cards and promised to keep in touch.

Coincidentally, Frank and I were also driving to D.C. that evening to attend NPCA's Annual Dinner. One of the first people we met at the dinner was Don Barry! By the end of the evening we had become firm friends.

I told Don that one way for us to increase the information in the black community was to involve black journalists in the mass media, and community leaders who helped shape public opinion. He was so excited about the numbers of people we had connected to the parks that he encouraged us to apply for a contract with the Park Service. In 2000 the Park Service accepted our proposal to take journalists of color and opinion leaders on familiarization trips o the national parks. By coincidence, NPCA's magazine, *National Parks*, carried a story about Frank and I winning the Marjory Stoneman Douglas Award. It caught the attention of a photographer at Miami's NBC-6 who got excited and showed it to Julia Yarbough, a reporter and avid outdoorswoman. They persuaded NBC to send a team to film one of our trips, and it just so happened that we were planning to visit Zion, Bryce and the Grand Canyon National Parks, some of the most scenic and beautiful in the country. We partnered with NPCA and the National Park System to supplement costs for several young people from California so they could make the trip.

We flew to Las Vegas, where all the participants met up at the MGM Grand. Most of us were strangers, but that was no impediment as we got together and ate, gambled a little bit and then strolled along the glittering Strip. Next morning, nine of us, including a 10-year old boy, piled into a 16-passenger rental van and took off for Zion. An hour and a half outside the glitz of Vegas, we arrived in Zion National Park.

Audrey Sawney, a physical therapist from West Palm Beach, burst out, "You mean I spent all that money to go to Europe and see Stonehenge when I could have come here instead?!"

It was so much fun to see the incredulous look on people's faces as we traveled through the grand monoliths of Zion, the vast acreage of lifelike shapes sculpted across Bryce Canyon, and the indescribably beautiful and varied natural formations of the Grand Canyon.

David Nieto, a young Latino man from Los Angeles, wondered aloud about all the foreign visitors we saw in the parks.

"How do they know about these places, living in Germany and Japan, when I live in L.A. and I never knew about them? People in my community need to see these parks," he said. "They need to know that places like this exist… that life is not just about going from the courthouse to the prison."

Chapter 18:

Ancient Mysteries at Bandelier National Monument

Iantha brought us all together again in year 2000 to develop the second national diversity conference, *Mosaic in Motion II*, in Santa Fe, New Mexico. On November 8-12, more than 400 people of Asian, African, Caucasian, Latino and Native American descent traveled to the conference. Nadine, who doesn't like to fly, drove from South Florida to New Mexico. She and a colleague drove through some very rough weather, including a tornado. Such was the importance we attached to the conference.

Representatives of the non-profit world, foundations, grassroots environmental groups and land managers from the national parks, forests and wildlife refuge systems shared our perspectives at the conference which was sponsored by NPCA and various federal land management agencies and foundations. Our keynote speaker, Charles Jordan, would later become Chairman of the Board of the Conservation Fund, a prominent non-profit that raises money and buys millions of acres to put in conservation. Charles was the first African American to hold such a position in the environmental non-profit sector.

The topics included: *"Defining Diversity for our National Parks and Programs: What is it and who is listening?" "People of Color and Minority Communities: Giving Ourselves Permission to be Conservationists/ Preservationists/Environmentalists in a world that says we are not," "National Park Diversity: Changing Perspectives through the use of the Media;" "National Parks and Public Lands; Whose Responsibility Is It Anyway?"* and *"Our Youth and America's National Parks: The Future is in Their Hands."*

We were addressing progressive topics with a diverse cross section of people from the urban and rural areas, the Park Service, the Forest Service and the Bureau of Land Management in one of the most dramatically beautiful cities in the country, in an area closely associated with Native American cultures and the Spanish invasion.

We visited nearby Bandelier National Monument, driving past the Los

Alamos nuclear complex to get there, and gaped in awe at the original cliff dwellings of Pueblo Indians who had thrived in the area as far back as 10,000 years ago. The vast cliff walls were pocked with openings leading into small caves where Native Americans had lived since the 13th century. We climbed the ladder and entered one of the caves, and found them quite spacious. After all those centuries, soot from the Indians' cooking fires still colored the roof. Once again, the lines between past and present appeared to blur. But I really got a chill when I noticed the ancient drawings of stick-like figures with elongated eyes and huge heads on the rock walls. They looked just like the pictures of space aliens we see today! What could that possibly mean?! I still don't have the answer to that question, but it leaves me open to the possibility that the history of our Earth is more mysterious than we might even imagine.

We visited one of the Kivas where the Natives practiced their spiritual rites and ceremonies, and mimicked grinding corn on one of the stone implements that their ancestors had used to refine their principal food so many years ago. Just walking on the trail that meanders through the forest brought me a sense of great peace and tranquility, even after learning that, for several years during World War II, the park had been closed to the public and the lodge used to house scientists and military people working on the Manhattan Project.

Like Mammoth Cave, Bandelier illustrated the transition that American culture has gone through. The Park Service tells the story of how Spanish settlers replaced the Native American populations in the area. "In the mid-1700's Spanish settlers with Spanish land grants made their homes in Frijoles Canyon. In 1880 Jose Montoya of Cochiti Pueblo brought Adolph F. A. Bandelier to Frijoles Canyon. Montoya offered to show Bandelier his people's ancestral homelands…"

I still don't know the story of how the park came to be named for Bandelier and what happened in the interim, but park documents illustrate how the park came to be established:

> …in late 1899, Commissioner Binger Hermann ordered J.
> D. Mankin, an agency clerk in New Mexico, to make an inspection of the ruins. Mankin was astonished to find himself
> in the midst of a lost civilization. "From a single eminence on
> the Pajarito," he wrote, "the doors of more than two thou-

sand [cave and cavate lodge] ... dwellings may be seen, and the number in the entire district would reach tens of thousands. If arranged in a continuous series they would form an unbroken line of dwellings of not less than sixty miles in length..."

Bandier National Monument was formally established in 1916 to preserve the historical and cultural artifacts as well as the ecological system. Between 1934 and 1941, the Civilian Conservation Corp worked in the park building a road into Frijoles Canyon, where many of the cave dwellings and miles of trail are located, along with a lodge and the current Visitor Center.

I wished that every American could see this place as it would help us appreciate the truth of Shakespeare's timeless words:

All the world's a stage,
And all the men and women merely players;

They have their exits and their entrances,
And one man in his time plays many parts...

We'd only spent an afternoon in the park, but I felt like I'd made and incursion into a time and place far removed from the ultra-modern city of Santa Fe.

Bill Watson, a member of the Nominating Committee for NPCA's board, had asked to meet with me after the conference. To my surprise and utter delight, he told me that I was being invited to join the Board of Trustees. I happily accepted. I'd served on the National Council the previous year, and our major activity had been to join the Board in Washington, D.C. in spring for Lobby Day. Members from all across the country troop up to Capitol Hill in teams from our respective states, and NPCA staff worked to get us appointments with our Congressional Representatives and Senators. But being on the board was the big time, and I was looking forward to being able to contribute on the highest leadership level to this organization which wields so much influence on behalf of the park system.

At the first meeting, the thing that no one acknowledged but was most obvious was that there were only two people of color at the table among nearly 30 people, and one of them was me. The other was an African

American man who was an executive with Georgia Pacific Company. Among the staff seated behind us around the room, only two were people of color, and one of them was Iantha.

The board included top business leaders from some of America's largest corporations and academic heavyweights from several Ivy League Colleges. It's lucky for me that I felt no shyness or reserve. The fact that I was one of only two African Americans made me relish the opportunity to pour my heart out and share the transformation that had occurred in me. I'd explain how the remnants of fear and the lack of information about these places was keeping people away. And how, with the proper invitation and a genuine interest in fulfilling the mandate of the Park System to maintain them "for the benefit of the American people," we could correct these conditions. Many people would flock to the parks and be inspired, and their spirit would be healed, as mine was, by the beauty and history within them. In turn, people would help protect the parks, because they'd know and value them.

I was impressed by the high level of scholarship and professionalism that the staff exhibited in briefing the board on current hot topics regarding the parks. When I began my first three-year term in 2001, the hot topic was the Bush administration's aggressive attempts to weaken rules protecting the parks, from reviving efforts to drill for oil in the Alaska National Wildlife Refuge to increasing pollution limits in the skies over our national parks.

After assessing the impacts of the administration's policies on the park system, including air and water quality, wildlife and funding to maintain the parks, the board concluded that the President had achieved the a "D."

I respected the deliberative process and the scientific methods that had been used to arrive at our conclusion. I was impressed with how much of the national media around the country carried the story. And I pressed the point that since our experience was that people of color for the most part did not feel a connection to the national parks, similar deliberation would be required as to how we connect these communities with the parks. Not only did the people need the parks, but the parks needed the people as well. As more people of color got elected to state legislatures and Congress, we could surely anticipate a slippage in support for the parks and public lands, especially when faced with competing needs such as funding for education and social programs.

At the Governor's Commission meetings in Florida I had clearly felt like an outsider. No one had "invited" us to participate. But on the board I had a different experience. I felt that many of the members were my friends, and we had wonderful relationships where we could talk passionately about the parks and many other interests. But when it came to the subject of *how* we would achieve the diversity we said we wanted, we affirmed that it had to be done, but had no *plan* to accomplish it.

Serving on the board gave me the opportunity to travel to more national parks across the country, since NPCA holds two of its meetings each year in a national park. The park managers valued the strength and independence that we brought as their advocates, and took pleasure in showing us special places in the parks and revealing the threats and problems they faced. From Valley Forge National Historical Park outside Philadelphia, where I first learned of the involvement of African American, Hispanic, Asian and Native American soldiers in the Revolutionary War, to the depths of the Grand Canyon where we spent a sublime night, it has been a magical time.

Over the eight years of the Bush administration, most of our efforts focused on beating back some of the most damaging proposals put forth, including a proposal to rewrite the mandate governing the park system and significantly weaken protections for the parks. It reminds me of some bizarre dance, where the administration puts forward a proposal so egregious and potentially damaging that it makes us all gasp. Eventually they retreat in the face of public opposition that we help mobilize. But before we can take a breath, they advance something else just as shocking, and the dance starts all over again.

The amount of time, energy and resources that this takes has been incalculable. It boggles my mind how elected officials who hold the public trust can direct the bureaucrats paid by taxpayers, to advance such ruinous programs against our society's interests. When they succeed, they enrich a few at the expense of our climate and our future. We have consistently advocated that there is a better way.

The big ingredient that has been missing from the equation is—the American people. For years we've pointed out that the average person—

and particularly Americans of color—knows little about the parks. This means that a combined total of almost 50 percent of the population is taken out of the loop when it comes to advocating for our public lands and the wild environment. Even if everyone in the other 50 percent were actively striving to save these places, it would still put the American people at a disadvantage.

I can't say that my message was heard or understood, because for a long time, I saw very little change. People still clung stubbornly to the old ideas of how "difficult" and "challenging" it was to get these communities involved. Meanwhile, Frank and I were having no trouble accomplishing just that, and were limited only by the unavailability of resources to support our efforts.

Chapter 19:

New Gov. Bush Says "Inclusion," Practices Exclusion

People who had never before been included in decisions about the environment were beginning to pay so much attention to the restoration and the district that at some pivotal meetings they were the majority in the room. At the District's budget hearings for Fiscal Year 2000, African Americans made history by turning out in unprecedented numbers. In Ft. Lauderdale, the majority of participants were African Americans, raising substantive water quality and outreach-spending issues with District representatives. Approximately thirty blacks showed up to a hearing later in Liberty City. When the District hired Frank Finch, a former officer of the US Army Corps of Engineers as their new executive director in 2000, the black press was well represented at his first press conference, clearly signaling that they intended to be included in the mix.

The burgeoning interest in the black community underscored our point that if they were presented with the information in a way that showed its relevance to their interests, they would become involved.

Soon after Governor Jeb Bush took office, a distinct chill fell over the effort to include African Americans in the restoration. Just after his election, the Florida governor was asked about what he intended to do for his black constituents. He responded, "Probably nothing." As ominous as that sounded, it was still shocking to see it play out in the restoration.

First, the governor jettisoned Eugene Pettis, who was in line to be the next Chairman of the District's Governing Board. Then, he created a nine-member board with no African American representative. Shortly afterwards, the District fired Leslie Wedderburn, the Director of Water Resources Evaluation, and a 19-year District veteran and internationally renowned expert in hydrogeology and large scale eco-system management. His job was then advertised for exactly the same qualifications and duties. Next, the District removed Trevor Campbell from his position as Deputy Executive Director and made him head of a support department, one of many he had previously led. Both men are African American. It was clear that the District was acting on the governor's orders. I was shocked at the speed with which a government agency could be politicized, but the District's top leadership rapidly fell in line behind its "leader" and abandoned any pretence about its inherent independence as a science-based arm of government.

The effect was catastrophic. Just a few months earlier, I had written a story about Dr. Wedderburn titled, "*Veteran black scientist key figure in restoration.*" I reported that as Director of the Water Resources Evaluation Department, Dr. Wedderburn was responsible for a staff of about 220 and a budget of more than $20 million. During his 19 years at the District he had held leadership roles in research, planning and regulation, and worked closely with several District Executive Directors and Governing Boards in developing programs that led to significant improvements in the way water was currently being managed.

I had written a similarly positive story about Trevor, who was held in great esteem by his colleagues. So their firing sent an ominous message to the black community. I shuddered to think how much knowledge and expertise had been sacrificed, when we needed our brightest and most experienced people for this massive water works project.

Naturally, we expected to see development into the Everglades taper off, but every time we drove on I-75 or U.S. 27 we'd see a new development going up in the swamp. The "restorers" hadn't called for a moratorium on development in the Everglades, so the Brownfields program gave them the best of both worlds. We found out later that the name "Eastward Ho!" was the brainchild of an executive Vice President of Arvida, the company that developed Weston, a gated community that was major barrier to the free flow of water in the River of Grass. We were flabbergasted when he was put in charge of the committee responsible for developing a public outreach campaign. Two years later, his committee produced a brochure called, "Is South Florida sustainable?" It had incorporated none of the information we said was vital to making African American and Latino communities feel included.

But people from the urban area were stepping into the gap. Al Calloway, a former leader of the Student Non-Violent Coordinating Committee that was so instrumental in the success of the Civil Rights movement, reacted viscerally after visiting the Everglades with us for the first time.

Civil rights veteran embraces Everglades at last
by Al Calloway

(*Pickup & GO!*, Vol. 4-8, January 2002)

It took Audrey and Frank Peterman to get me out into the Everglades.

I had seen documentaries on public television with Marjory Stoneman Douglas, and had skimmed through her definitive book, *The Everglades: River of Grass*, but as an African American veteran civil rights activist who has survived "action" in both the southern and northern arenas since 1960, oh, no, not the Everglades!

Too many souls in The Movement who failed to master how and when to avoid or engage crackers, rednecks, or white people in general, lost their lives because of it, and conventional wisdom had it that African Americans were not the boaters, campers, hunters, or fishermen of the 'Glades. So, while I have been spiritually and intellectually drawn to the Everglades since my South Florida arrival in 1979, I never tried to find or organize a group that would venture into them.

Thank God for the Petermans. Since last year, I've been to the Everglades National Park three times, the Big Cypress National Preserve, the Dry Tortugas National Park, and twice to Higgs Beach (where Africans are buried in a mass grave), and the Henrietta Marie exhibit at the Mel Fisher Museum in Key West. Each trip has been an awesome experience shared with wonderful people, all brought together by the spiritually led mindset and work of Audrey and Frank...

A member of the executive leadership of the Fort Lauderdale branch NAACP, Al promptly organized an Environmental Justice Task Force at the branch, with the intent of taking these environmental issues to the national level.

The Task Force issued a White Paper over Al's signature as Chairman, and Frank's as Co-chair, declaring, among other things,

If Everglades restoration is to be successful, the human

needs of the poor and disadvantaged must be addressed. These people are as much a part of the species diversity of the area as are rivers, reptiles, bears, birds and trees. Restoration must not be a matter of "flood and mud" and "stick and brick." It must be an integrated program calculated to assure a good quality of life for all citizens while ensuring protection of the environment for future generations.

In April 1998, the Task Force coordinated with the Miami-Dade branch to bring a groundbreaking NAACP Environmental Justice Conference to the New Birth Baptist Church in the heart of Miami-Dade's black community. More than 150 people showed up to hear speakers that included: Lt. Gov. Buddy MacKay; Dr. Brad Brown, head of the National Oceanic and Atmospheric Administration; Col. Joe Miller, Chief of the Army Corps of Engineers responsible for the restoration; Dick Pettigrew, chair of the Governor's Commission; Thomas Sadler, Policy director the National Audubon office; Doug Yoder, Director of Metro-Dade's Department of Environmental Resource Management; Leola McCoy and Dr. Bullard. From 9:30 a.m. to 3:30 p.m., there was an exhaustive discussion of environmental and related issues facing the black community. Participants were interested and vocal about wanting to be participants in the process.

Amusingly, an e-mail on the Everglades list serve revealed how some environmentalists viewed our efforts:

> I choked on my coffee this morning as I read an article in the Miami Herald announcing that the Ft. Lauderdale and Dade Chapter of the NAACP will co-sponsor the first NAACP Environmental Justice Conference Saturday (today?) from 9:30 a.m. until 4 p.m. at New Birth Baptist Church, 13230 NW 7 Ave, North Miami. Bishop Victor T. Curry reportedly will host the conference.
>
> Astonish (sic) - I re-read it several times to make sure -the article indicated the conference is being held to give more than 300 environmentalists and NAACP leaders from across the state a forum to discuss the negative impact Everglades restoration may have on Blacks and other minorities.

To obtain more information, the article suggested calling (954) 764-7604 which is the phone number for NAACP Ft. Lauderdale branch.

Do any of my colleagues in the environmental/conservation community have any idea what this is all about? Has any among us received advanced notice of this 'environmental' meeting or an invitation to speak? Is this as bad as it sounds or could inclusion of the word 'negative' in regards to impacts be a misprint?

Does anybody detect a faint whiff of Sugar in the air?

The e-mail came from a member of a group called the Everglades Coordinating Council. The implication was that Big Sugar was pulling the strings and the NAACP and people involved with the conference were mere puppets. This was a particularly distorted view, since a year earlier, we had vocally supported a proposal to add a penny-a-pound tax on sugar to pay for the restoration, and our county was one of the few in the state where the proposal passed by an overwhelming margin.

Thankfully, two of our white colleagues, Kim Swatland and Mary Munson, responded with e-mails that set the record straight, sharing that they had been part of the conference and were impressed with what had been accomplished.

When the Corps turned over the report of their "Restudy" as required by Congress in July 1999, Frank and I attended the ceremony on Capitol Hill, thanks to our Audubon partners. Members of the Clinton Administration, including Vice President Gore, were on hand to accept the road map for the restoration. But the process by which we knew it had been developed gave us no confidence that anyone in authority had any real concerns about the issues of minorities and the general public. In fact, they seemed far more inclined to dismiss "those people" and their rights.

But we couldn't give up, and the fact that Congresswoman Carrie Meek took the issue seriously gave us a boost. In 2000 she decided to call a Town Hall Meeting in Miami on the subject, *"Everglades Restoration: Our Lives Depend on It"* which would provide information to the community as well as hear the local people's concerns. We worked with her office to organize the event, and more than 500 people showed up. The meeting starkly illustrated the difference between the way government agencies and environmentalists perceived the project, and how members of the black community perceived it.

One of the speakers was Deputy Assistant Secretary of the Army Michael Davis. Earlier that year, I'd gone to his office at the Pentagon to try and persuade him to come to Miami and meet with members of the local black community. He had agreed, and our company arranged a meeting of community leaders including black publishers and other business representatives.

A member of the Water Management District's Governing Board and a representative of the Greater Miami Chamber of Commerce rounded out the panel. While Mr. Davis and the panelists talked about the scientific soundness of the restoration project and what a boost it would be to the environment and economy, members of the black community were concerned about how the restoration would affect people's health and ability to remain in the neighborhoods that were targeted for redevelopment.

"This project is not as cut and dried as they'd have you believe," said Cynthia Laramore, from Belle Glade. "In my neighborhood, they're planning to dig hundreds of ASRs, (Aquifer Storage and Recovery Wells) around Lake Okeechobee to store water. This lake is a sick body of water. Yet, it is where our communities get our drinking water. We already have an extremely high incidence of kidney stones and gall bladder problems. But I haven't been able to get the Corps [U.S. Army Corps of Engineers] or the [South Florida] Water Management District to tell me how they have factored the impact on our health and well-being into this plan!"

> "Everglades restoration is a $7.8 billion dollar mega-project that will have a tremendous impact on Miami's urban core," said Wayne Rawlins.
>
> Urban planners are anticipating an increase in South Florida's population of an estimated 2.1 million people over the next 15 years, thus creating a need for the redevelopment of the inner city. Normally, redevelopment of the urban core has meant gentrification. The residents of urban and rural communities need to have a major share in the redevelopment activities.
>
> Seven point eight billion dollars equates to a lot of jobs and

a lot of contracts. Where are the mechanisms to transition the poor people in the urban and rural areas to meaningful participation in Everglades restoration? While we are planning to roll out the welcoming mat for our new South Floridians, let's not slam the door on the face of those that live in the prime properties of Overtown, Liberty City, Florida City, Sistrunk or Belle Glade.

We cannot push out these forgotten people but instead we need to create access for them to the opportunities that Everglades restoration presents. Now is the time to advocate to our Federal, State and local elected officials and policy makers to demand meaningful participation of minority businesses and poor people in the Everglades project.

As soon as the mikes opened for questions, people flocked to them, asking how the restoration will change the area, and how they could participate.

Congresswoman Meek was fascinated by the number of new issues raised, and pledged to investigate them further. True to her promise, the Congresswoman took up the mantle. Frank crafted the specific language that she included, almost verbatim, in the Water Resources Development Act of 2000. For the first time, the federal bill governing the conservation and development of water and related resources included a section on Community Outreach and Assistance. It stated:

(1) Small business concerns owned and operated by socially and economically disadvantaged individuals.

In executing the Plan, the Secretary shall ensure that small business concerns owned and controlled by socially and economically disadvantaged individuals are provided opportunities to participate under section 15 (g) of the Small Business Act (15 U.S.C. 644 (g).

2. Community Outreach and Education

In General – the Secretary shall ensure that impacts on socially and economically disadvantaged individuals, including individuals with limited English proficiency, and communities are considered during implementation of the Plan, and that such individuals have opportunities to review and comment on its implementation.

Provision of Opportunities – The Secretary shall ensure, to the maximum extent practicable, that public outreach and educational opportunities are provided, during implementation of the Plan, to the individuals of South Florida, including individuals with limited English proficiency, and in particular for socially and economically disadvantaged communities.

It was a tribute to Congresswoman Meek's clout on Capitol Hill that she was able to get this section included, even though it's a far cry from what we anticipated. Congresswoman Meek's bill was opposed by even some of her colleagues from Florida, but she eventually won them over. To our astonishment, the Everglades Coalition, including our ally Dr. Strahl, vigorously opposed the inclusion of the provision, on the grounds that if we "burdened" the bill with these requirements, it might jeopardize the entire funding package for the Everglades.

But Congresswoman Meek knew that if the bill didn't include specific language dealing with minorities, there would be no way to hold the leadership accountable. The Act required the leadership to report back to Congress every five years. On this basis, members of the community had some leverage, since the report must show how they've carried out these responsibilities. Unfortunately, as we came to learn, there are lots of laws on the books that would improve things for society. But without the political will to enforce them and without pressure from the people, they remain impotent.

The magic of the national parks kept us going. The places we discovered, the amazing history we were finding, and the incredible natural high we experienced from being in the places where our ancestors had lived, walked and worked, created a wellspring of pride and joy. As an African American who grew up in a predominantly black country, I felt that I could hold my own with a king or a pauper. But I also know many black people who suppress feelings of shame about our beginnings in this country, because the history they know consists only of the pain and shame of slavery. In the parks, we were finding the other stories—the stories of brilliance, heroism, and courage under impossible circumstances. We desperately wanted to get these stories out into the wider public.

Thankfully, around the end of 2000 the National Park Service accepted our proposal to research stories about African Americans in the parks in South Florida, and then introduce them to journalists of color and community leaders. To fulfill the contract, we arranged several trips to national park units across Florida.

In the March/April 2001 issue of *Pickup & GO!* I described our "Living Heritage" trip:

> In mid-January, a group of 10 from Broward County, Florida, on a Millennium Mission to experience our black heritage, walked into the First African Baptist Church that our ancestors rebuilt on Cumberland Island National Seashore, Georgia, in 1937. Observing the labor of our forbears' hands, the rough, serviceable wooden benches, and the small altar with a proud, affirmative cross made of two sticks lashed together, we could almost feel the anguish, the hopes and dreams, the faith and love that have been poured out into this sanctum.
>
> As we gaped in awe at the First African Baptist Church, I wondered: Could our ancestors have dreamed that their descendants would come back and be TV producers and reporters, publishers, writers, attorneys, musicians, educators, health administrators? That we'd be educated? Affluent? Have the world at our fingertips?
>
> The same weekend, at the Timucuan Ecological Reserve and Kingsley Plantation outside Jacksonville, we touched the ruins of the cabins our ancestors built and in which they lived. Our group listened in awe as our African American guide, National Park Service Ranger Martha Rozier, spun a tale of African life on the Kingsley plantation. Its mistress, Anna Madgigine Jai, a Wolof princess from Senegal sold into slavery, ran the plantation in her husband Zephaniah's frequent absences. Of her, he said, "Her management abilities rival my own..."
>
> "People today seem to think that if you were a slave, that meant you were stupid," Rozier said. "Every aspect of life on

the plantation illustrates the vast range of talent and ingenuity that our people possessed… They had to know architecture. They had to know science—they made this incredibly durable material called tabby—a mixture of seashells and sand that is still standing today. The plantation… was an economic engine and a self-contained version of society. The enslaved Africans were the most integral part of creating a functioning, economically successful plantation…"

"I'm not the outdoor type, or so I thought," says Fort Lauderdale resident Pearl Mozie. "I really enjoyed myself and, in the process, I learned more in those three days than I could have by reading a thousand books… I hope to experience another adventure in the near future."

On this trip, we carpooled up I-95 from Fort Lauderdale, making our first stop at Canaveral National Seashore. This unit of the park system shares space with the Merritt Island National Wildlife Refuge and the Kennedy Space Center. To get to the Space Center, we drove through the refuge, ogling the vast numbers and varieties of birds in the marsh. It was just like driving across the Everglades. We were intrigued to discover the Eldora House and its museum, including exhibits honoring the contributions of the African Americans who had been part of that community since the House was built in the 19th century.

We drove a little further up the coast and stayed in St. Mary's, the gateway city to Cumberland Island. Early next morning, we took the 45-minute ferry ride across the river to the island. We had met the park's superintendent, Art Frederick, some years earlier. He told Frank and me that he'd chosen the Park Service for his career because when he was a little boy of about 7, he had been fishing in the Everglades with one of his male relatives when a Park Ranger came by to talk with them. He said it made such a profound impression on him that he'd made up his mind then and there that he would become a park ranger, too.

Very little motorized transportation is allowed on the island. From where the boat deposited us at the dock, we would have to walk the 15 miles to the other end at Half Moon Bluff, site of the old African American community. Superintendent Frederick was very supportive of the effort to introduce new constituencies of people to the parks, and he arranged for us to have transportation up to the settlement.

The First African Baptist Church was where John F. Kennedy married Carolyn Bessette in 1996. When we walked in, we marched up to the pulpit and spontaneously broke into a spirited rendition of "We Shall Overcome," which I changed to "We HAVE Overcome."

Chapter 20:

"Pahson" Jones and
"The Sage of Porgy Key"

Besides the incredible natural beauty that we were finding in the park system, we started learning amazing stories about the history of people of color that are not found in the history books or taught in school systems. We came to the realization that the park system is a repository of the American experience, and many of the places it protects are the site of pivotal incidents in the development of our country. Since people of color were integrally involved in building America, it follows that our history is interwoven within the parks.

One of the most remarkable stories we discovered about the contributions of people of color to the National Park System was in Biscayne National Park, approximately an hour south of where we lived in Fort Lauderdale. I first heard about "Pahson" Jones and the Jones family after we had been involved with the parks and the Community Partners for a couple of years. At a retirement party for Everglades Superintendent Dick Ring, I met Brenda Lanzendorf for the first time. A petite blonde with laughing eyes that met mine, we were immediately drawn to each other. It took only minutes for me to find out that she was the Chief of Cultural Resources and a Marine Archaeologist at Biscayne National Park, and for her to learn that Frank and I were involved in promoting the national parks. From that moment we became allies and collaborators.

Brenda was piecing together the story of the Jones family, African Americans who at one time owned two islands outright, and part of a third island in the park. She was studying Porgy Key where the foundations of the Jones family house stood, and found many relics from the family's isolated life in the middle of the bay. She was eager to engage people in the local community in the effort to research and document the family's history, and to have their story highlighted as a feature of the park. For our part, it was a thrill to learn about the Joneses and to help publicize their incredible achievements.

Shortly after meeting Brenda, we made plans to visit Porgy Key with members of the Community Partners, who were of course highly excited.

As Brenda steered our small NPS motorboat through the deep blue waters of the bay, she narrated what she knew of the Jones family story. The details would be supplemented later by researcher Carolyn Finney, who was in the process of completing her doctoral thesis on the relationship between African Americans and the National Park System.

As we skimmed across the bay, Brenda began to regale us with stories about the Joneses. The patriarch of the family, "Pahson" Lafayette Jones, was born in 1858 in Raleigh, North Carolina, presumably into slavery. After emancipation, he moved to the seaport of Wilmington, N.C. where he worked as a stevedore and learned to sail small boats. In 1892, he made his way south to Orlando, Florida, where he tried his hand at growing oranges. But an unexpected freeze wiped out the orange fields, so he continued south to Miami, where he went to the prestigious Biscayne Bay Yacht Club in Coconut Grove to get a job. The Commodore, Ralph Monroe, told him to come back the following day and demonstrate what he could do. Lafayette was such a skilled sailor and boat handler that after his try-out, he was hired on the spot.

A capable, reliable and industrious and a man who took pride in working with his hands, Lafayette so impressed Commodore Monroe that he helped him get work as a builder and later as a caretaker on the property of Walter S. Davies, a wealthy landowner who had received a land grant from the British Crown. Lafayette subsequently went to work as a foreman on a pineapple farm, where he became proficient at growing limes and pineapples.

In 1895, Lafayette married Moselle Albury, a woman with Bahamian roots whom he met while working at the Peacock Inn in Coconut Grove. They had their first child in March 1897, and named him King Arthur Lafayette Jones. That same year, the Joneses invested $300 of their hard-earned savings in property, buying the entire island of Porgy Key, one of the small outlying islands in Biscayne Bay. In 1898, they purchased Old Rhodes Key, the same year they welcomed a second son, Sir Lancelot Garfield Jones. Sir Lancelot was reportedly born in the bottom of the boat as Lafayette frantically sailed his wife toward Miami and Jackson Hospital. The group listened in rapt attention. About 40 minutes away from the Visitor Center at Convoy Point, Brenda steered the boat between two mangrove islands, cut the engine and there, on the port side, we saw the remnant of a garden, and a path leading up to a concrete structure. It was the last place you'd expect to see signs of human habitation.

There was no dock, so we got off the boat and into the water, walking carefully on the slippery stones. When we got onto the island and set foot on the path, I felt as if I was walking on sacred ground. It ran a short way through coconut trees past a flaming pink oleander bush. The foundation of a building appeared, with solid concrete steps leading up to a concrete floor. Some parts of the walls were still standing. A bronze plaque was attached to the entrance wall identifying it as "The Jones Family Homesite," placed there by "Friends of the Jones Family."

We walked reverently through the site, while Brenda pointed out the sophisticated methods that the Joneses had employed in building their home and in farming the coral-based island. We climbed the sugar apple trees (known in Jamaica as naseberry) and marveled when she showed us how skillfully the Jones family had protected the tree roots, packing coral rock around them to hold in the moisture. She told us that it was a unique practice the Jones employed that had contributed mightily to the success of their enterprise.

As we toured the small island, we mused over what life may have been like for the family when they moved here at the dawn of the 20th century. The coral rock island would have been covered with gumbo limbo trees, palmetto palms and thorny vines that could slice through the skin. The island had no source of fresh water source and in the Florida heat, would have been thick with mosquitoes. But the Joneses set about clearing the land and making it home. In their kingdom, far away from the rest of the world, they built a house with a sophisticated water catchment system and developed a sizeable key lime and pineapple plantation.

Within two years of their arrival, the industrious family was producing enough pineapples and limes to turn a profit, and they eventually became the biggest suppliers to markets on the east coast of Florida. But that was just the beginning of their resourcefulness. Back on the boat, Brenda pointed out the channel that the Joneses had dug in the coral using pickaxes and other hand tools in order to get their boat close enough to the island to load and unload their produce. She said the channel can still be seen in satellite images today.

The Joneses continued adding to their holdings, buying nearby Totten

Key in 1911. Their sheer industriousness would have been remarkable by itself, but Israel, the family patriarch, was also a deeply spiritual and community-minded man, which explains his popular title of respect, "Pahson." He supported Mt. Zion Baptist Church in Miami, and helped create a Negro Industrial School in Jacksonville, which would eventually become Florida Memorial College, relocated to Miami in 1968. King Arthur and Sir Lancelot had a tutor who lived with them on the island in their early years, finishing at Florida Industrial College in St. Augustine.

The boys grew up free and in harmony with nature, tending to their plantations and becoming expert in the fish and marine life in the surrounding waters. After their mother died, and later their father (in 1932 at age 73,) and facing increasing competition from lime producers in Mexico, the brothers became fishing guides. Wealthy industrialists including the Firestones and Honeywells had built the ultra private Cocolobo Club just across the channel from Porgy Key. The Jones brothers supplied stone crabs and lobster to the club, and became guides to some of the most notable leaders in America, including Herbert Hoover, Lyndon Johnson and Richard Nixon who were in pursuit of the wily bonefish.

When Arthur died in a Veterans Administration Hospital in 1966, after serving in both World War I and World War II, Sir Lancelot remained on his island paradise, alone but not lonely. Having lived on the bay his entire life, he was intimately attuned to its secrets. The lanky, affable naturalist became known as "the Sage of Porgy Key," welcoming school children from Miami and informing them about the environment with the same aplomb with which he greeted presidents and statesmen.

But the real mettle of this gallant knight was tested and proved in the 1960s, when developers looked at the pristine tropical paradise of Biscayne Bay and visualized another city, similar to Miami Beach, with high rise development, shopping centers and an oil refinery. Well-funded and politically connected, they set about creating "Islandia," and got 14 of the 18 registered voters on the surrounding islands to vote in favor of this development.

But Sir Lancelot refused to vote for it or to sell his land to the developers. He provided the impetus for a counter movement which opposed the development. The "Islandia" plan was eventually defeated, and in 1970, Sir Lancelot and King Arthur's widow, Kathleen, sold the ancestral island to the federal government to be protected as part of Biscayne National Monument. His only request was to be able to live out the rest of his life on the island.

"All in all, the monument is a good thing," he is quoted as saying at the time. "Some people would like to make this Miami Beach No. 2, but I think it is good to have somewhere that people can go and leave the hustle and bustle behind and get in the quietness of nature. I like the name 'monument.' It means that things here are going to stay pretty much as they are today."

Sir Lancelot remained on the island until 1992 when park rangers plucked him off just ahead of Hurricane Andrew's arrival. The hurricane caused further damage to the property, and Sir Lancelot spent his remaining years in Miami, where he died in 1997 at age 99.

Since our first visit to Porgy Key, growing numbers of the Community Partners worked with Brenda and others from the park to clean up the home site. We took black journalists from press and television to the park and Porgy Key in particular to learn the story of the Jones family. In 2001, Professor Gene Tinnie, a member of the Community Partners, an artist and historian, organized a conference in Miami that brought descendants of the Seminole Indians who had been force marched from Florida to Oklahoma on the Trail of Tears, as well as academics from the Bahamas Antiquities, Monuments and Museums Corporation which operates the Pompey Museum in Nassau, and Archivist David Wood, author of a guide book on the Seminole Settlement in Red Bay Bahamas. The visitors from the islands presented information on the Underground Railroad from the Bahamian side, highlighting the relationship between the Seminole Indians and freedom-seeking Africans who ploughed south through the wild Everglades to find safety in Cuba, Haiti and the Bahamas.

Titled "*The Other South Florida History*," the conference was held at the Historical Museum of South Florida and was widely publicized as part of the 2001 Pan African Bookfest and NPCA's Miami Community Partners Program. It included an evening program at the historic Lyric Theater in Overtown, one of Miami's most famous black neighborhoods, and featured a panel discussion and open forum led by the Seminoles and Bahamian guests. The program brought in many local people who were amazed to learn this rich history on their doorstep that they'd never heard before.

As part of the event, Brenda organized an outing to Porgy Key that was covered by Julia Yarbough at NBC, who had become passionate about the parks and took every opportunity to promote them on her station. Mrs. Rosetta Finney, Chairperson of the Dosar-Barkus Band of Black Seminoles, was so moved by the Jones story that she broke into tears. At the time, her tribe was facing a challenge from the Seminole leadership in Oklahoma where the families had been relocated after the Trail Of Tears. The tribes were trying to restrict who could be considered a Seminole, in what was widely seen as an effort to rob the Black Seminoles of the ability to participate in designated federal funds. The piece that Julia aired, together with stories in the *Miami Herald* and the *Westside Gazette*, drew wide attention and helped achieve our mission to get more information to the public.

Brenda also reached out to Homestead High School and engaged seniors in a research project to collect historical facts about the Jones family. After weeks of enthusiastic research at the Historical Museum of Miami, on their own time on Saturday mornings, they presented a stirring report to the park which has since been included in the display at the Convoy Point Visitor Center. One young man, who said he'd lived his entire life on the outskirts of the park but never felt a reason to venture in, summed up his experience in this pithy statement:

"This story shows us that it's not only about the opportunities that are given to us, but the opportunities we can create for ourselves."

Chapter 21:

Restoration Frustration Boils Over

With things progressing so nicely on the parks side, our experiences on the restoration side were incredibly frustrating. In March, 2001, I wrote an article titled, "I need an army!" published in the *Westside Gazette*, in which I laid out the manipulative, disingenuous, dismissive actions of the government agencies and NGOs as it relates to involving communities of color and urban people:

> ... For five years we have advocated to the District, the Corps and two incarnations of Governors Commissions that they needed to invest money in black and minority communities—which will be overwhelmingly negatively impacted by Everglades restoration—to increase the level of information and involvement, and to develop businesses and skills so that the local community that is at the bottom of the socioeconomic ladder, can come up to par with the rest of the society. This, after all, is the true meaning of 'sustainability.' The process under which this could happen is by implementing the federal Executive Order on Environmental Justice, 12898, signed by President Clinton in 1994.
>
> As we have told you many times in these pages, the agencies have ignored, overlooked, side-stepped and finally paid lip service to these issues as long as they can, while other communities such as the agriculturists and the developers who massacred the 'Glades, constructed the restoration policy. Now that the CERP (Comprehensive Everglades Restoration Plan) has received federal and state authorization, the District and the Corps are forced to comply, and even at this late date, when black and minority communities are at least four years behind the curve, the Corps and the South Florida Water Management District continue to pay only lip service and token gestures to the black community.
>
> At a focus group of "selected" people held at Florida Memorial College March 11, to hear the Draft Public

Outreach Management Plan and Draft Socio-Economic and Environmental Justice Management Plan put together by the District and the Corps, Leola and I were almost beside ourselves to see the level to which 'environmental justice' had been trivialized and propagandized. Thankfully, many others who are even new to this issue pointed out that both plans were insulting as to their lack of specificity on how to achieve unclear goals. To illustrate the intent to merely 'propagandize' our communities, without giving us any real information about how the process will affect us and how we will participate, the black-owned company, which has been selected, clearly had not a clue.

Therefore, when Bonnie Kranzer, Ph.D. from the District and Stu Appelbaum form the Corps describe what sounds like a beautification plan that will keep the water flowing and everyone nice and happy in the environment, without ever mentioning the potential for urban removal and gentrification, they have no idea that people are not getting all the information. When Kranzer et al stare raptly at Black participants and devour their suggestions and concerns, promising to '… take that back and include it…' they don't know that we've been there, done that, for five years! And all of this rhetoric is more delay! Delay! While the real issues are ignored.

So it's up to me and you, army! Here's what you need to do right now: Rewrite the following letter, or cut it out of the newspaper, sign your name, copy it and mail it to the following people: U.S. Rep Carrie Meek, Alcee Hastings, Peter Deutsche, E. Clay Shaw, Sen. Bob Graham and Bill Nelson; the Florida Congress of Black State Legislators, the Florida House and Senate Natural Resources Committee, and the Everglades Committees, and to Gov. Jeb Bush…

The sample letter stated that the development of the CERP without input from the community was a problem that would only grow into a bigger problem down the road. It synopsized the threats to the community in terms of displacement, health, and the lack of opportunity to participate in the process and gains from the restoration.

Senator Bob Graham's office received so many letters from community members that they called to find out what was going on, and precisely what we wanted. We had worked with the Senator on many issues connected to the national parks and even attended one of his strategy meetings about the future of the park system in Yellowstone, so his staff was receptive to our concerns. But even for them, trying to make a process inclusive that had been designed to be exclusive was arduous, and we didn't feel that we were making progress anywhere close to the amount of effort the community was putting out.

Yet the concept of "opportunities we create for ourselves" was being expressed in our lives. Our dedication to our mission, and our willingness to take advantage of every opening that presented itself, led Frank and I to some unexpected places. For example, since hearing about the Buffalo Soldiers and the national parks from Ranger Shelton Johnson at the Racial Justice Conference in Denver, we had become even more intrigued. Shelton was stationed in Yosemite National Park, where he had found records showing that the Buffalo Soldiers had been assigned to protect the park in 1899. We had the opportunity to visit Yosemite, reconnect with Shelton and learn more about the Buffalo Soldiers when I was invited to join an Advisory Board of Delaware North Companies, a concessionaire operating hotels and amenities in the National Parks on a contractual basis. Richard Stephens, President of Delaware North, had served with me for a year on NPCA's National Council, and I guess he was struck by my passion to see all Americans using and benefiting from the parks.

The board included a former U.S Ambassador to Australia, high-ranking officials in the National Park Service and representatives from some leading conservation organizations. A year later, Charles Jordan joined the Board, which formed a Diversity Committee that we both served on. We recommended strategies for them to use to connect with black Americans in particular and Americans of color in general. But they took the same approach to diversity as the non-profits: They listed it as a priority, but assigned no budget, no staff, and developed no plan to achieve it.

The company advertised periodically in *Pickup & GO!*, and paid all expenses for Frank and me to attend the Advisory Board meetings in

Yosemite, where we stayed in the stately 4-Star Ahwahnee Hotel, directly overlooking Half Dome, one of the most famous views in the park. We were able to explore and visualize the park as the Buffalo Soldiers may have seen it so many years ago, and Shelton wrote an article for *Pickup & GO!*, "*Letter to Dead Soldiers,*" in which he recounted the Buffalo Soldiers' history that he had pieced together from military reports.

> From records in this office I find that the park was under the control of Lieut. W. H. McMasters, Twenty-four Regiment of Infantry, with a detachment of 25 men of the Twenty-fourth Infantry, he being relieved June 21, 1899 by Lieut. William Forse, Third artillery, with a similar detachment of that regiment.

> *And:*

> I am unable to find any records as to the operations of these troops outside of the monthly reports rendered to the Interior Department, but from the present condition of affairs I am convinced that the park was as well guarded and protected as possible considering the small number of men detailed for the purpose. (E.F. Wilcox, Captain, Sixth Cavalry, Acting Superintendent of Yosemite National Park, October 1899)

The men were charged with protecting the scenic, rugged and lofty landscape in the high Sierra Nevada Mountains that helped cement the concept of "Manifest Destiny" in the American psyche. Yosemite was the third National Park established, and since the National Park Service was not founded until 1916 to manage them, in the interim the job of protecting the parks became the responsibility of the U.S. Army.

The Buffalo Soldiers patrolled the ruggedly beautiful American treasure, keeping in check the stockmen who wanted to use the land for grazing and the timber men who wanted to turn the prized giant sequoia trees into so many board feet of lumber.

In October 2002, Frank and I were in Yosemite for a meeting of the Delaware North Advisory Board. I was sitting on the balcony of the Ahwahnee, when my cell phone rang. That was a surprise, because I almost never have my phone on in the parks. It was our friend, Don Barry, calling from Washington, D.C. At the end of the Clinton administration, he had become Executive Director at the Wilderness Society, a conservation group founded in 1934 with the sole purpose of protecting wilderness on public lands. I was surprised to hear from him, and even more surprised by his first question.

"Audrey, do you and Frank have to be in Florida to do what you do?" he asked.

"No," I responded. "Why?"

"Because we have a position in Atlanta that Frank would be perfect for. If you are flexible, he should apply."

"Well, we are not looking for a job," I said haughtily. "We have our own company and what we're looking for is contracts. But here's Frank."

I handed the phone to Frank and listened to his end of the conversation. When he hung up, we looked at each other in stunned silence.

We had two daughters and a grandson in Atlanta. For years, my daughter Lisa Martin had been trying to persuade me to move to Atlanta, and I had laughed off the idea.

"What would I do in Atlanta? There's no beach!"

I had a serious need to be close to the water. Even if I didn't go to the beach for months, I liked knowing that it was there. Atlanta was five or six hours from the nearest beach. But suddenly, here was Atlanta on the table as a possible option. We liked what we knew about the Wilderness Society, and we had the utmost confidence in Don. Atlanta was considered a Mecca for African Americans, so if there was anywhere in the country where a movement for environmentalism could take off among black Americans, it would be Atlanta. And we'd be close to the children!

By December 2002, after several interviews in Atlanta and D.C., Frank accepted the job as the South East Regional Director of The Wilderness Society. Shortly before we left, two unusual occurrences confirmed that we had made the right decision.

I'd just filled the birdfeeder and gone back into the kitchen when Frank came in, bug-eyed.

"Baby," he breathed. "A pigeon just ate out of my hand. I just had the impulse to walk over to it with a little bit of seed in my hand, and it stepped right off the fence onto my hand."

We'd lived on the ranch seven years and never had this kind of close encounter.

A few weeks later, we were sitting on the beautiful canopied swing looking out over the peaceful meadows where horses and cows grazed in the fields. I got up and went inside the house to get us cool drinks. I returned minutes later to find Frank in that wide-eyed state that told me something amazing had just happened.

"I was just sitting here and I saw this blue jay coming toward me," he said. "I thought it was coming a little low to make it over the top of the swing. But it came straight under the roof and perched on my head!"

"So what did you do?!" I couldn't believe I had missed this sight.

"Nothing. What could I do? I just sat here quietly until he got ready and left."

We took this as a sign that the powers that had guided us from the first day we set out on the road had given their stamp of approval on the move to Atlanta.

In January 2003, after a big send off party at the ranch, we said "so long" to Florida and drove to our new home in Atlanta.

Chapter 22:

Move to Atlanta – the Black Mecca

I was thrilled by the energy of the city and the fact that there was so much racial diversity. Black people were visible in every area of life and in every capacity. We had heard about the horrendous traffic in Atlanta, and we decided that we wanted to live no more than a couple of miles from Frank's office. Fortunately, the office was in Midtown, and we found an apartment that was only a seven-minute drive away, and close to Centennial Olympic Park. One block over was a plaza with a supermarket, a dry cleaners, a bank, a drugstore and a post office.

A little over a mile away is the Martin Luther King Jr. National Historic Site, and the Carter Center, including the Jimmy Carter Presidential Library and Museum, is approximately two miles away. Our upstairs bedroom window faced the Civic Center across the street, and four months after we moved in, we watched an incredible Midtown Music Festival performance where we could actually see the performers from our bed!

The first few environmental meetings we went to were as uniformly white as when we'd first started in Florida. Here was the one arena where diversity had not penetrated. The occasional other black person we saw usually worked for one of the government agencies. In almost 20 years in Atlanta, the director of the Wilderness Society's office had always been a white man. So when Frank showed up, it was a big change in an arena where the leadership was exclusively white, and predominantly male. At some meetings, it felt like we were back in that bar in Gillette, Wyoming.

But some members of the community immediately embraced us and made us feel welcome. At the first reception we were invited to, almost nobody met our eyes or returned our smiles. Thank God we ran into Nan and Britt Pendergast. This couple, married (64 years at the time) still treated each other like lovers. He was attentive to her every whim, and she still had the bearing of an elegant young woman. They were long-time environmentalists who had lived in Atlanta more than 70 years, actively supported the Civil Rights Movement and were close to Dr. King. They invited us to their home in Buckhead, and generally made us feel very welcome. Knowing we had their support was a huge boost.

Frank has a knack for setting people at ease, because he is so much at ease with himself. He's elegant, knowledgeable, prepared, and has great breadth of life experience and wisdom to draw from. Shortly after he started at the Wilderness Society, a group from North Georgia called to ask for the organization's help in securing wilderness designation for a section of the mountains. Frank agreed to drive up to Ellijay, an hour and a half north, to meet the group.

The meeting was set for a barbecue restaurant in a predominantly white area where the owner was known as a big supporter of the Republican Party. Once a year he'd go to Capitol Hill and put on a big pig roast for members of Congress. His restaurant was the gathering place when Republican leaders came to town. As we walked in, I wondered if he knew we were black. The walls were covered with photos of Republican politicians posed with the owner, and I was relieved to see a photo of one black person, Congressman J. C. Watts of Oklahoma. At least one other black person had been here.

I think the owner was surprised when we walked in, and even more surprised when Frank was introduced as the representative from the Wilderness Society. I could almost hear the walls cracking.

The group had a very collegial discussion and Frank laid out the various strategies that could be used to achieve their goal. They agreed on the best course of action, and we left Ellijay feeling like we made some new friends and allies. That meeting eventually led to the introduction of a bill in Congress (HR 707) to conserve the area under the designation of the Mountaintown National Scenic Area.

The overwhelming majority of members of the Wilderness Society across the country—perhaps as much as 95 percent—are white. In carrying out its mission "to ensure that future generations will enjoy the clean air and water, wildlife, beauty and opportunity for recreation and renewal provided by pristine forests, rivers, deserts and mountains," the Society focused on science and politics. But Frank felt that the focus also had to be on people. Otherwise, who were we saving those places for? He felt strongly that there should be more emphasis on engaging the community in preservation, and especially citizens who were unfamiliar with public lands. Unless Atlanta's large black population was invited into the enjoyment and conservation of the wild lands around them in the Southeast, the chances of being able to achieve the mission would be greatly reduced. He persuaded his peers and management at TWS that outreach to the urban population would benefit the people as well as the resources. He pointed out that logically, if people didn't know and love the land, protection would be impossible and unsustainable.

The organization allowed its regional directors some autonomy, so even as he was working to persuade his head office in D.C., Frank was also moving forward nationally and locally. Part of his duties was to work closely with the Congressional Black Caucus, (CBC) to get their support for wilderness issues. The CBC has the most pro-environmental voting record in the entire Congress, but somehow this is not communicated to their constituents. The Congressmen and women said they voted for the environment as a matter of conscience, but they were focused on their constituents' most urgent concerns, seeking equity in such areas as education, employment, health care and a generally good quality of life.

There are hundreds of people lobbying Congress on behalf of the environment, but only a handful of them are black. It was a novelty for them to see Frank representing an environmental organization, but they established an easy rapport born of their shared Southern heritage and Civil Rights backgrounds. Lucky for us, our Congressman was none other than the Hon. John Lewis, whose leadership in the Civil Rights and Human Rights movements was legendary. Imagine our surprise to learn that he also had an incredible record in the environmental movement! His office was bulging with awards, many of them from environmental organizations. Having a black man come to talk with them about wilderness made them see that the wilderness might be relevant to blacks after all. They were glad to see that at least one salary in the environmental segment was going into the black community. Many complained that the environmentalists took their votes for granted, spending lots of money in support of white candidates' campaigns, and none at all with African Americans who actually vote for the environment.

I thought that environmental organizations in Atlanta would be receptive to Earthwise and use our consulting services to help bridge the obvious gap in communications between the races. I went with Frank to many of his meetings, where at least 95 percent of all participants were white.

I also went to a meeting of the Atlanta Community Partners which was still struggling to find its footing, and 90 percent of the participants were people of color. I went to environmental justice meetings and they were all black, except for the people representing the agencies. The difference was so stark. I was introduced to many leaders, who I immediately told about the service I had to offer, and sometimes followed up with written communication. Still, there were no takers. I got the feeling that people didn't realize anything was wrong, that this was the status quo.

But nothing could burst my bubble. Frank was being paid to do the work he loved, and I reasoned that eventually things would have to change and business would pick up for Earthwise. I knew that the condition of our environment wasn't likely to improve until we literally had a condition of "all hands on deck," with everyone in America fully knowledgeable and doing their part to keep our planet livable. Frank traveled frequently and I often went with him, especially if it was a road trip. It gave me the opportunity to learn on the spot what he was doing, and we enjoyed each other's company. It was always a pleasure to be on the road together.

It was a joy to be in such close proximity with our daughters Lisa and Andrea and their families. Lisa's son Yero was 8 and we were thankful to be part of his life at an age when he was still impressionable, and we became very close. Many Sundays our home was filled with family and lots of Jamaican jerk chicken, rice and beans, collard greens and corn-bread that I made. On holidays, Frank took over the kitchen, often working through the night before Christmas to produce a feast of turkey and dressing, a standing rib roast, a whole snapper stuffed with shrimp and crab meat, and pies made from scratch. He joked that he had his bottle for company, as he'd pour a bit of wine into something he was making, and then pour some into himself.

"A little wine for the food, a little wine for me," he'd joke.

Shortly after we got to Atlanta, I was invited by Delaware North to attend the Celebration of the Buffalo Soldiers Centennial in Sequoia National Park, where DNC was the concessionaire. They offered to put me up at the Wuksachi Lodge, which they ran, and generally made the trip affordable for me. Who could resist? I flew into Fresno/Yosemite International Airport, picked up a rental car and drove the winding, scenic road up to the giant trees.

When I passed through the entrance station and was greeted warmly by the ranger on duty, I felt like I was coming home. I always get a surge of pride when I hand over my National Parks Pass, which identifies me as a regular. When I hand over that pass, I am telegraphing the message that I know the park system and value it. It's an insider's club open to everyone in America, and I feel that it affirms our common humanity and shows respect for nature.

Chapter 23:

Buffalo Soldiers, the 'Beach Lady,' a Princess and a Queen

Sequoia National Park is twice the size of New York City and almost six times as large as Washington, D.C., in the High Sierra Mountains. As I drove up the winding mountain road, with spectacular views on either side as far as I could see, a shiver ran through me as I thought of the Buffalo Soldiers who rode steadily for 16 days from the Presidio to get to the park. Deployed to protect the park in the summer of 1903, the men of Troops I and M of the ninth U.S. Cavalry and three white officers arrived at the park in June under the command of Captain Charles Young. The third African American to graduate from West Point Military Academy, Captain Young said later that the worst he could wish for an enemy would be to make him a black man and send him to West Point.

A poet, musician, and a veteran of U.S. wars against Native Americans in the American West and against natives in the jungles of the Philippines, Captain Young arrived in Sequoia in June 1903 with 93 Buffalo Soldiers from Troops I and M of the Ninth U.S. Cavalry, and three white officers. In a brochure provided by the park I read:

> Young and his troopers arrived in Sequoia after a 16-day ride to find that their major assignment would be the extension of the wagon road. Hoping to break the sluggish pattern of previous military administrations, Young poured his considerable energies into the project, and dirt and rock began to fly. By mid-August wagons were entering the mountain-top forest for the first time. Still not content, Young kept his crews working and soon extended the road to the base of the famous Moro Rock. During the summer of 1903, Young and his troops built as much road as the combined results of the three previous summers.

The wagon road enabled wealthy, influential people to visit the park for the first time, and to show their appreciation and support by lobbying Congress for funding to adequately protect it. But once the road was finished, Captain Young observed people trampling the shallow roots of the giant trees, and he built a fence around the most exposed trees to protect them. He also sought to acquire more land to expand the boundaries of the park, but was unsuccessful, and the Park Service later acquired much of the same property at a far higher price.

Captain Young and the Buffalo Soldiers so impressed the citizens of nearby Visalia that community leaders insisted that one of the giant sequoias should be named in his honor. Col. Young refused, asserting that these lofty 2,000-year-old living beings should not be diminished by the attachment of any human's name. He capitulated only when it was agreed that the person honored would be Booker T. Washington, who was his contemporary.

The Booker T. Washington giant sequoia tree had fallen into obscurity until early in the 21st century when George Palmer, a newly-retired Californian, learned about the Buffalo Soldiers story and pressed for the park to observe the centennial of their service in Sequoia. He wrote letters informing President Clinton, Interior Secretary Bruce Babbitt, his California senator, Diane Feinstein, and Oprah Winfrey. When the National Park Service agreed to hold the Centennial Celebrations in 2003, the park's archivist, Ward Eldridge, began searching for records from the Buffalo Soldiers' time in the park. That's when he stumbled upon information about the Booker T. Washington tree, and set about identifying it among the Giant Grove of Sequoias. The story he told gave me the chills:

"I was talking with Floyd Thomas, who is the curator at the National Afro-American Museum and Cultural Center in Wilberforce, Ohio, where Col. Young spent a good deal of time.

"Floyd asked me, 'Have you ever heard of the Booker T. Washington tree?' I hadn't, but Floyd faxed over a historic photograph from Col. Young's papers of a giant sequoia bearing such a sign. And the search was on.

"It took almost a year, but in the spring of 2000 Bill Tweed, the park's chief naturalist, suggested that I check along the Moro Rock Road. 'Given the time they spent building that road in 1903, Capt. Young would have had a chance to select a large sequoia there,' he said.

"Working from the faxed image, I made my way down the narrow road.

I was focused on a number of large sequoias near the Auto Log, but I was having no luck making a match with the photo. Finally, I turned away and there, across the road, stood the very sequoia in the photograph with the bark furrows that twist slightly up and to the right. The clincher was a feature of another sequoia to the left—a horizontal ridge of bark ringing the tree some 30 feet from the ground.

"I was so happy. I got in touch with Booker T.'s great-grandson, Ted Jackson, who is a district superintendent with California State Parks. I invited him to go see the tree with me, and as we're driving up the mountain, he asked me if I get out much into the Sequoia back country. He seemed to be terribly familiar with the environment here. Then I found out that he used to be a ranger here at the park and still camps out frequently in the backwoods.

"I took him to the tree—I'd really only just found it—and the image I'd used to find it was a fax of a Xerox, so it is quite low quality. But, it had a couple of distinguishing features. So we're standing at the tree, and he looks at the picture and says, kind of incredulous, 'Is this the picture you used? Are you sure this is the right tree?'

"I got a sick feeling in the pit of my stomach. Then, at almost the same instant, Ted looked up at the trunk, and there, exactly where the photo shows that a sign had hung, was a large old nail. That was the clincher. It was an unbelievable experience."

The entire time he was telling this story, my heart was pounding with excitement. It reinforced my belief that unseen forces come to our assistance when we commit ourselves fully to a task. Besides, I had no doubt that our ancestors are pleased that these stories are being uncovered and are helping us in the process.

At the Centennial Celebrations, I met Col. Young's descendants, Mr. and Mrs. Dennis Russell and their son, Kevin, and a number of Booker T.'s descendants, including his granddaughters Mrs. Margaret Washington Clifford and Mrs. Gloria Washington Baskin, and his great grandson, Ted Jackson. When I asked Mr. Jackson how it felt to know that his great-grandfather had been honored with a giant sequoia 100 years ago, he said he was less impressed with that than by knowing that the Buffalo Soldiers had been instrumental in managing public lands 100 years before him.

"In this position I'm often considered a trail blazer," he told me, "and now I find that I am just following in the footsteps of those ancestors."

In the heartfelt tributes that poured out that day, the Deputy Director of the National Park Service, Don Murphy, proposed that a giant sequoia should finally be named after Col. Young. The Colonel Young tree was selected and named in 2004.

The base of the giant sequoias look like feet with toes curled in the act of walking, and their massive red trunks loom straight up for more than 300 feet before sprouting branches. The first time Frank and I visited Sequoia, I was skipping ahead of him on a trail when I came upon bear scat, so fresh it was still steaming. I stopped in my tracks, and immediately we began to talk louder and sing, telegraphing our presence to any nearby bears. Black bears tend to avoid people, but there are also grizzlies and mountain lions aplenty in the mountains. It made me admire Captain Young and his men even more for being able to negotiate this environment and accomplish so much a century earlier when the land was even more wild and untamed.

On the other side of the country, on the Atlantic Coast just north of Jacksonville, Florida, we became aware of another force of nature, the redoubtable MaVynee Betsch. MaVynee learned about Frank becoming the Southeast Regional Director of the Wilderness Society, and one of the first pieces of mail Frank received was a letter from her. She welcomed him and enclosed a check for a subscription to *Pickup & GO!*, and also included a copy of a newspaper article featuring the renowned ethno botanist, Dr. Anthony Andoh, and his wife, Mrs. Kali Sichen Andoh. The Andohs lived on their 20-acre forest retreat in College Park, an Atlanta suburb. MaVynee encouraged us to connect with them, but it didn't happen until years later when MaVynee came to Atlanta with film producer Erica McCarthy from Nowhere Productions, which was doing a documentary on MaVynee. It was a most joyful get together, as we were on one vibration about nature and the importance of caring for our world.

With her seven-foot-long gray-streaked dreadlocks which she wore in the shape of the continent of Africa and carried slung over one arm, and her long nails that made curlicues around her finger, the six-foot tall former opera singer, descendant of an enslaved African princess and the white man who married her, was every inch a diva. Her rich voice and strong persona communicated her lineage and we all looked up to her.

Dr. Andoh, whose legacy of indigenous knowledge of the plants of the world dates back generations and whose father, like himself, was educated at the peerless Royal Botanic Gardens at Kew in England, has written 10 books about plants and their uses by different cultures of the world. MaVynee, we learned, had dedicated the fortune she inherited from her wealthy forebears, to support more than 60 groups that preserve nature and some of the world's most vulnerable people, including pygmies in Africa and rainforests in South America. She had an Audubon Society Handbook for Butterfly Watchers dedicated to her, and a right whale named for her.

A descendant of Anna Kingsley and Zephaniah Kingsley, MaVynee had grown up playing on the sand dunes of American Beach, the resort town her grandfather built for African Americans in the 1930s. Her grandfather, A. L. Lewis, was Florida's first black millionaire, and the founder of the state's first insurance company. MaVynee was very attached to the dunes, which she grew up calling "Nana," and for the past nine years focused on getting the dunes protected by the National Park System as part of the Kingsley Plantation and Timucuan Ecological Preserve, 17 miles south.

MaVynee had a relationship with the plantation that we believed to be an excellent model of how the parks can work with local communities. Every year, she was the star attraction at the Kingsley Heritage Celebration, which brought descendants and from all over the country and members of the local community into the park. The event included tours of the original plantation house, the kitchen house, barn and 23 tabby slave cabins, as well as the small plot where the unique "Sea Island Cotton" was grown for demonstration. Craft demonstrators in period costumes reenacted plantation life.

The celebration was grounded in the experiences of members of the African American population that had historically lived on the barrier islands off the coasts of Florida, Georgia and the Carolinas. The Gullah-Geechee people were proud of their heritage, and the opportunity to re-energize it by sharing it with others. One of the most famous contributors was Marquetta Goodwine, who describes herself as an "art-ivist." We had met Queen Quet, as she is known, and been entranced by her at the Mosaic conferences. Queen Quet has been the ambassador for the preservation of her culture and people, and testified before the United Nations in Geneva about the development and other pressures threatening their very survival.

These two powerful women—MaVynee and Queen Quet—were instrumental in getting land and territories added to the park system, and in the process show how the system is a living, dynamic entity. MaVynee, educated at the Oberlin Conservatory, moved to Europe where she bowled the Germans over with the opera "Salome" which she performed in German. Her sister, Johnetta Cole, became renowned as a college president in America. In the mid-80's, when developers turned their eyes on American Beach, MaVynee recognized the threats to her precious haven. With the A.L. Lewis Historical Society, she focused on preserving American Beach, and got the area placed on the National Register of Historic Places. In 2004, she succeeded in persuading the Amelia Island Plantation (which had bought up much of the land around American Beach) to transfer the sand dunes she calls "Nana" into the care and protection of the National Park Service. The dunes were added as an expansion of the Timucuan Ecological and Historical Preserve and Kingsley Plantation.

Queen Quet worked closely with South Carolina Congressman James Clyburn to get a Geechee Heritage Corridor established as a unit of the park system. It comprises many of the offshore islands from Florida to North Carolina that represent the Gullah Geechee culture. Congressman Clyburn subsequently appointed Queen Quet to the 15-member Gullah Geechee Cultural Heritage Corridor Commission in Charleston, South Carolina. The Commission will help determine how the Corridor is managed.

Chapter 24:
"Keeping It Wild" Soars

Back in Atlanta, things began to turn around in our second year. Frank's predecessor had commissioned a booklet called *"Why Wilderness: What the Last Remaining Wild Lands of the Southern Appalachians mean to the People of the Southeast."* It included lots of scenery and the preface was by Congressman John Lewis, who talked about his roots in rural Alabama:

> Walking through fields, smelling the wildflowers, touching the ancient oaks, poplars and pines, I learned wonder. Drinking from a fresh water spring, I learned purity. Fishing with a simple cane pole, I learned contemplation and patience. Feeling the dirt and pine straw between my toes, I learned the wilderness is a part of me—I cannot and never will separate myself from its beauty and peacefulness...

> Part of the problem we have in our society, particularly in urban centers, is that we don't lose ourselves to what is natural. In our rush to progress technologically and to grow economically, we sometimes forget about the things that give people a sense of fulfillment and happiness. People have busy lives and difficult priorities—raising families, educating their children, trying to get ahead. But it shouldn't be an either/or choice when it comes to protecting wilderness. We must be willing to move beyond our own selves and our own problems and consider the larger impact of our actions and the legacy we leave for our children. If we don't, we will lose a part of our humanity we can't replace...

Frank inherited hundreds of copies of the attractive and informative booklet, and worked with Kathryn Kolb, the photographer, to create a photography exhibit at the Fernbank Museum in Atlanta. About 150 people attended the opening reception, approximately 50 percent of whom were black.

This success led him and Kathryn to develop a program that gave people the opportunity to explore the woods in organized groups. Called

"Keeping It Wild," the program rapidly attracted African Americans and people of different races from Atlanta and the suburbs. They embraced the experiences, which ranged from ecological walks in downtown Atlanta led by a forest archaeologist, to hikes in old growth forests in the mountains of North Georgia.

The program was managed by a Steering Committee made up of volunteers from some of the major conservation organizations such as The National Wildlife Federation, the Conservation Fund and the Wilderness Society, as well as local organizations including Trees Atlanta, the predominantly-black West Atlanta Watershed Alliance which had succeeded in preserving more than 400 acres of forest in their Cascade neighborhood, the Edge of Night Camping Club, and our own Earthwise Productions, Inc. We partnered with some of the major academic institutions including Morehouse and Spelman colleges, and Emory University to provide seminars that explored the history and contributions of African Americans. We wrapped up our first year with the "Keeping It Wild Gala" held at Clark-Atlanta University in October 2005. Congressman John Lewis, our keynote speaker, mesmerized the crowd of approximately 200 racially diverse participants with tales about growing up in Alabama, and his experiences in the Civil Rights Movement, many of which are detailed in his book, *Walking with the Wind: A Memoir of the Movement.*

By the following year, the program had grown so much that attendance at the Gala doubled. Keynoting the event, Charles Jordan said that of all the environmental events he has been to around the country, this was the first truly racially diverse gathering he had ever seen. He said that this should become a model for the country.

Our co-chairs for the Gala, Laura Turner-Seydel (daughter of media mogul Ted Turner) and her husband Rutherford Seydel were so impressed with the racial diversity of people involved with Keeping It Wild, that Laura approached us with a proposition. The Seydels' agreement to co-chair the event was a coup since, as Atlanta's most prominent environmental couple, they were in high demand. This arrangement had been achieved through the deft strategy of steering committee member Susan Kidd, Senior Vice President of the Georgia Conservancy, and Felicia Davis, who is one of the most influential black women in the environmental movement in Atlanta and the country. The racial diversity of these two women who had access to Laura and whose recommendation she trusted, and the communities they bridged illustrates why "Keeping It Wild" is so successful.

Laura, a passionate supporter with deep ties to the Civil Rights Movement in Atlanta, had a dream for the Civil Rights Movement and the environmental movement to unite and ignite the sort of sweeping changes that characterized the Civil Rights movement of the 1960s. With her support, "Keeping It Wild" presented the *"First National African-American Earth Day Summit: Stewardship and Sustainability"* at the Martin Luther King, Jr., International Chapel on the campus of Morehouse College, April 19, 2007. It brought together African American leaders of the conservation community, mainstream environmentalists, business and religious leaders, and members of the academic community to focus on solutions to the problems posed by global warming and climate change. The President of the Wilderness Society flew down from Washington, D.C., and a wide cross section of people from across the economic spectrum flocked to hear the message.

National speakers included Jerome Ringo, Immediate Past Chair of the National Wildlife Federation and President of The Apollo Alliance, and Nia Robinson, Chair of the Environmental Justice Climate Initiative. The Rev. Gerald Durley, Senior Pastor of Providence Missionary Baptist Church in Atlanta and a friend of Laura's, said he had become "a missionary for the environment," after seeing the movie, "The Great Warming".

"When Laura invited me to see that movie, I thought, 'Oh these environmentalists...' but because I respect Laura, I decided to go. And it changed my life."

Jerome and Nia emphasized the changes brought about by climate change and pointed to the destruction of the Gulf Coast and the devastation of its population, particularly the aged and the poor who were overwhelmingly black. They pointed to the Climate Change Report issued by the Congressional Black Caucus which warned that climate change would have a disproportionately high impact on communities of color around the country. Many people who were already at risk due to being at the lower end of the socio-economic scale would be further victimized by flood, drought, hurricanes, tornados and fire.

Nia and Jerome gave examples of what needed to be done to change that future, including personal conservation in our homes and government-driven changes to reduce the effects of climate change. Charles made it personal by talking about his grand-daughter Mia, and his unwillingness to pass on to her an environment so depleted that she would lack the things we take for granted: clean air, abundant energy and water, and a quality of life that enables her to achieve her potential.

Southern Company, the chief financial sponsor of the KIW Gala, gave us 2,500 energy efficient light bulbs, which we distributed to participants at the Summit, in cloth bags supplied by REI (the well-known acronym for giant retailer Recreation Equipment, Inc.) and paper bags we got from Whole Foods. Those bulbs would spawn a movement bigger than we ever dreamed.

That Earth Day, Rev. Durley asked three of his associate ministers to provide their insight into what it means to care for the Earth. He said it was the first time in 20 years at the church that he had ever celebrated Earth Day, because he hadn't seen its relevance before. Several other participating ministers in the Concerned Black Clergy of Metropolitan Atlanta preached Earth Day sermons, emphasizing that we have a moral responsibility to care for God's creation.

A week later, Laura told us that she went to an Earth Day function in Washington, D.C., where House Speaker Nancy Pelosi was the keynote speaker. When the Wilderness Society's President, Bill Meadows, gave the closing remarks, he mentioned that he had been to a lot of Earth Day celebrations but had never seen anything close to the diversity and the energy he experienced at the African American Summit in Atlanta.

Rev. Durley subsequently wrote a letter explaining the transformation he had gone through:

> **My total perspective on the environment and life in general, was drastically altered**
> **by Rev. Dr. Gerald Durley**
>
> I have, for a number of years, regarded myself as an informed, enlightened, educated and involved human being when it comes to critical issues which negatively impact the lives of people. In college, I became deeply committed to the civil and human rights movements, as we fought for the dignity and equal rights of all who call themselves Americans.

Championing the cause for social justice and racial equality virtually consumed my life as I completed my undergraduate and graduate school education.

Becoming a psychologist and a pastor in the African American community afforded me the opportunity to make a significant, positive difference in this segment of society. I was satisfied that I was completing my calling until I was invited to view a film entitled, "The Great Warming." As far as I was concerned, the invitation was just another event which was sponsored by a group of "environmental alarmists" attempting to solicit support and raise funds. But, since I was invited by someone I highly respect, I reluctantly consented to attend.

On May 18, 2006, my total perspective on environmental issues and life in general was drastically altered. I became a concerted devotee of doing everything in my power to speak truth to the issues which can change the man-made, exploitative behavior which is literally destroying the environment which God created for us to live in, enjoy, and have our being.

What was so EARTH-shattering about that fateful day in May? I learned, for the first time, about the carbon dioxide which is not being absorbed by trees because we have cut them down, therefore less oxygen for healthy air is being emitted. I was shocked to see and hear about our self-serving demands that lead to massive fossil fuel burning. Yet, we continue to dig for more and more coal, rather than seek alternative energy sources. This depleting and defoliating simply fuels our greedy need and malicious overuse of precious natural resources.

Environmentalists tell us that the world is warming. At the same time, the global appetite for energy is rising rapidly. The U.S. Department of Energy says that global energy consumption will grow by 50 percent during the first quarter of the century, all of which has serious implications for global climate change.

So, what does all of this mean to an African-American pastor in Atlanta, Georgia, who is concerned every day with the elimination of poverty; curtailing homelessness; improving and providing health care; decreasing unemployment; lessening teenage pregnancy; reducing crime; cubing violence; eliminating racism; and trying to assist people through another day?

It became crystal clear to me as I watched "The Great Warming" that environmental concerns must become an integrated, active part of the life-sustaining messages in the African-American community. These essential messages must be mandatory teachings throughout all faith traditions, if we are to survive.

The faith community consistently prides itself on being in the prevention and healing business. Therefore, if we are serious about what we teach and preach, our message must speak clearly and boldly to:

1. What we can do to reduce levels of energy consumption

2. Learn how to effectively join forces with those who are more knowledgeable about improving environmental conditions; and

3. Discuss in sermons, seminars, workshops and lectures about health issues, weather conditions, economic concerns, and the negative impact of global warming which are all connected to how the environment is regarded.

There is so much that *can* and ***must*** be accomplished when we know what is happening to our environment, and its direct impact on each of our lives. No one person, group or organization can bring about complete awareness and comprehensive change alone. The faith community must become a far-reaching, consistent voice, from pulpits, to exhort the masses to understand, get involved, speak out, and be converted to "SAVE OUR WORLD… FROM US!"

Armed with this information from the source, reflecting a very influential person who was using his influence on behalf of the environment, we tried to impress upon the environmental segment that the greatest requirement was to get more information out to the public. We warned that the presumption that everyone knows what's happening and that people just choose not to get involved was a fallacy, and it was dangerous because it perpetuated the ignorance. In the same context, I had to correct white park advocates over and over again when they talked about the parks saying, "All Americans have fond memories of our times in the parks," and I'm literally screaming, "How many times do I have to tell you that's not true?"

Moreover, numbers from all the polls taken and studies done showed that more than 70 percent of African Americans and Hispanic people said that the lack of information about the parks—where they are, what to do and what to expect—were the chief reasons they didn't go. But many of the people at the pinnacle of the parks movement were so entrenched in their belief systems, they simply couldn't—or wouldn't—get past their preconceived ideas.

In 2003 we were alarmed to learn that the Environmental Protection Agency's report on the state of the environment had been edited by the White House to dilute and in some cases remove those parts of the report that described the risks from global rising temperatures. We reported on it in an article in *Pickup & GO!:*

> Among the deletions were conclusions about the likely human contribution to warming from a 2001 report on climate by the National Research Council that the White House had commissioned and that President Bush had endorsed in speeches that year. White House officials also deleted a reference to a 1999 study showing that global temperatures had risen sharply in the previous decade compared with the last 1,000 years. In its place, administration officials added a reference to a new study, partly financed by the American Petroleum Institute, questioning that conclusion.
>
> Meanwhile, in an astonishing announcement on global warming and extreme weather, the World Meteorological organization signaled in early July that the world's weather is

going haywire. In a startling report, the WMO, which normally produces detailed scientific reports and staid statistics at the year's end, highlighted record extremes in weather and climate occurring all over the world in recent weeks, from Switzerland]s hottest ever June to a record month for tornadoes in the United States—and linked them to climate change. – *Pickup & GO!* Vol. 5, Issue 5.

At NPCA board meetings that included visits to the national parks, we learned that global warming and climate change were already affecting the landscape. For example, although the Great Smoky Mountains National Park is a long ways from the coal-fired power plants that supply the southeast, the emissions still make their way up the mountains creating a toxic haze that harms plants and wildlife. Some days the air in the park was reported to be worse than in downtown Washington D.C. In NPCA board discussions, the question arose as to whether we'd restore the Everglades only to have large segments of it submerged under rising seas.

By December 2004 when a tsunami washed over 12 countries killing more than a quarter of a million people and displacing millions more, the handwriting on the wall was heartrendingly clear. The world's leading climatologist, Dr. Rajendra Pachauri, Chair of the Intergovernmental Panel on Climate Change (which would later share the Nobel Peace Prize with Vice President Al Gore) warned: "Climate change is for real. We have just a small window of opportunity and it is closing rather rapidly. There is not a moment to lose."

Dr. Pachauri cited measurements showing that levels of carbon dioxide, the main cause of global warming, increased over the past two years suggesting that climate change may be accelerating out of control. He said that because of "inertia" built into the Earth's natural system, the world was only now experiencing the results of pollution emitted in the 1960s, and much greater effects would occur as the increased pollution of later decades worked its way through the environment. He concluded, "We are risking the ability of the human race to survive."

By then, I had practically begun to rant. Recognizing the urgent need for action, I pointed out to the boards I served on that it was more vital than ever to devise programs that got information to the public and let them know what we were facing. Obviously, we couldn't afford to leave anyone on the sidelines anymore. I took every opportunity to speak to groups that were not involved with the environment, often speaking for free, and joining competitions that provided me with an audience, telling people about the urgency of the situation and the need for all hands to get on deck.

But the people were not seeing that message reaffirmed in the media or in the sources where they get their information. Many people dismissed it as an issue that rich white people had created and considered it the responsibility of "those people" to take care of the problem.

The devastation of New Orleans and the Gulf Coast in 2005 from the combination of multiple hurricanes and a failed levee highlighted for the world the very real jeopardy facing people as a result of the environmental changes taking place. A lot of the devastation resulted from the development of the off-shore barrier islands, which, while in their natural state would have protected parts of the shore from the storm surge, but could no longer serve that function.

In their report, *Climate Change and Extreme Weather Events: An Unequal Burden on African Americans*, the Congressional Black Caucus pointed out:

> The recent hurricanes, Katrina and Rita, that devastated the gulf region is in part a result of the warming of the environment. According to the Intergovernmental Panel on Climate Change, (IPCC) (2001a-Figure 2-6) a consistent, large-scale warming of both the land and ocean surface occurred over the last quarter of the 20th century. The report also provides evidence that warming in some regions is linked with observed changes in biological systems on all continents...
>
> ...The overwhelming loss of life and property by the poorest residents of the gulf region provides another example of how climate change is devastating communities and families of color who are unable to afford Flood Insurance and other necessary protections that will allow them to rebuild and restore their lives as they were before the disaster...

Frank and I felt like it was déjà vu all over again, and this catastrophe really illustrated why "sustainability" is unattainable unless we take care of the poorest and most vulnerable among us. But even after the horrific experiences played out before our eyes—as our friends including Felicia rushed to help in Mississippi and we saw Atlanta's homeless population swell with people displaced from New Orleans—the message still did not seem to have penetrated either camp. The environmental segment continued much the same as usual, and people of color seemed no more or less inclined to deal with the environmental factors that made it increasingly likely that we would see such devastation again and again.

Chapter 26:
Transformative Personal Experiences in the Parks

One discrete area that reflects the environmental sector's failure to engage the public, and it's potentially damning consequences, is the Arctic National Wildlife Refuge. It was a primary concern for NPCA and other environmental groups such as The Wilderness Society to protect the Refuge from oil drilling. At more than 19 million acres, the Refuge is the foremost jewel in the system of protected lands, being so remote that its natural processes have been little affected by humans. Consequently, it is also a potent force in helping regulate our climate.

Native American tribes that have lived on the land for more than 10,000 years still co-exist in relative harmony with the large mammals that have historically supplied their needs. The refuge contains substantial oil deposits, and has been at the center of a tug between environmentalists who want to protect its ecological integrity, and major oil companies which want to extract the oil reserves.

The push to develop the Refuge's oil deposits greatly increased under the Bush administration, but the public's resistance to drilling in this icon of American wilderness forced Congress to vote against it time after time. Two Native American tribes in Alaska directly connected to the issue are the Gwich'in Athabascan community which opposes drilling, and the Inupiat tribe, which supports it.

The issue of what was at stake in the Refuge was so little known and so misunderstood that, as energy prices shot up in the 2000s, for the first time we started seeing letter writers to the local papers complain that they didn't care if a couple of animals were hurt in the Arctic – the important thing was that drilling should take place so they had gas to get to work.

We got a whole different side of the picture in 2003 when Charlene Stern, a member of the Gwich'in, joined Frank at an event sponsored by the Wilderness Society in Birmingham, Alabama. She spoke passionately about her early days in her village, when her grandfather would sit on the porch with his binoculars, carefully scanning the mountains for any sign of migrating caribou. The Gwich'in depend upon the caribou for more than 70 percent of their diet. But the very area targeted for oil drilling is the breeding ground of the caribou, and the Gwich'in people were alarmed that drilling would not only disrupt the environment, but it would also affect the herds' health and well being. They visualized their entire way of life disappearing.

Frank and I were actively engaged with helping to protect the refuge, contacting our congressional representatives, writing and speaking in support of keeping one of the last remaining great wild places in America wild and natural. Appreciating the value of wilderness, we were convinced that our country should be exploring ways to produce energy that was renewable and sustainable, especially wind and solar energy. Drilling into the reserve to fulfill current needs would be like raiding our children's college fund to support a drug habit. It would produce relatively little oil, and would require the development of infrastructure such as roads and drilling and extraction machinery that would completely change the area.

At the Mosaic conference in Atlanta in 2002 Juan Martinez, a young Hispanic man who had recently been exposed to the outdoors through a Los Angeles conservation program, had put the problem in stark terms for us.

"You can talk about oil drilling all you like," he'd said. "But to a person who has never been out of the city, who has never seen wilderness and who has no idea what you're talking about, it makes no difference whatsoever. The best way to get people involved is to expose them to the outdoors, and it doesn't have to be Alaska. I get what's happening with the Refuge because I've actually been into the woods in California."

We brought that message back to the environmental sector, once again emphasizing the need to reach people through the media they use. The groups continued to vigorously oppose drilling in the media they traditionally used – the magazines and newspapers that reached the same demographic groups that they had always appealed to. So while the controversy over the reserve raged, the vast majority of people in urban areas people remained uninformed about its value, and were not engaged with protecting it.

In June 2006 we flew to Alaska for a meeting of the NPCA board. We took a small charter plane to Skagway and Klondike Gold Rush National

Historic Park. Our companions in the five-passenger plane were the Chairman of the NPCA Board, president of the Los Angeles Goldman Sachs, and his five-year old son. It was a smooth flight over stunning views of the glaciers. The town of Skagway is situated at the northern-most point of the Inside Passage in southeast Alaska, and there were huge cruise ships just off shore.

The park includes many of the buildings in this frontier city, and the National Park Ranger leading our tour was pointing out the historic buildings when we heard him mention the Buffalo Soldiers. Then he continued just as if he hadn't dropped a bomb in our midst.

As Frank and I were sputtering, "The Buffalo Soldiers were here? And that's all you're going to tell us?" another board member, who has almost fulfilled his lifetime goal of visiting every unit of the park system, said, "What was that about the Buffalo Soldiers?"

It was a relief to see others showing interest in the stories of people of color in the parks. The ranger told us that they were still doing research about the Buffalo Soldiers and their contributions, and didn't know very much. We emphasized that that just wasn't good enough, as equal priority should be given to unearthing and publicizing these stories as the others told at the park.

We had an ace in the hole in the form of our dear friend, Ranger Sandy Snell-Dobert, who had helped us arrange and lead urban expeditions when she worked at the Big Cypress National Preserve in South Florida. We've found people in the National Park Service to be very high caliber public servants who love the resources and are dedicated to their preservation. But there's something very special about the relationships we've formed with people who really get the spirit of the Park System and the fact that it belongs to the American people. Sandy was one of those people.

Imagine our surprise to find that the Buffalo Soldiers played a pivotal role in maintaining law and order in the frontier town for the Gold Rush in1898! Sandy sent me this excerpt from the *Daily Alaskan*, Feb. 4, 1902, ("It Was Swell," p.2):

> The terms of enlistment of many of the men in Company
> L. have about expired, and as an au revoir to the soldiers who
> will soon leave the post, their comrades gave an elaborate
> dance at Anderson's hall last night. The entire colored colony

of Skagway were (sic) at the dance. The ladies were radiant in party dresses, and they were gallantly swung to the best dance music that Skagway could afford. The hall was an unremitting scene of jollity and merriment. The affair was swell.

At that same board meeting, I got a chilling reminder of the fact that some people actually viewed the integration of the park system as fraught with danger. I was having breakfast at the lodge in Glacier Bay National Park, looking out at amazing glaciers and recollecting the words of the Native Americans who had greeted us the night before with the reminder that this was originally their land, and they were happy to have developed a good working partnership with the Park Service.

My companion that morning was a white colleague who heads up a prominent environmental foundation. He began to express to me all the difficulties he saw associated with bringing more Americans of color into the national parks. He said that Latino families, for example, tend to gather in large numbers, and that this would require parks to modify their parking lots, picnic sites and restroom facilities.

"OK," I said, "and the problem with that is…?"

I suggested that it would be a small concession to make in exchange for the happiness, self-esteem and freedom that it would promote. I said that our company had personally introduced thousands of people to the parks, and all had expressed similar feelings of awe, amazement and delight.

"So does that mean everyone has to go to the parks?" he snapped. "Does that mean we have to have the boom boxes and everything?"

Aha! So there's the problem! I thought. We had visited more than 100 units of the park system by that time, and we've never heard a boom box or had any incident of noise pollution in the parks. Moreover, I pointed, fear of a "boom box" is a little outdated since everyone uses an iPod these days.

Duh! It made me wonder just who some conservationists have in mind as they're seeking to "protect" our natural resources and environment.

The following month, Frank and Iantha and I joined the American Hiking Society for a Volunteer Vacation that took us to San Francisco to repair hiking trails. The Hiking Society arranges these vacations across the mainland and Hawaii, matching people with projects in the national parks, forests and other publicly owned lands. For the cost of membership ($30 per year) and a payment of $100, the Society will match you with a project of your choice, and takes care of lodging and food. Imagine our delight to find that we'd be staying at the Presidio of San Francisco! That place had a magical allure for me ever since I learned that the Buffalo Soldiers had been bivouacked there. We were thrilled to see plaques displayed prominently around the fort with photographs of the Buffalo Soldiers and their contributions. Miraculously, we found Buffalo Soldiers brochures produced by the Park Service in the Visitor Center and book-store, with a synopsis of their service to America in assignments across the U.S., Cuba and the Philippines.

In September of that year, I took a group of nine people on a tour of Yellowstone and The Grand Teton National Park. They included Monica, who'd produced the piece on our 2000 Grand Canyon trip for NBC, and her friend Imelda, Audrey Sawney, who'd also been on that trip and brought her fiancé Daryl and her sister; my friend Sharon, and Iantha. Our friend, Betsy Robinson, a wildlife biologist and naturalist guide who lives in Bozeman, Montana and her husband Steve, led the tour. For five days and four nights, our group was spellbound.

As Betsy drove us through the parks, telling us stories about the animals, the ecology and the history of what we were seeing, our eyes drank in wondrous sights: grand mountain views, flowing rivers, rushing waterfalls and gaping canyons; 100-strong herds of buffalo; bugling bull elk with enormous antlers guarding their harem; our first pronghorn antelope— one of the last herds remaining in the wild—cautiously waiting to cross the road; a grizzly bear striding across the mountain in the Lamar Valley, flushing a herd of antelope resting under the trees; a mother and baby moose lying by a stream along the highway; and finally, the stunning sight of the wall of mountains known as the Grand Tetons, across a glassy lake…. Wow!

"Oh my God! Oh, My God!" Everyone was gasping. Sharon collapsed into her seat and said, "Oh my God! All this beauty is wearing me out!"

Daryl said the trip was the perfect bridge between his old life and his new life, since he and Audrey were on the verge of getting married. He said, "My idea of recreation is mowing the lawn, so it really took a lot for Audrey to persuade me to come on this trip. But I can't tell you how it has broadened my world. It's like a bridge between my old life and the new life Audrey and I are going to build together." They were married two months later.

Since then, Sharon has called many times, overflowing with excitement whenever she sees the mountains in a TV commercial.

"I didn't know they were real before. I couldn't imagine anything so massive," she exclaims. "It made me feel that God must really love me to have created so much beauty for me to enjoy, and I'm glad I have a friend like you to encourage me to take that trip."

Imelda said that after a couple of days back home in Los Angeles, she began to feel that she really needed some outdoors.

"I went out to the Santa Monica Mountains National Recreation Area not far from where I live," she said, "and I had the best time. But I wouldn't even have thought about going there if I hadn't gone to Yellowstone."

By then, Iantha had left NPCA and established her own consulting company, The Kenian Group, Inc. She was still focusing on the issue of diversity, and called the expanded planning team together again in 2006 to plan a Summit in Charlotte, North Carolina, in October 2007. To my amazement, one of the most electrifying speakers at the Summit, Tony C. Anderson, a senior at Morehouse College, said that he had only recently gotten involved with the environment, as a direct result of the energy-saving light bulb he'd gotten from our African American Summit. To maximize the impact of the Summit, Felicia Davis and Na'Taki Osborne, both members of the KIW Steering Committee and leaders of environmental programs, had arranged to take advantage of Nia's presence in town and hold a special session for students on the Atlanta University Campus. Tony was so impressed with what he had learned that he said he had a thrilling moment when he realized that the light bulbs were a means to reduce electric costs as well as to protect the environment.

"I immediately talked with some of my peers and we decided to launch an initiative to raise one million energy efficient light bulbs, and distribute them to low and moderate income families around Atlanta. Not only would we distribute the bulbs, but we would educate the recipients about the environmental and economic benefits of using these bulbs, and we'd remove the old bulbs at the same time. We recognized that if people had to choose between an energy efficient bulb that cost $7 and a regular bulb that cost $2, they were most likely going to go for the cheaper bulb. We had to show them the benefits and make them feel like part of the solution."

They called the program "Let's Raise a Million," (LRAM) and in short order had raised and installed more than 5,000 bulbs. Wow! Talk about an unexpected consequence.

The Summit brought together nearly 100 participants, a mix of every race, class and age group, who were all taking leadership roles in efforts to protect the environment and sharing insights into how to get the demographic group they represented to be more involved. The Summit was supported by the Wilderness Society and NPCA and featured a host of speakers from racially diverse communities.

My other most striking memory from that Summit came from a young black woman working with The Conservation Fund. She had come to the Summit direct from a meeting of another major land conservation organization of over 2,000 people. She told us how relieved she was to be with our diverse group, since she'd been one of only a handful of people of color at the other meeting.

"How does a 250-pound black woman become invisible?" she asked, and answered her own question. "Go to a white environmental meeting. I was wearing my name tag so I was clearly part of the gathering, but I couldn't meet anyone's eyes, and nobody seemed to notice that I was there at all."

That was particularly odd because at every meeting we went to, we heard how necessary it was for people of color to be more involved, and how desperate the environmental segment was to become more diverse. Talking to one of my white friends later who was at the conference, she said, "Well, a lot of people come to those meetings and they're looking forward to seeing other people they know, so it becomes kind of cliquish. Besides, if you went over to speak to someone you don't know, wouldn't it seem like you were singling them out and making them feel different?"

"Well, they are different," I responded. "Think of it this way: If you're having a party and someone new comes to your house, wouldn't you go over and introduce yourself and make them feel welcome? Would you think that makes them feel 'different?' It's the same thing. If the person is new to my setting, you better believe I'm going to make a point of helping them feel like part of the group! "

Chapter 26:
Honoring "The Sable Guides of Mammoth Cave"

In October 2007, I was at an NPCA board meeting at the south rim of the Grand Canyon, and after our meeting at the El Tovar hotel overlooking the Canyon, I went to the communal computer to check my e-mail. To my surprise, there was an e-mail from Linda Canzanelli, the former Superintendent of Biscayne National Park. I opened it and read to my amazement, that our friend Brenda had been diagnosed with terminal cancer, and had only a few months to live.

I got on my cell phone immediately and called Diana Blank, one of my closest friends on the board. I told her I was coming over to her hotel and we needed to have a drink right away. She met me in the lobby, which was sumptuously appointed, with a blazing fire, and a bar at one end. We went to the bar and got a stiff drink, and then I told her what I'd just learned. She was very compassionate and supportive. We sat and talked for a long time, staring into the fire as if it held the answers to all life's mysteries.

Fortunately, next morning we were planning to hike down into the canyon and spend the night. We hiked four-and-a-half miles to Indian Gardens, an oasis 3,000 feet down. The superintendent, his wife and several staff members were along for the trip, and we would be allowed to use housing that's usually kept for the rangers in the back country. My fellow travelers opted to continue hiking further down to where they could see the Colorado River. But being in the middle of the Grand Canyon, with an indescribably beautiful view everywhere I looked, I didn't feel I needed to go anywhere else.

I had the entire 360 degrees of the canyon to myself. I lay back in a folding chair and let the peace of the canyon seep into my bones. I let my tensions float out of me, atoms of concern about Brenda's condition floating out to join the canyon walls. The canyon evolved over millions of years and still it remained. Countless life forms from the dinosaurs to the Native Americans had passed this way, acting briefly on this stage of life before passing on, and still the canyon remained, impassive, timeless, and ancient.

By the time my friends came back, the sun was slowly withdrawing its rays from the canyon walls. Later we watched the moon come over the cliffs and the heavens come alive with stars. Next morning I was the first one up and outdoors to see the sunrise, and I was rewarded with a show I will never forget. When we came out of the canyon, I was feeling quite serene. This too shall pass, I thought. I only asked that Brenda did not suffer terribly.

A week after I got back to Atlanta, it was time for the Third Annual "Keeping It Wild" Gala. Our Keynote Speaker, Majora Carter, was founder and Executive Director of Sustainable South Bronx and winner of a Genius Award from the MacArthur Foundation. The $500,000 award distributed over a five-year period allowed her to build the organization, help reverse environmental degradation in her South Bronx community and create green jobs. Her presentation, "Protecting Your Environment: The Power of One" was so powerful that one influential person told us that he had quit his job as a result of hearing her, and gone on to do the non-profit work that was his passion. Others told us that they had increased their community involvement and volunteerism, and one of our KIW Steering Committee members whose membership had lapsed because of other commitments, rejoined our group.

Shortly after, Frank and I drove to Florida to spend Thanksgiving with his mother, and we made time to go see Brenda at her home in Homestead, just outside Biscayne and Everglades National Park. She was her usual sunny self, although she was undergoing a course of radiation and chemotherapy. We went to the local Cracker Barrel, her favorite breakfast place, and it was just like old times. Brenda was single at the time. She told us about a wonderful man she had met on a trip to Ireland, and they'd fallen madly in love. He called her every morning at 5 a.m.

"Peter is so wonderful," she said.

It really tugged at our heart that our wonderful friend might be in her last days, but I couldn't help thinking how lucky she was to be riding on the wings of love at such a time. I didn't want to think how Peter might manage after she was gone.

I told Brenda that we would be happy to come and stay with her whenever she needed us, and that we would keep our schedules flexible so we could come to her at a moment's notice.

She was touched, and told me how much it meant to her when Frank said "All I need is my laptop and Blackberry, and I can work from anywhere."

"You guys really took a load off my mind," she said. "I wouldn't want to die alone."

Die!! The thought I was so certain I'd come to terms with was suddenly inconceivable.

Once again, the National Park System came to our emotional rescue. As luck would have it, just about that time I received an invitation from Mammoth Cave National Park to an event honoring "the Sable Guides of Mammoth Cave" in Kentucky. For years we had been hearing about these "Sable Guides" and were intrigued by the story that young, enslaved Africans had been the primary explorers of the longest underground cave system in the world. The event was being held in February 2008, and my building anticipation distracted me from thoughts about Brenda's illness.

Our 13-year-old grandson Yero Winborne and I drove up from Atlanta for the weekend. Once we turned off the highway after the five-hour trip, the road wound through a thick forest with calming leafy views on either side. We emerged after a couple of miles into a developed area comprising the Visitor Center and the Mammoth Cave Hotel. We checked into the hotel, but found it unsuited to our taste, (a little too old and rustic) so Yero and I decided to spend the following night at a hotel in the nearby town of Cave City.

We learned that Jerry Bransford, the great-great grandson of Mat Bransford, one of the original "Sable Guides," had recently returned to the park to guide tours in the summertime. We met him that evening, and I was struck immediately by his gentle personality and his humility. He was very proud of his ancestors and their relationship to the cave, and was pleased that they were getting the recognition that had been denied them for so long.

It gave me the chills to be able to tour the cave system with him and Yero. I could hardly have constructed a better emotional bridge for myself. Being in the cave with Jerry, feeling his ancestors all around us, and having my grandson with me made me feel as if I was part of a long chain of life stretching backwards and forwards. Somehow, it made Brenda's imminent passing feel a little less tragic.

"I grew up in Glasgow, a little community at the edge of the park," he said. "When I came back to work for the park in 2003, I was a little emotional, because I remember my father taking us to the park when I was a kid, from the time I was about 8 years old. We'd go up on the ridge and sit in the place where he was born. I didn't understand then that he was coming back home. He had lived here his first 21 years, until our property was bought up from under us through eminent domain in 1937. He'd tell us stories of how he ran around as a kid, and how black and white families used to live fairly close together.

"We'd go to the restaurant, and even though it had become a national park, we couldn't sit down. Some of the folks there knew my father since childhood, and they made it clear that they would bring the refreshments to the back door, and we'd have to take it and go off. My father never said a negative word about it, but I was old enough to know it wasn't right."

The story of the Bransford family and the experience of the black cave guides at Mammoth Cave was like a microcosm of the American history involving the exploitation of African Americans for unpaid labor, the impregnation of black women by their white "owners," and the fate of their offspring as disposable chattel. It also showed the amazing ability of the enslaved to take lemons and make lemonade, and contribute to the advancement of our country in many different sectors.

Jerry's great-great-grandfather, Mat Bransford, was the son of the wealthy white farmer, Thomas Bransford, born to a young enslaved woman named Hannah. Bransford "leased" Mat and his brother Nick, to the man who bought Mammoth Cave and was looking to make it into a tourist attraction. The two teenagers and another of their peers, Stephen Bishop, are said to have had a spirit comparable to today's most extreme cavers. They squeezed their bodies through narrow cracks in the rock, hung suspended from ropes that they used to navigate over chasms, and generally went above and beyond the call of duty to explore the caves under the most hazardous circumstances. Their inscriptions have been found in some of the most inaccessible parts of the cave.

As our group entered the cave, I was astonished by the lofty height and expanse of the entrance cavern. It looked like a great cathedral, subtly lit by well-placed electric lights which barely held back the darkness. Passageways meandered off to the side and we could even see what appeared like lofts above the main avenue. As the park ranger led the 20 or so people in our group deeper into the cave, explaining some of the physical characteristics and the history of exploration in the cave system, I felt a little extra confidence because Jerry was beside me. It was as though his ancestors, who had explored these caves in the thick gloom, were walking beside us and so we were doubly protected.

At the time the cave was purchased by attorney Frank Gorin in 1838, only 20 miles had been explored. Gorin brought Stephen Bishop, and Mat and Nick Bransford, whom he "leased," to work in the cave. The three young men were taught the cave routes by two earlier guides, J.C. Shackelford and Archibald Miller, but they probed farther and deeper into the subterranean world. In 1938, Stephen was the first person to cross the great chasm, opening up more of the cave that was eventually found to be more than 300 miles long.

When Gorin sold the property about a year later, its new owner, Dr. John Croghan proceeded to develop amenities including a hotel, to publicize the cave system and attract guests. Stephen, Nick and Mat continued to explore the cave under the same economic system Gorin had established, namely with no money accruing to them. Tourists to Mammoth Cave at the time were mostly wealthy, educated white people. Professors, scholars, writers, scientists and world travelers toured the cave under the guidance of the enslaved Africans. Before going underground, they were instructed to follow the instructions of their black guides instantly and explicitly, as it could mean the difference between life and death. As a result of the expertise they'd developed and the responsibility placed on them for the tourists' safety, Stephen, Nick and Mat occupied a unique position in American life: slaves above ground, they were masters underground.

References to the Sable Guides that have survived include a visitor who wrote: "In most regions of the cave, it is hazardous to lose sight of the guide. If you think you walk straight ahead, even for a few rods, and then turn around and return to him, you will find it next to impossible. So many paths come in at acute angles. They look so much alike, and the light of a lamp reveals them so imperfectly, that none but the practiced eye of a guide can disentangle their windings."

Another stated: "The services of a guide cannot be safely dispensed with, and guests should respect his authority, for the law holds him responsible for the safe return of those put under his care."

The enslaved black guides had no opportunity for formal schooling, but soaked up the information they got from visitors to the caves.

Tourist Maria Child wrote of Stephen Bishop:

"His vocation has brought him into contact with many intellectual and scientific men and as he has great quickness of perception and a prodigious memory, he has profited much by intercourse with superior minds. He can recollect everybody that ever visited the cave, and all the terms of geology and mineralogy are at his tongue's end."

Frank Gorin wrote that Bishop's talents were "of the first order," and said that he considered him trustworthy, reliable and companionable.

"He was a hero and could be a clown. He knew a gentleman or a lady as if by instinct. He learned whatever he wished without trouble or labor."

According to one account, Mat had acquired "a considerable degree of culture … by contact with scholars and professors of every science, especially of geology and mineralogy."

Jerry sent me the following letter, a copy of which is at the Tennessee State Museum in Nashville. It was written by Union Officer James Fowler Rushling in July 1864, following his visit to Mammoth Cave and a conversation with Mat Bransford that rings with feeling:

> We gleaned the following facts concerning his personal history, which I record here as a lively illustration of the "peculiar institution." It seems he was born a slave, and is now the *property* of one Thos. Bransford, of Nashville, Tennessee, a wealthy slaveholder, resident in Edgefield, who turned traitor among the first and with his two sons and son-in-law, is now either in the Rebel Army or at all events within its lines. His family, it is said, still lives in Edgefield, and, it is understood, regularly draws pay from the proprietor of the Cave for the services Uncle Mat renders.
>
> As a guide to the Cave, Uncle Mat has been going in and out, now about 26 years—at an average of two to three times a week, and it is computed by one of his friends that in that time he (sic) has traveled in all nearly 20,000 miles in the Cave. He is married, and in his time has had four of what

Christians call children, but Kentuckians—chattels. Three of these, two girls and a boy have been sold from him; he has one boy still left, a lad about ten years old, who—thanks to the Rebellion—will probably be left to him. Two of his children, a boy and a girl were sold from him, when only about 7 or 8 years old. A man named Shaw bought them both; but he soon become bankrupt, and they both went to the auction block, whence they were sold by the Sheriff to the highest bidder – one to one purchaser, as it happened, and one to another. The other girl was sold at another time, as she grew up, to a man named John Coates, who with a meanness worthy of a dabbler in human flesh afterwards removed to Illinois, and then returned and sold her!

Said I, "Uncle Mat, I don't suppose you missed these children much? You colored people never do, they say."

"Sho, Cap'n! Don't you 'blieve dat. Culled folks has feelins, jus de same as white folks! 'Course I'se a man, and can bear sich things, do it went mighty hard at fust, But it's most killed do old woman, dat's a fact! Sho went roun kind o'crazy like, for long time; but what can niggahs do? 'Twont no use, no how, and so we come at last to bear it. When it cum to takin way de oder child, wc's older, and'd seem so much of dis ting, dat we just gub her up to wunst, and bore it best we could."

I asked him where his wife was now.

"For sev'ral years now, she's been a livin' near me – only two miles and a 'half o so off. I saved money enuff from what gemmen give me, for goin in de Cave, to pu up a little house. Massa Doyle, whar she lives, don't charge us any ting for rent of ground—and so we just lives dar. Got a good house, and plenty furniture. Would get 'long nice, if we only had de chillen back."

"And how does Mr. Doyle treat your wife? Is he a good master?"

"'Why, yes: Massa Doyle's not so bad. Mighty close, tho: makes her step round lively, and keeps her at it. Would *fight* her sometimes, reckon, if he dared."

"You mean he would whip her?"

"Jus so: only he's afeared I'd run her off. You see I'se been wid white folks a heap and talked so much about de Norf, dat I could cut away any time, ef I only pleased. Massa Doyle knows dis, mighty well, and so he leaves us 'lone."

I told Mat that slavery was about over; that he and his wife and children would soon all be free; that before another year rolled round an amendment to the Constitution would blot the institution – no, not institution but diabolism – from the face of the continent. I wanted him to come to Nashville, and be free at once; but the old man said he couldn't part with the cave. "It seems most like a child now, you know, we've been togedder so long."

Mat found creative ways to earn money, including selling some of the cave fish and crawdads to tourists. In the 1870s, he donated the land for the Mammoth Cave school, where many of the Bransford children and the children of other black cave guides learned to read and write.

Stephen Bishop died in 1857, but Mat, Nick and their descendants thrived. Mat's grandson Will was a guide at the cave for more than 40 years, and was chosen to represent Mammoth at the Chicago World's Fair in 1893. Another grandson, Matt Bransford opened a hotel for black visitors who were barred from the Mammoth Cave hotel and its dining rooms. The couple marketed their facilities through postcards that they made up and handed out as they traveled to places like Niagara Falls.

But the legacy of these intrepid black explorers, entrepreneurs and survivors were virtually obscured from public view until very recently.

When the Kentucky National Park Commission bought the estate, including the caves from the last of Groghan's heirs in 1929, their goal was to persuade Congress to add it to the federal land treasury as a national park. But while the National Park System had been established "for the benefit of the American people," there apparently was no room in the system for the fabled black guides.

Jerry says his father told him that, after more than 100 years of continuous service at Mammoth Cave, the black cave guides were called into a manager's office and told that they would lose their jobs when the

National Park Service took over.

"Boy, this thing is coming out of my hands. I can't keep you on when the park comes in, so you need to be looking around for what you're going to do," Jerry remembers his father saying the black cave guides were told.

In 1931 there were 11 black men, including 8 Bransfords, among the 20 guides at Mammoth Cave. At least five of the white men continued as guides with the National Park Service, but none of the Bransfords remained.

"Our land had been taken from us by eminent domain, and many people in our family had trouble buying new land and resettling," Jerry Bransford told me.

Coming around full circle, in the latter part of the 20th century, the white side of the Bransford family was also looking to connect with their black relatives at Mammoth Cave.

"About 21 years ago, a woman named Pat Davis came to Glasgow on a mission. She has the three original business ledgers that her great-great-grandfather kept. We have the same great-great-grandfather. He made it clear in the ledger that he fathered Mat from a little slave girl named Hannah. It's almost as though she was meant to come here. I was already looking, so my interest was sparked. Pat and I recognize that we have kinship, and that's just the way it is."

But the story of the Sable Guides might have remained in obscurity were it not for Joy Lyons, an enterprising young ranger at the park who became intrigued by the number of stories that persisted about one black cave guide, Steven Bishop. She began to wonder whether the stories were about one man, or several different black men.

"I went over to the curatorial room one day to look at photographs," Joy explains, "and noticed that a number of black guides were identified as being Stephen Bishop, even though they were obviously different people. One of the photographs had a car in it. But Bishop had died in 1857. I thought, What is the deal—was every African American man here called Stephen Bishop, no matter what the date? So I started looking for family descendants and reading historical accounts and newspapers, anything I could get my hands on."

From that beginning, Joy has reconstructed the historical record which she presents in the book, *Making their Mark: The Signature of Slavery at Mammoth Cave.* She has also been instrumental in getting the story of the Sable Guides publicized, and *American Legacy* magazine and other publications have written copiously about it. Like Brenda had brought out the Jones story at Biscayne, Joy illustrates that one committed person can make a huge difference in what stories are revealed and emphasized at a national park. Although there is only one history, there are multiple stories and perspectives, but many remain dormant until someone has the passion to explore and publicize them.

By a stroke of good fortune, Jerry Bransford retired from a career with Dow Corning and was also retracing his history at the same time Joy was looking to highlight his ancestors' story. She invited him to come back to Mammoth Cave, and he returned in 2003. Today, after a hiatus of approximately 70 years, a Bransford once again leads tours at Mammoth Cave, though only in the summer.

"I am the only employee at Mammoth Cave today that has direct ties to some of the first people in the cave," Jerry observes. "This is not fiction. This happened to my family. The last one of the black cave guides to leave, Louis Bransford, turned in his keys in 1937. Some say they considered hiring him, but the general understanding was that no black person was going to become a national park ranger. There wasn't a black national park ranger at Mammoth Cave until the 1970s."

Chapter 27:
Everyday Heroes Won "Some Victory for Humanity"

We kept track of how the Everglades restoration project was going by means of a list serve that circulated everything about the restoration printed anywhere in the country. It was plagued by such contradictions that it just began to seem idiotic. For example, the U.S. Corps of Engineers actually gave permits to businesses to develop quarries around the edge of the Everglades, which a little bit of commonsense would indicate must be contrary to the goals of restoration. This would force the environmentalists to have to oppose it in court, so it was a consistent tug of war. We could see why the restoration "leaders" would want to keep decisions to their small clique, because if communities really knew what was happening, they wouldn't stand for it. Obviously, someone was benefiting from the delays and contradictions, while the price to us taxpayers continues to swell.

We continue to get the *Westside Gazette* delivered, and I've noted with chagrin the glossy inserts from the Water Management District promoting the restoration, but giving the community no real information and nowhere to get a toehold in the process. A superficial PR campaign was a cynical way to fulfill the letter of the law to inform and involve minority populations. It certainly did not live up to the spirit of the law.

On April 1, 2008, I flew back to Miami to be with Brenda. Frank had been offered the opportunity to do a week-long session for executives at Harvard, and we agreed he should take it. Months earlier Brenda and I had agreed on this time, because members of the National Association of Black Scubadivers were coming to the park from all across the country for the annual "Diving With a Purpose" event, in which Brenda taught them underwater archaeology and they helped her map the shipwrecks on the bottom of the bay. She would no longer be able to dive with them, and she was getting weaker so she wanted me to be present to help make the event a success.

A few weeks before, we were putting the finishing touches on this story, and it occurred to me that we needed to get on record what her aspirations were for the site. Mindful of her illness and reluctant to disturb her, I nevertheless followed my heart and called her at 6 a.m., the time we'd been most likely to talk before. She got on the phone, her usual perky and enthusiastic self, and I recorded her words verbatim:

"Oh God, Audrey. There is so much to this story and this site. They are inextricable parts of each other. I want people around the world to hear about this family and say, 'I have to go see this site.' We have to stabilize the ruins and develop a visitor plan that allows people to visit the site without destroying the natural resources. We could put in a floating dock, so that people have access without changing the character of the island. It needs to be on the National Register of Historic Places. I want everyone to know that in a time when there were so few opportunities for African Americans, this family created a heritage and a legacy at the turn of the 20th century that can still inspire us today."

She was well enough to pick me up at the airport, with a friend from the park driving. We went to her beautiful home where her two beloved dogs, Maggie and Brandy, greeted us effusively. We went out to a new Japanese restaurant for dinner that night and when we came home, Brenda mentioned that Dayton Duncan had sent her a DVD of the segment on the Jones family that would be in the movie. By a stroke of good fortune, I was seated next to Dayton Duncan, Ken Burns' producer, at an NPCA dinner in Washington, D.C. in 2001, and bent his ear all evening with the Jones story. At the time, Duncan was working with Ken Burns on a documentary about the National Park System for release in September 2009. I was gratified when he sent me a note almost two years after our meeting telling me that the documentary will include a segment on the Jones story. Brenda had invited Frank and me down to Biscayne when Ken Burn's researcher Susan Schumacher came to scope out Porgy Key, and we had a wonderful time on the island with Susan and her young daughter. When Ken and Dayton learned that Brenda was terminally ill, they sent her a DVD with a preview of the Jones segment in the documentary, "*The National Parks: America's Best Idea*." We watched it together at her home two nights before she went to the hospital for the last time, and she was grateful that the story would live on beyond her.

We watched, spellbound, the beautiful photography and the loving re-telling of the Jones story. The piece focused mostly on Sir Lancelot Jones, and Brenda said wistfully that she wished it had spent more time on Pahson Jones, as that story had such historical value because it went back more than 100 years. I was just happy to see the story on video, because I knew that thousands of people who saw the documentary would want to know more about the story, and we had plenty to present. I was most grateful to Brenda because it was her passion that had brought the story to light. I was thankful for the compassion shown by Burns and Duncan to send the DVD to her, with strict instructions not to circulate it.

By the end of the week, Brenda's condition had accelerated and she was admitted to the hospital. I slept at her bedside, relieved periodically by the legions of her friends from the park and Peter, who hastened to her side. Ken Stewart, founder of the Diving With a Purpose Group, loved Brenda like a sister and was frequently at her bedside, along with members of her family. She made her transition April 15, and the following week Frank and I flew to El Paso, Texas, enroute to a long-planned birding trip with some of our friends from the NPCA Board in Big Bend National Park.

As I've often said, the parks are my heritage, my therapy and my inspiration, and that was affirmed once more when we visited Fort Davis National Historic Site enroute to Big Bend. Since I'd learned about this park, it had taken on almost mythical proportions in my mind. I choked up when I saw the craggy rock formations close to the fort and realized that the Buffalo Soldiers had looked at exactly this same view more than 140 years ago, when they were based at the Fort from 1867-1885.

It contains the Buffalo Soldiers' barracks, their beds, clothing and armory among other relics of their service, but for me, the most poignant thing was to observe the same views that they looked out on more than 140 years ago. Supt. Chuck Hunt was graciously taking us on a tour of the fort, and then tried to show me into the hospital, which he said was the only one of its kind in the Park System.

I balked. I had just returned from Florida, keeping vigil at Brenda's bedside until she died. I'd had too much of hospitals that month, so I stepped off the back porch and into the outdoors to calm my feelings. My eyes went first to the large tree that was buzzing with warblers. But then I turned to the right, and I froze when I saw the rows of black "hoodoos," on the mountains. The granite formations resembled a dignified people frozen in time as they looked implacably into the distance.

My eyes pumped out hot tears as I thought about how many times the Buffalo Soldiers would have looked at this view which communicated the eternity of nature and emphasized the relatively short span of human life. I thought how, being so far away from home and their loved ones, often suffering the racial slights and disrespect of the men they served with, and fighting for a land that did not fully accept them as human beings, the soldiers might have taken comfort and assurance in their destiny from this view.

Then Supt. Hunt completely burst my bubble when he told us that the adjoining lands that I could see from that very spot were up for sale. If they were bought by a developer, which seemed likely, no one would ever again be able to have the experience that I had just had. The Park Service was working with The Conservation Fund to help secure the property, and we resolved to do everything in our power to spread the word that this property was an invaluable asset of American history that it was vital to preserve.

The National Park System gave me a true appreciation of the Buffalo Soldiers' invaluable contributions in the forefront of westward expansion, mapping the wilderness, building forts and roads, protecting settlers, and participating in every aspect of exploration and conquest accomplished in that time.

The most serious problem faced by the Army during the Indian War period was desertion. In 1868, the desertion rate for enlisted personnel was approximately 25 percent. Desertions among White regiments were roughly three times greater than those among Black units. Also, both African-American cavalry and infantry regiments had lower rates of alcoholism than their White counterparts. While in the field, both the troopers and their horses faced not only hostile Indians and outlaws, but also extended patrols of up to six months and covering more than 1,000 miles. Adding to their ordeal was the scarcity of water and the extremes of weather common to the southwest. When not on patrol, the Buffalo Soldiers were engaged in endless drills, parades, and inspections. At Fort Davis in 1877 a dress parade, complete with the post band, was held each evening except for

Saturdays. Regarding the African-American troopers, the Post Surgeon noted that: "the troops seemed especially proud of their uniform and of their profession as soldiers. (National Park Service)

When we left that park, my equilibrium had been restored. I had made peace with Brenda's passing and shed my tears, mixing them into the ground where the Buffalo Soldiers' secret tears may have also fallen. I saw how the strivings of each human being creates a bridge to the future, and I was just happy to be a link in that bridge.

Little did I know it, but Brenda's passing would be the first in a series of losses that came in rapid succession. Three months later, on July 29, Frank's mother Veta passed away peacefully at home, four weeks after her 90th Birthday. Frank was the only person in the room with her, as I had been the only person in the room with Brenda when she died. We had driven down to Fort Lauderdale when the family told us mom said she was tired and ready to go home. Until that week, she'd walked an average of six miles around the neighborhood every day, and still lived on her own. Her funeral was a glorious celebration, led by four of her grandsons who are ministers and one of our daughters who is also a minister. Each of them credited their spiritual awakening to her.

Less than a month later in August, I received a call from Leola's daughter Deatra, informing me that Leola had died. That cut me to the quick, because I knew how valiantly she had fought, and how deeply she had suffered. And it was all for the love of her people, those who were neglected and discarded. Leola was able to see everyone's humanity and respect it as her own. She believed in justice, and was uncompromising in her pursuit of it. In 2006, Nova Southeastern University had awarded her an honorary law degree from the Shepherd Broad Law Center.

As Lisa and I barreled down I-75 South from Atlanta to Florida the Friday night before her funeral, our car was practically being lifted off the road by winds from the outer bands of Tropical Storm Fay. Thank God, I'd had a chance to spend some quality time with Leola the previous Mothers' Day, when I visited her at home and her daughters Verenda and Deatra and her granddaughter Joi came over. We had an impromptu celebration with much food and drink together with her family. I couldn't help thinking how often Leola and I had driven the Florida Turnpike from Fort Lauderdale to Tallahassee to press for environmental justice. In August (1999) we'd learned that Florida's State Department of Environmental Protection was holding a series of forums on contaminated soils, and the standards to which they should be cleaned up. Since the contaminated soils were mostly in areas where people of color and the poor lived, Leola and I had a serious interest in being part of the discussion. We'd only learned about the first forum days before it took place, when a memo came across Frank's desk at the Audubon Society. Parts of the eastern Everglades were on fire that summer, and we literally drove through smoke and flames on the turnpike to get to Tallahassee.

Lee made an indelible impression on the discussions, as we provided the only counterpoint to the business lobbyists and consultants who argued that the standards should be relaxed to leave higher levels of pollution in the soils, or it would cost their employers money. Our position to the Department of Environmental Protection was that the soils should be cleaned up to the point where it was most supportive of human health.

Dr. Richard Gragg represented Florida A & M University's Environmental Sciences Center, which was recently awarded just over $650,000 by the State Legislature to put into effect an environmental justice program. State Rep. Josephus Eggelleton represented the district where the Wingate Superfund site was located, and had spearheaded the creation of the EJ program at FAMU. Attorney David Ludder from the Legal Environmental Assistance Foundation, also supported our position, and the organization was advising Leola on the cleanup of the Wingate Superfund site. Leola and I were later appointed to the Advisory Board of the Center, but we felt that it wasn't moving as aggressively as it needed to, given the extent of the problem.

It was appropriate that we should be speeding down the turnpike in a storm to attend her funeral. Leola always said her husband Mac was the most loving, supportive husband and father in the world, and she couldn't imagine being without him. When he died of prostate cancer in 2004, Leola filed a lawsuit against the City of Fort Lauderdale.

"I had to do it, Audrey," she told me. "I had to let them know that his life mattered. And his death mattered. They can't just poison us like rats without somebody standing up to them."

Our beloved MaVynee died in 2005, a year after she succeeded in getting her beloved "Nana" sand dunes added to the park system, and just months before she was to have an audience with the Dalai Lama. I was happy that Carolyn Finney, Nadine Patrice and I had celebrated her accomplishments at her 70th Birthday Party where the feature length documentary, "The Beach Lady" was shown and she was given the accolades that she so richly deserved. In his book *American Beach: A Saga of Race, Wealth and Memory*, author Russ Rymer poignantly captures her life and her tremendous contributions. The A.L. Lewis Historical Society is continuing her family's legacy.

I miss these friends and relatives terribly, but my feelings are mitigated by the fact that each of them contributed their very best to the struggle to help America live up to her ideals. As Hedwig Michel instructed, each of them had "won some victory for humanity."

Part Three:

It's Time to Discover Our Parks

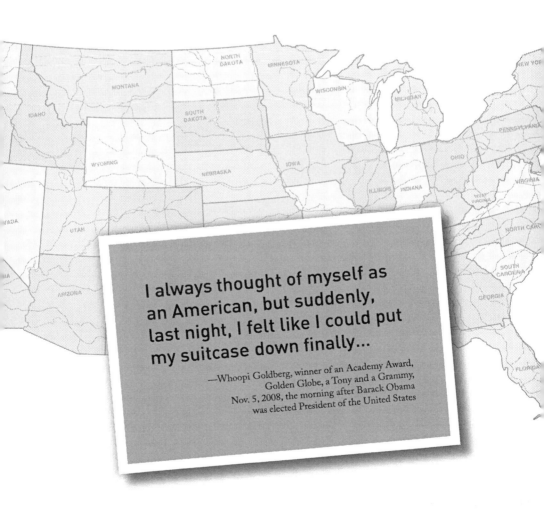

I always thought of myself as an American, but suddenly, last night, I felt like I could put my suitcase down finally...

—Whoopi Goldberg, winner of an Academy Award, Golden Globe, a Tony and a Grammy, Nov. 5, 2008, the morning after Barack Obama was elected President of the United States

Epilogue

Connecting the Parks and the American People

Many Americans of color have a tortured relationship with our country. We are her sons and daughters, yet we never feel quite at home. There are large swaths of the country where we feel unwelcome, or which we mentally write off as the domain of white people. We are hopeful that the ascendance of an African American to the highest leadership of the land will shift people's perspectives and enable them to feel a greater sense of belonging. According to talk show host Whoopi Goldberg on Nov. 5, 2008, the morning after President Obama's election, "I always thought of myself as an American, but suddenly, last night, I felt like I could put my suitcase down finally..."

In our experience, the National Park System offers the simplest and most direct way for all Americans to connect with nature and with the idea of America as our country. In the national parks we see and feel that we are one family, as the parks memorialize the Native American cultures, black explorers, Asian builders, Hispanic ingenuity and white accomplishments in the creation of our country over the past 400 years. As Frank said at Yellowstone, people who grow up visiting the national parks have a larger view of the country, and what it means to "own" it.

It is past time that the barriers obscuring the parks from the people are brought down. Those barriers include the failure of federal land management agencies and mainstream environmentalists to carry out their mission of promoting the parks to the American people. If the national parks are to be managed "for the enjoyment of the American people," it stands to reason that when more than fifty percent of the people do not know parks exist, public land managers should know they are failing at their jobs.

A first step towards accomplishing the mission is to welcome hundreds of environmental leaders of color around the country that are prepared to serve as consultants, contractors and role models for our communities. It is an overwhelming challenge to break into the funding stream, with the result that our growth is stymied although we invest superhuman efforts every day. The public lands managers have to abandon the falsehoods that they "can't find people of color who are interested or qualified," while deliberately ignoring the expertise we bring.

The survival of the National Park System depends upon the public's support. While timeless formations such as the Grand Canyon don't need human management, Congress allocates the money necessary to maintain buildings and roads, study the effects of change on the ecosystem, and protect artifacts. But in tight budget years, when faced with choices between funding social services and national parks, people who don't know the parks and have no idea of their benefits may be inclined to sacrifice these places. Therefore, the stewards of public lands must make sure that the parks have a large constituency among the American population that values them and what they represent.

The negative perception that some environmentalists and land managers have about non-white people must be exposed and dealt with before we can achieve the necessary changes. For example, while visiting the Glacier-Waterton International Peace Park linking Montana and Canada as part of an NPCA board meeting, one of our white colleagues came over to us and congratulated us on how well we'd handled ourselves. Since we'd been enjoying guided tours and staying in lush accommodations – at that moment the luxurious Prince of Wales Hotel - Frank and I looked at each other, briefly puzzled, then shrugged. What were we, UFOs? Why would the way we handle ourselves stand out? But evidently, in this gentleman's thinking, we were way out of our league this far from our "natural" habitat in the urban core.

In May 2008, our friend Charles who'd been an executive in the environmental segment returned to the field after a 10-year hiatus. After his first meeting, he called us, in a state of shock.

"It was like I'd just stepped out for a cigarette, or taken a bathroom break," he said numbly. "Nothing has changed. It was the same people sitting in the same rooms talking to each other, with one black guy and one Latino guy. The concerns we expressed about the lack of diversity weren't even mentioned by the executive who summarized the day's events."

The exploitative and extractive measures promoted by the Bush administration over eight years in office contributed to a rapid decline of our most pristine places. The "Healthy Forests" Initiative was a shield that led to large areas of our national forests being cut down, and the "Clear Skies" Initiative actually weakened the laws protecting the amount of emission released into the air. To effectively resist these initiatives requires a nationwide effort by concerned citizens, writing their congressional representatives and the president. But the effort was never made, and environmental leaders continued to do what they've always done, which essentially kept the public face of the movement white. They talked about the goal of inclusion, but failed to use their resources and influence to achieve that goal.

At the heart of the problem is the control of money and power, as white environmental groups compete with each other for funding. Where logic would demand a unified approach in addressing the most fundamental problem of our times, non-governmental organizations are often locked in competition and pursue programs that will help their group raise the most money. If a program falls out of favor with funders, that's the end of it, as we learned when NPCA suspended its diversity program in 2003 on the basis that the funding to support it had dried up. Programs targeted to the mainstream community remained in place and in some cases increased.

Grassroots leaders including Roger Rivera, president of the National Hispanic Environmental Coalition, consistently argued for a higher percentage of environmental dollars to be spent in communities of color. A 1999 study of foundation grants showed that *less than half of one percent* of the multi-million dollars they give to environmental groups each year goes to groups of color.

Recent research showing a strong connection between the reduced amount of time children spend playing in the outdoors and the increase in attention deficit disorder, hyperactivity and other imbalances, emphasize the human need to connect with nature. But instead of supporting grassroots groups which are engaged in this work, mainstream white groups develop their own programs focusing on "urban kids," in which they parachute in and take young people of color into the outdoors for a day or a week. However, this mainly serves to cement in the young people's mind the fact that this is something white people do, since they don't see outdoors role models in their community.

To what degree does the subconscious fear of white leaders that the iconic vistas of the national parks will be overrun and trashed by Americans of color act as a barrier to the integration of our publicly-owned lands?

To what extent does the inability to conceive of the masses becoming engaged in environmental protection retard the environmental movement?

Environmental leaders who consider themselves liberal, progressive and evolved, and who by virtue of their self-perceived "noble" calling are convinced they are above reproach, will be appalled to be confronted with the idea that their actions are based on racial prejudice and exclusivity. Yet this view is widely held among leaders of color who repeatedly raise pressing issues that need to be addressed, only to be overlooked time after time in favor of retaining the status quo. The extent to which this has deprived us of the opportunity to build greater public involvement and the momentum needed to address global warming and climate change is appalling. Only history will determine the amount of damage done to our environment that may have been avoided if there was true leadership and respect for the potential of all Americans to contribute to solutions.

Many people of color tune out the environment as "a pastime for rich white people who don't have anything else to worry about." Unfortunately, that works to our detriment because black, poor and urban people are more likely to live in polluted environment that jeopardizes their health, often without knowing it. The effects of environmental disasters on the black and poor can be seen on the hurricane-devastated Gulf Coast. Global warming and the price of gas determine whether poor families can afford air conditioning or suffer in airless homes. Atlanta, the "Black Mecca," was declared the "Asthma Capital" of the country for 2007.

We have seen government agencies such as the Army Corps of Engineers marginalize and dismiss the interests of poor and minority communities, and sabotage the efforts of their leaders to protect the local environment.

In Florida, we saw the City of Fort Lauderdale create their own "community group," in support of the *polluters* instead of the affected people. The Waste Management Corporation brought in a black consulting firm which organized a group of citizens from the Wingate area, who supported exactly what the officials said. The Superfund site was ultimately "capped" with plastic, and the black commissioner whose district included the site pressed for it to be developed into a banquet facility and golf course.

We saw the potential for the Everglades restoration, Eastward Ho! and the Brownfields program to positively remake the face of South Florida reduced to a shell in which a couple of select public relations firms benefitted by providing glossy, superficial communications to the community. Not only was the Environmental Justice Order not implemented, but it was essentially gutted by the Bush Administration.

An example of the result was evident in a May 4, 2008, story in the *Miami Herald*. It made us feel like déjà vu all over again:

Everglades project lacks black input

Officials are hard pressed to draw blacks into the debate over plans for the restoration of the Florida Everglades.

by Peter Bailey

A public meeting last month in Liberty City failed to draw blacks into the conversation surrounding the Florida **Everglades** restoration plan.

Planners held the open discussion at the African Heritage Cultural Arts Center to garner feedback from residents on proposed recreational activities that would be suitable for lands within the plan.

With a price tag between $8 billion and $10 billion, the project calls for an extensive network of canals to improve water management by channeling storm waters to much needed areas.

"The plan can definitely improve the quality of life in the inner city," said Shauna Allen, project manager of the Central Florida Restoration Branch. "Without getting input from the community, we can't know what improvements they desire."

Proposed canals through Miami's inner city may lead to the creation of linear parks, lined by park benches, said Allen, who is black.

"There are usually very few African Americans at our meetings," said Allen. "There is a definite barrier we face in getting blacks involved with the project."

At the April 21 meeting that drew about 15 people, mostly white, participants listed camping, hunting and riding all-terrain vehicles as activities they wanted included in the plan.

A similar meeting in Florida City held a week earlier was equally unable to draw a large number of Hispanics.

Activists argue that planners have failed to make the project relevant to minorities.

"The problem is the issue has not been framed where blacks feel they have a dog in the fight," says Alison **Austin**, a board member of the North America Association of Environmental Educators. "Blacks don't see the **Everglades** as part of their environment."

Austin said officials so far have focused solely on environmental education without making the issues relevant to the community.

"Blacks will join in the discussions when officials connect the issues to topics like gentrification and environmental justice," she said.

Austin, director of the Belafonte **TACOLCY** Center in Liberty City, was recently awarded a grant geared toward teaching teenagers the significance of building urban forests.

Meanwhile, Allen said her group has enlisted a marketing firm to focus primarily on garnering minority participation.

Allen, who grew up in Alabama where her father was an avid hunter, calls the campaign "personal."

"I really want to see more of us engaged in the issue because we have a lot to gain from this project," she said.

Ironically, 10 years ago Allison was part of our group that had great success in getting African Americans interested and attending meetings about the restoration and Eastward Ho! But as people saw that there was little real opportunity for them, they lost interest. Since there is virtually no accountability, "leaders" can continue to pretend that they're actually trying to accomplish "inclusion" while effectively just spinning their wheels.

Our relatives and friends had fully expected us to meet with racial hostility in the raw outdoors, and we hadn't. But a more subtle form of racism permeates the halls of power in the environmental segment. It is not overt. It can be very genteel. It is the conviction of well-meaning people that they know what's right for "those people." They assume a God-given prerogative to "save the environment," with little appreciation for the people who are part of the environment. Many of those who support the environmental movement made their fortune from the extraction of natural resources and the exploitation of labor. We first have to accept that all have contributed, to a greater or lesser extent, to both the bad and the good. Finding answers to global warming, climate change and developing healthful practices that sustain human health and the environment are the biggest challenges facing humanity now and in the near future. Americans comprise four percent of the world's population, consume 25 percent of its resources and contribute approximately 40 percent of the waste. While these numbers seem bleak, we are in a very advantageous position to affect the outcome of these issues.

It's not really a mystery to us how the descendants of people who were brought to this hemisphere because of our deep connections to the land today claim proudly, "Black people have nothing to do with the woods." Black researchers such as Cassandra Johnson of the US Forest Service and Carolyn Finney at the University of California/Berkeley have explored how the role of memory, fear, and cultural identity shape African American perspectives of the natural environment.

But there is a need to reconcile these conflicting emotions, particularly in light of Richard Louv's findings in *Last Child in the Woods, Saving Our Children from Nature Deficit Disorder*, in which he shows that inadequate exposure to nature is a major contributor to obesity, attention deficit disorder and depression in children. Why wouldn't this be true of adults, and especially for people who have broken their close connection to nature in only a few generations? The national parks were set aside by our ancestors who could not have conceived of the hectic pace at which we live now. But even in the 19th century, they recognized that we would need places where we could get away and reconnect to our humanity, to our very selves and to each other.

The antidote to the misinformation that has put African Americans, Latinos and other people of color at a disadvantage in America can be found in the national parks and our public lands system. "History is written by the victors," but the irrefutable information of what happened on this continent can be found on the land. Only then will we be able to visualize our country as one America, in which every citizen can claim the rightful and honorable place secured by the lives of our ancestors.

The National Park System will celebrate its Centennial Anniversary in 2016, in a country that is far more racially diverse that when it was established. To fulfill its mission of serving the American people, all Americans should ideally know and love their irreplaceable, God-given "Birthright."

When Frank and I reminisce about the incredible adventure that our life has become, and the contributions we have been allowed to make in moving things forward, he teases:

"I told you... the places we shall go and the things we shall do!"

But even he admits that there is no way he could have foreseen the extent of how far we've traveled. "A journey of a thousand miles begins with a single step," said Lao-tzu. If we had ignored our hearts' desire to go out and explore the parks when we had the opportunity, our world might still be limited to the cities and suburbs. We could have taken our friends' advice and aborted our plans or gone out in fear with a gun. We could have quit when the finances got tough, or when we found out the hypocrisy behind "environmental protection."

But something kept drawing us forward: The spiritual awakening we experienced in the parks, the kindness of strangers such as Midge Hainline (we lived on the ranch with her seven years!) and the fact that we were united in this dream. Most important, we both trust in a benevolent God who guides us if we let Him, and who has only the best desires for our life. With gratitude, I realize how our faith and work are used to "win some victory for humanity."

Appendix #1

Helpful Hints for the Aspiring Explorer

One common impediment to exploring our public lands is the misconception that you have to "rough it" in the Great Outdoors. Nothing could be further from the truth.

I was on the phone with one of Frank's classmates from Morehouse College, on the occasion of their 50th Class Reunion. He was telling me about the trip he and his wife had taken to Egypt in 2007, and I mentioned the similarity I saw between the natural formations in Badlands National Park and the pyramids of Egypt. Of course that launched into a rhapsody about Yellowstone and the Grand Canyon, when he said, "Yes, I saw a commercial about that tribe that built the glass platform over the Grand Canyon. We thought about going to see that, but you know, my wife doesn't like to camp."

"Huh?!" I sputtered. "Are you telling me you think you have to camp if you go to the Grand Canyon?"

"Are you telling me we don't?" he responded.

And there my heart broke. Because I imagined how many Americans literally go looking for happiness the world over, yet are insecure or know too little to explore our own backyard. It made my resolve even stronger to help change that.

From the establishment of the National Park System, park advocates recognized that they would have to make it relatively easy to get to the parks, and provide comfortable accommodations suitable for the wealthy patrons who could affect Congress and public opinion. As the Buffalo Soldiers built the road into Giant Forest at Sequoia National Park to make travel easier, so the first superintendent of the National Park System, Steven Mather, sought to create inviting lodging. One of the hotels Mather was instrumental in building was the Four-Diamond Ahwahnee Hotel in Yosemite, whose warm wood tones and winter fires have welcomed presidents and royalty into its understated opulence. Like the Ahwahnee, Old Faithful Inn in Yellowstone National Park is a National Historic Landmark with soaring cathedral ceiling made of wooden beams, just steps away from Old Faithful Geyser.

Whatever your budget, and no matter how remote the park, you can find hotels and restaurants in the parks or in the gateway city nearby. The big nature parks offer many choices from expensive to mid-priced lodges, cabins and campgrounds.

We wouldn't trade the experience of driving across the country in one continuous loop for anything, because it gave us the opportunity to see the landscape unfold before our eyes, and the amazing physical differences. From impenetrable cliff faces on the northeast coast to the incredibly fragile skin of the earth at Yellowstone, to the verdant rainforests on the Olympic peninsula, we could see how diverse and beautiful the land is.

But you can get equal satisfaction from an afternoon visit to the Martin Luther King, Jr., National Historical Site, a weekend trip to Mammoth Cave in Kentucky, or a five-day tour of Zion, Bryce and the Grand Canyon. Wherever we're going on business or pleasure (I say our business is pleasure), we check to see if there's a unit of the park system enroute or nearby.

Recently, we traveled to Greensboro, North Carolina, so Frank could attend a meeting of the Board of Visitors of the Nicholas School of the Environment, Duke University. As we neared the town I began to see signs for Guilford Courthouse National Battlefield. Wow! I had never even heard of that! Immediately I resolved that while Frank was in his meeting, I'd go visit that park. I spent only hours there, but after watching a computer simulation of the battle of the Revolutionary War Battle of Guilford Courthouse that was fought there on March 15, 1871, I left with a soaring feeling of pride in my breast. The site commemorates the place where Major General Nathaniel Greene, Commander of the American forces, outwitted and outfought superior British forces led by Lt. General Charles Earl Cornwallis.

The parks are a cost-effective buy for the most frugal family. In 2006 the Park Service raised fees from $50 for a National Parks Pass, which covers entrance for a year to every unit, to $80 for an Annual Pass which allows entry to every national parks, forest and wildlife preserve for a year. Some parks charge no entrance fees at all. Buy an Annual Pass at the first park you visit that charges entrance fees. If anyone in your party is 62 years old or older, that person can purchase a Golden Age Pass for a mere $10. It's good for a lifetime and allows a carload of people entry into the parks.

When planning your trip, decide what is most important to you. Is it stunning natural beauty? Black, White, Native American, Latino or Asian history in the park system? In some units such as Valley Forge National Historical Park outside Philadelphia, you can find all of the above linked in the story of America. Is your priority beauty and/or history close to home? Activities for the children? Many of the parks offer an exciting mixture that will meet and exceed your expectations.

Your first stop might be the National Park System website, a good source of information about the location of the parks, fees, hours of operation, best time of year to visit, accommodations, programs, and the parks primary features. Most of the units are open all year round, although some areas may not be accessible in winter, and we recommend that swampy parks such as the Everglades are best enjoyed in the cooler months when there are fewer mosquitoes.

Check out nearby cities or convention bureaus for competitive prices on accommodation that match your budget. They can also give you ideas about what else is in the area that you might want to experience.

If the park has an entrance station, you either buy your parks pass or show the one you already own. At many units you can also buy a day pass or a weekend or week pass. At that point you will be given a color brochure about the park, and some parks publish newspapers that tell you what is going on in the park that season.

Once you enter the park, make the Visitor Center your next stop. Visitor centers have large bathrooms and exhibits, as well as a gift shop and bookstore featuring publications and media about aspects of the park. The Visitor Center often shows free movies that provide an in-depth look at what you can expect to see at that unit and an appreciation of why it was designated as part of the park system.

Park rangers are available to answer questions and make suggestions about what activities and programs are available. Don't miss the ranger-guided walks and talks that have been a staple of the park experience for generations.

So what do you do at the parks? Our son Frankie put it poetically, "The view is what you do." In the big nature parks, the view is so enrapturing that you don't need to do anything, except drink it all in. Whether you're taking a casual walk or a strenuous hike, watching wildlife in their natural habitat, horseback riding, bicycling, mountain climbing or canoeing, you are always in close touch with the spectacular expanse of nature working its subtle magic on mind, body and soul.

The National Park Service is beginning to expand the stories of the contributions of African Americans, Latinos, Asians, Hispanics and Native Americans into the stories they tell in the national parks. When we first started visiting the parks, the displays we saw and the stories we heard promoted the exploits of white Americans, mostly men, with just a passing reference to the contributions of other races. But the Park Service is responding to the community's demand that they tell the full stories, and in some cases it is quite uncomfortable for the agency.

Particularly in the South, people still cling to the notion that the "War of Northern Aggression" was never about slavery. The Park Service takes a lot of abuse from these people when it interprets a Civil War Battlefield or other historic site where the facts do not conform to the image they have of the past. At Fort Davis National Historic Site in Texas, the Superintendent told us that many visitors who came expecting the site to be devoted to Jefferson Davis were sorely disappointed and upset when they realize that it commemorates the legacy of the Buffalo Soldiers who were stationed there.

The most important thing to remember is that the parks belong to you and your family. If your experience is unsatisfactory in any way or if you find that the stories are presented in a way that is insensitive to the contributions of non-white people, put your concerns in writing and send it to the park, as well as to the Director of the National Park System in Washington, D.C.

On our first trip to Harpers Ferry National Historical Park, I almost fell dead on the ground when one of the park's foremost historians who was leading our tour said, "And Stonewall Jackson is my hero. He was the greatest...."

There was a rushing in my ears as I tried to process what I was hearing, who it was coming from, and where I was. Only three of us were black among the group of twenty or so leading advocates for the national parks.

I wasn't that confident of my American history, but I do know that if Stonewall Jackson, a Confederate General in the Civil War had prevailed, my world would have been very different right at that moment.

I shuddered between two worlds, the now and the "what if?" And the speaker continued his story passionately, obviously unaware that he had wounded me to the core.

Frank and I were looking at each other with bug eyes.

I was too stunned to respond. I was so angry I was afraid I might burst into tears.

As soon as I could get him aside, I told the historian I didn't understand what he meant when he said, "Stonewall Jackson is my hero."

He seemed surprised. "What do you mean?" And he started once again to express his great admiration for Jackson.

I told him I appreciated his right to choose his hero, but he should be aware that his "hero's" success would have meant my enslavement and the continued enslavement of people who looked like me. I was almost desperate to give myself an out that we could both live with, because I couldn't stand to think of him as a racist, and I was heading in that direction.

"You mean you admire his military skills, right?"

He looked at me and said, "Right."

I drew my colleagues' attention to the incident, and told them that, for a black person just being introduced to the parks, this kind of experience would turn them off forever. The parks should incorporate the stories of all the participants and give the context in which they were happening. Above all, presenters should be professional and refrain from injecting their personal biases into the stories.

When we take people for their first visit to a national park, we choose one that's overpoweringly scenic so they get the immediate impact on their senses. If there are children and young people involved, we select a park where there is lots of wildlife, which inevitably captivates their attention.

It is difficult to dislodge today's young people from their electronic toys, and in some of the more remote parks cell phones don't work. Some of the more rustic accommodations in the parks don't have television sets.

If you have a teenager who would be uncomfortable in these conditions, you might want to book into one of the chain hotels outside the park. When we take our grandchildren to the parks, ranging from age 4 to 16, we rent an RV and stay in campgrounds, and we've seldom even turned on the TV that comes with it. The children are more interested in playing in the outdoors, frolicking around the campfire, "helping" us make meals and roasting marshmallows and 'smores. Whatever your youngsters need, be gentle with them and remember that it's a new experience for them, and one they probably would not have chosen. You may be pleasantly surprised to find that they begin asking to go to the parks.

Frank's Camping Tip

If you choose to go camping, camping magazines and catalogs are great sources of information about the outdoors. They probably share mailing lists, because soon after we picked up a catalog at the local Army Navy Surplus store and I ordered a camping knife, the catalogs started rolling in. As members of the Sierra Club and the Audubon Society, we regularly got their magazines about the state of the environment and the publicly-owned lands. I also subscribed to a camping magazine, and even though I seldom had time to read them thoroughly when they arrived, I'd glance through and make a mental note of the things I really wanted to get back to.

Although I have no fear of the woods, since I'm a country boy from Alabama who grew up following my grandfather down to the sloughs in search of herbs, sassafras, wild persimmons and blackberries, it increased my comfort level to know the prevailing thoughts and equipment that were out there. I could have chosen a hunting magazine too, since I grew up fishing and hunting with the men in my family, but I had long ago decided that there was enough killing going on in the world without me actively participating.

So if you're not already an active outdoors person, spend some time acculturating yourself and getting yourself mentally comfortable before you go out camping. You can do it through books and video or, more enjoyably, by spending a few hours on the weekend exploring a state or local park or National Wildlife Refuge, where you can be close to nature and close to home.

Appendix #2

Official 'Black' Units of the National Park System

Twenty of the 391 units of the National Park System have been designated as specific to the black experience, but we've found connections in dozens more now that we've visited 152 units. Called "The African American Experience Fund," these units are:

(1) The African Burial Ground National Monument in New York City commemorates the 15,000 free and enslaved Africans who built Wall Street, and were discarded unnoticed underfoot until a 1991, when groundbreaking for a federal building at Broadway, Duane, Elk and Read streets revealed their skeletons. The monument opened in October, 2007.

(2) The Boston African American National Historic Site, commemorates the African American patriots in Boston, Massachusetts, and includes the Black Heritage Trail, a 1.6 mile walking tour of 14 sites that were part of Boston's free black community in the 19th century.

(3) Cane River Creole National Historical Park in Natchitoches, Louisiana, preserves 62 acres of the original landscape where enslaved Africans lived and worked on the plantations along the Cane River. The multicultural legacy of the Caddo of Oklahoma, the Clifton Choctaw/Appalachia, the Tunica Biloxi and the descendants of the communities of color can also be experienced here.

(4) The Frederick Douglass National Historic Site, Washington, D.C., preserves the home where the great abolitionist lived from 1877 to1895, walking the 6 miles to his office in the Capitol every day. Mr. Douglass bought the 21-room house when he was 60 years old, and his commanding presence can still be felt in the home, thanks to the fact that his second wife, Helen, devoted herself to preserving the memorabilia associated with his life. It is the only unit of the National Park System containing more than 90 percent of the original artifacts.

(5)   The Booker T. Washington National Monument in Hardy, Virginia, includes a replica of the kitchen cabin that was home to Booker T., his mom and his brother and sister while he was a small boy, and which he wrote about in his autobiography, *Up From Slavery*. A quarter-of-a-mile walk winds through the historic area showcasing the tobacco farm where he was born in 1856 and lived through the Civil War. The site includes a 1.5 mile nature trail.

(6)   The New Orleans Jazz National Historical Park, in the heart of the French Quarter, celebrates the history and evolution of jazz, the quintessential American music.

(7)   The Maggie Lena Walker National Historic Site, Richmond, Virginia, includes the opportunity to visit her 28-room home where she lived for more than 30 years and the Jackson Ward Community in which she worked. The first woman to charter a bank (St. Luke's Penny Savings Bank) in 1903, she served as its president until 1929.

(8)   The Paul Laurence Dunbar State Memorial/Dayton Aviation Heritage National Historical Park, Dayton, Ohio, includes the poet's last home, which he bought for his mother in 1904. It showcases many of his literary masterpieces, personal belongings and his family's furnishings, as well as the places where Orville and Wilbur Wright made the great advances in flying, including the Huffman Prairie Flying Field where their first airplane, the 1905 Wright Flyer took to the air.

(9)   The Nicodemus National Historic Site in Bogue, Kansas, is one of the last remaining all-black towns formed by African American pioneers who pushed west after Reconstruction. Many descendants still live in the town, and preserve the memories of their ancestors' relationship with the Buffalo Soldiers and American Indian cultures to which some are related, and whose gifts of meat helped them survive the early years.

(10) Natchez National Historical Park, Natchez, Mississippi, spans the spectrum from the Melrose Mansion, depicting how prosperous whites lived in the "Cotton Kingdom" to the William Johnson House, built by the free black barber, who owned enslaved Africans. This park provides examples of lifestyles in the antebellum South.

(11) The George Washington Carver National Monument, Diamond, Missouri, includes a replica of the cabin in which he was born toward the end of the Civil War. Among the woodlands, streams and tall grass prairie of this 240-acre site, visitors discover Carver's timeless story and his unquenchable thirst for knowledge. You can literally walk in the great man's footsteps in his secret garden.

(12) Tuskegee Institute, Tuskegee, Alabama, preserves the legacy of Booker T. Washington, including his home, the Oaks, and many of the buildings constructed by students under his tutelage in the 1880s. The legacy of George Washington Carver, including his garden and the multiple products he developed from the peanut, are on display in the museum named for him. The school officially opened as the Tuskegee Normal School in 1881 and has educated African Americans continuously in its 127-year history.

(13) The Mary McLeod Bethune Council House, Washington, D.C. Between 1943 and 1949 this was the residence of the famous educator, civil rights activist, federal official, founder of the National Council of Negro Women and Bethune-Cookman College, who advised four presidents on African American affairs. Some of the original furnishings remain although the house has been modified. The National Archives for Black Women's History, which preserves Mrs. Bethune's legacy, is located on the premises.

(14) Tuskegee Airmen National Historic Site, Tuskegee, Alabama, commemorates the achievements of the trail-

blazing Tuskegee Airmen, whose outstanding performance as the first group of black men selected to train as pilots and support staff paved the way for integration of the Armed Services.

(15) The National Underground Railroad Network to Freedom connects the buildings, trails and "stops" used by more than 100,000 enslaved Africans in their pursuit of freedom in the years spanning the American Revolution and the Civil War. It includes approximately 200 sites across the U.S., north to Canada and south to Mexico and the Caribbean.

(16) The Selma to Montgomery National Historic Trail commemorates the route taken by marchers on "Bloody Sunday."

(17) The Martin Luther King, Jr., National Historic Site, Atlanta, Georgia, is dedicated to the life and work of the great Civil Rights leader, and includes the home on Auburn Avenue where he was born.

(18) Brown v. Board of Education National Historic Site, Topeka, Kansas. The former Monroe Elementary School was one of the segregated schools that African Americans were forced to attend before the Supreme Court's ruling in 1954. Interactive exhibits provide a timeline and explain the complex events leading up to the decision.

(19) Little Rock Central High School National Historic Site, Little Rock, Arkansas. Walk in the footsteps of "The Little Rock Nine" as they fulfill the promise of the Supreme Court's Brown v. Board decision, and are met by mob violence. The events of fall 1957 forced President Dwight Eisenhower to use federal troops to assure that the black teenagers could attend the all-white school. In September, 2007, the "Little Rock Nine" were all present to dedicate a new Visitor Center at the site.

(20) The Carter G. Woodson Home National Historic Site, Washington, D.C., is where the "Father of African American history" lived from 1915 until his death in

1950. The house has been closed pending restoration, and in the interim, programs featuring Dr. Woodson's life are given at Mary McLeod Bethune Council House, just a half-mile away.

Appendix #3

Untold Stories

Other parks we have visited that reflect the contributions of black ancestors include:

FLORIDA

- The Big Cypress National Preserve in South Florida was once a near-impenetrable forest of 600-year-old big cypress trees. In the middle of the 20th century, teams consisting mostly of African American, Native American and white laborers cut the Tamiami Trail through the muck, linking Tampa and Miami by road for the first time in 1928. In the middle of the 20th century, black men worked in alligator-and-snake infested water, sometimes up to their necks, using a two-handled saw to cut down the cypress trees to produce wood that was used to build barracks, docks and other infrastructure. The women farmed, worked as cooks, organized schools for black children and developed a sense of community. Little evidence remains of their community, but the natural splendor of the Big Cypress ecosystem can be observed by taking a drive across the Tamiami trail, with its plethora of wildlife, visible in the spring, fall and winter.

- Cape Canaveral National Seashore. Home of the Kennedy Space Center, this seashore also includes the Merritt Island National Wildlife Refuge and the Eldora House, which showcases the contributions of African Americans to the area.

- The Kingsley Plantation/Timucuan Ecological and Historic Preserve, in Jacksonville. We had the luxury of touring the plantation with MaVynee Betsch, one of the descendants of the original owner, Zephaniah Kingsley and his wife, Anna. This site is profoundly unique, as Anna, born a Wolof princess, was captured and sold into slavery in Cuba. She was "bought" by Zephaniah Kingsley, who made her his wife, and left the plantation and other business interests in her capable hands while he traveled extensively. The plantation includes original "slave cabins," made from a combination of sand and shells, and is just a few miles away from American Beach, established in 1935 by MaVynee's great-grandfather, A. L. Lewis, as resort for African Americans from across the country. A year before her death in 2005, MaVynee, one of the world's most committed environmentalists, succeeded in her 12-year effort to get eight-and-a-half acres of the sand dunes where she had played as a child, affectionately known as "Nana," included as part of the National Park unit. The legacy is carried on by the A.L. Lewis Historical Society.

GEORGIA

- Cumberland Island National Seashore, St. Mary's, Georgia. The 15-mile- long island is accessible only by ferry or private boat, and is book-ended on the south by the ruins of the Carnegie family's Dungeness mansion, and the First African Baptist Church and the black settlement at its north end. The African Americans were in service to the Rockefellers and Carnegies, and walked the 15 miles back and forth each day. The island still retains a forest of live oak trees, some as many as 600 years old, and herds of wild horses, wild turkeys, wild pigs and armadillos make for exceptional wildlife viewing. The First African Baptist Church was re-built in 1937 after a fire demolished the original building, and includes the rough, serviceable wooden benches, and the small altar with a proud, affirmative cross made of two sticks lashed together from that period.

- Kennesaw Mountain National Battlefield Park, Kennesaw, Georgia, preserves the site of one of the defining battles of the Civil War. From encampments on these leafy hills, General Sherman and his Union troops defeated General Johnston and the Confederate troops in the Atlanta Campaign of 1864. Earthwork trenches and some of the cannon remain as vivid reminders of the struggle that ultimately led to freedom for African Americans.

SOUTH CAROLINA

- The Gullah/Geechee Cultural Heritage Corridor stretching from Jacksonville, Florida, to Wilmington, North Carolina, was created in 2006 to preserve the history of the Gullah/Geechee people dating back to the arrival of the Africans at Jamestown in 1619. Spearheaded by Congressman James Clyburn of South Carolina, the designation as a Heritage Corridor enables diverse groups to work together to highlight the culture, and to get federal funding support.

- Fort Sumter National Monument, Sullivan's Island, where the first shot of the Civil War rang out April 12, 1861, is only accessible by ferry. One of the few forts that remained under Federal control after South Carolina and six other southern states seceded from the Union, it weathered the 34-hour bombardment launched against the federal troops garrisoned there since 1860. Park Service rangers led us on a tour through the fort's storied history, including descriptions of how it was used in support of World Wars I and II. Nearby Fort Moultrie was instrumental in our success in the Revolutionary War, as it rebuffed the bombardment of British ships for nearly two years.

WEST VIRGINIA

- Harpers Ferry National Historical Park preserves this small town at the confluence of the Potomac and the Shenandoah rivers, including the fort where John Brown launched his attack in 1859, precipitating the Civil War. It includes Storer College, where W.E.B. Dubois and other founders launched the Niagara Movement in 1909, the forerunner to today's NAACP. In honor of John Brown and his band of men, including enslaved Africans and his own sons, the Niagara leaders removed their shoes and walked barefooted and reverent across the dewy grass.

PENNSYLVANIA

- Valley Forge National Historical Park, in Valley Forge, is where General George Washington's Continental Army—made up of black, white, Latino, Asian and Native American men—weathered unbearable cold, starvation and disease in the winter of 1778. Incomprehensibly, they hung on until the weather abated and food began to trickle in. It is still considered a mystery today how the enigmatic German, Baron von Steuben, managed to get regular supplies started again and drilled the men into a fighting force within a couple of months. They streamed out of Valley Forge as a fighting force, and the encampment is considered a turning point that helped America win the Revolutionary War. Walking across the fields I was filled with admiration and pride for my African American ancestors' suffering at this place, and their survival that helped establish the country we know today.

MASSACHUSETTS

- The New Bedford Whaling National Park in New Bedford tells the story of the whaling industry and the large percentage of whalers who were African Americans, Cape Verdeans, West Indians, and Polynesians, along with Native American Indians and white people. Affiliated with the Inupiat Heritage Center in Barrow, Alaska, it commemorates more than 2,000 whaling voyages that sailed out of New Bedford to Alaska and joined natives from Barrow and other regions in whaling activities. More than 75 percent of the crews were men of color and the most prosperous black whaling entrepreneur, Paul Cuffee, built whaling ships commanded by his relatives and manned by black crews. He supported the Back to Africa Movement, and completed one trip transporting free Blacks to Sierra Leone before the War of 1812. He traveled to Britain and was received by Members of Parliament and the Duke of Gloucester, before returning home and succeeded in making another successful journey relocating 38 people to Sierra Leone.

MISSOURI

- The Jefferson National Expansion Memorial in St. Louis, includes not only the giant, 60-story Gateway Arch, the symbolic gateway to the American West, but the Dred Scott Courthouse, where in 1846 Dred and Harriett Scott filed charges of false imprisonment against their "owner,' which went all the way to the Supreme Court and helped precipitate the Civil War. A 4-minute train ride inside the arch deposits you at the top, where on a windy day, I felt it sway. The Old Courthouse preserves the courtroom where the Dred Scott trial was heard June 30, 1847, was renovated in 1855 and divided into two rooms. Extensive newspaper reports and photographs provide insight into the case, and a museum of Old St. Louis is housed downstairs in the same building.

CALIFORNIA

- The Golden Gate National Recreation Area includes 16 superlative natural and cultural areas, as impressive as the Presidio, as forbidding as Alcatraz and as wildly scenic as Marin Headlands, Muir Woods or Angel Island. As part of a Volunteer Vacation offered by the American Hiking Society, in 2006 we stayed in the Presidio in return for repairing trails in the Tennessee Valley. Overlooking the Golden Gate Bridge, the Presidio depicts the history of the Buffalo Soldiers who were once posted there, through plaques and displays at the Visitor Center.

ALASKA

- Klondike Gold Rush National Historical Park. The Buffalo Soldiers kept peace in this frontier town consumed with gold lust, as prospectors made their way to the gold fields of the Yukon.

About the Authors

As a boy, **Frank Peterman** followed his grandfather into the fields and meadows of southeast Alabama, gathering roots and herbs, hunting with his .22 caliber rifle, fishing in the streams and creeks. His grandfather cautioned him never to shoot at anything he didn't intend to kill and eat. As a young man, he worked with his father in South Florida's orange groves, where his dad insisted that a portion of the grove be left for the animals to eat. Currently, his focus is to get the last remaining wilderness areas in America protected, and he believes that the only way to assure that is when the American people know and appreciate what they own.

An only child, **Audrey Peterman** grew up with her grandmother in Summerfield, Jamaica, a small village as happy as its name. No one was a stranger, as everyone's roots went back generations, and the children enjoyed chores and pastimes together, carrying water on their heads from the standpipe or running off to mango fields to eat succulent fruit at the peak of perfection. Today her passion is to connect Americans to the National Park System as a means of awakening civic pride, self-esteem, and engendering a sense of responsibility toward the planet and future generations.

The couple co-founded Earthwise Productions, Inc., a consulting and publishing company in 1994. Shortly after their life-changing initial excursion to several national parks, they began publishing a travel newsletter, "Pickup & Go," and in 2009 they founded a national conference, *Breaking the Color Barrier in the Great Outdoors*. Audrey also belongs to the boards of the National Parks Conservation Association and the Association of Partners of Public Lands. Frank is also Director of Public and Political Awareness for the Wilderness Society, Eastern Forest Program. Together, they help steer the Wilderness Society's "Keeping It Wild" program, a widely noted effort that raises awareness about the value of natural lands while building partnerships among diverse groups and individuals interested in conservation.

Praise for the Authors

"When my friend told me that her well-known environmentalist friends were coming to Accra, Ghana, and I should take care of them, I assumed they were white, because the only environmentalist of color I know is my good friend, Wangari Maathai [2004 Nobel Peace Prize winner]. Since I met Audrey and Frank I feel connected with the universe in a deeper way… I find myself looking at the trees, the birds… things I never noticed before I am seeing in a whole new light of appreciation."

—Ambassador Dr. Erieka Bennett,
Founder, the Diaspora African Forum;
2009 Trumpet Award Honoree

Index

A

Acadia National Park, v, ix, 4, 6, 9, 217-218

African Americans, ii, v, x-xi, xiii, 32, 46, 53, 57-58, 65, 68, 75-77, 82-83, 87, 89-90, 107, 109, 111-112, 119, 122, 124, 130-131, 133-134, 143, 147, 154, 157, 162, 164, 176, 184, 196-198, 203, 208-209, 211-212, 214, 218

Alaska National Wildlife Refuge, 119, 218

Anderson, Tony C., 171, 218

Andoh, Anthony, 153, 218

Anhinga Trail, 60, 101, 218

Anne Kolb Nature Center, 90, 218

Applebaum, Stu, 218

Arapaho, 19, 218

Arctic National Wildlife Refuge, xii, 166, 218

Armstrong, Cheryl, 96, 218

Asians, x-xi, 48, 75, 78, 203, 218

Attention deficit disorder, xiii, 194, 198, 218

Audubon Society, 55, 57-59, 62, 64, 73, 82, 88, 101, 112, 154, 188, 205, 218

B

Badlands National Park, v, ix, 16-18, 200, 218

Ballard, Joe, 89, 218

Bandelier National Monument, vi, 116, 218

Bar Harbor, 6-7, 218

Barry, Don, viii, 113-114, 142

Bass-Dillard Neighborhood Issues and Prevention, Inc., 70, 218

Bates, Katherine, 97, 218

Bear Mountain State Park, 99, 218

Betsch, MaVyne, 218

Big Cypress National Preserve, 100, 102, 124, 168, 211, 218

Biscayne Aquifer, 72, 86-87, 218

Biscayne National Park, 59, 102, 108, 133, 173, 218

Black Hills, 18-19, 218

Black Publishers' Summit, 110, 218

Blank, Diana, viii, 173, 218

"Bloody Sunday", 76, 209, 218

Bock, Lisa, 58

Borglum, Gutzon, 19

Bowser, Gillian, 95, 218

Bransford, Jerry, 175, 181-182, 218

Bright Angel Trail, 42, 218

Broward County Department of Community Affairs, 218

Broward County Department of Natural Resources, 73, 218

Broward Times, viii, 75, 110, 218

"Brownfield", 66, 218

Brown, Brad, 125, 218

Brown, John G. and Barbara, 60, 218

Browner, Carole, 88, 218

Buffalo Bill Cody, 22, 218

Buffalo Ford, 26, 218

Buffalo Soldiers, vi, 141-142, 148, 150-152, 168, 170, 185-187, 200, 203, 207, 215, 218

Bullard, Robert, 70, 218

Bureau of Land Management, xi, 77, 116, 218

Burns, Ken, 184, 218

Bush, George, 218

Bush, Jeb, vi, 110, 122, 140, 218

C

Cadillac Mountain, ix, 7, 9, 50, 218

Calloway, Al, viii, 111, 123-124, 218

L

M

N

Quick Order Form

Please copy, complete and mail

Postal Orders: Earthwise Productions, Inc. 450 Piedmont Avenue, Suite #1512, Atlanta, GA 30308, USA. Telephone: 404 875 1375

Please send _____ copy(s) of **Legacy on the Land: A Black Couple Discovers Our National Inheritance and Tells Why Every American Should Care**. $19.95 each

Sales tax: Please add 8% tax for copies shipped within Georgia.

Priority Mail Shipping and handling fees: U.S. $6.00 for first book; $2.00 for each additional copy.

Please send more FREE information on (check your selection):

- ☐ *Pickup & Go!* travel newsletter
- ☐ Speaking/Presentations
- ☐ Consulting
- ☐ Mailing Lists
- ☐ Print or video proceedings from the historic *Breaking the Color Barrier in the Great American Outdoors* conference, held September 23-26, 2009, in Atlanta, GA [call 404-875-1375 for titles]

Name: _____

Address: _____

City: _____ State: _____ Zip: _____

Telephone: _____

Email address: _____

Payment: Enclose check or money order, payable to: Earthwise Productions.

For additional information visit our website:
www.earthwiseproductionsinc.com/legacyontheland